ENGINEERING MATHEMATICS
WITH MAPLE

International Series in Pure and Applied Mathematics

ENGINEERING MATHEMATICS WITH MAPLE

John S. Robertson

Professor of Mathematics and Computer Science
Georgia College

McGraw-Hill, Inc.

New York   St. Louis   San Francisco   Auckland   Bogotá   Caracas
Lisbon   London   Madrid   Mexico City   Milan   Montreal   New Delhi
San Juan   Singapore   Sydney   Tokyo   Toronto

ENGINEERING MATHEMATICS
WITH MAPLE

1 2 3 4 5 6 7 8 9 0 DOC DOC 9 0 9 8 7 6 5

ISBN 0-07-053120-X

The editors were Maggie Lanzillo and Jack Shira;
the production supervisor was Phil Galea.
R. R. Donnelley & Sons Company was printer and binder.

The illustration shown on the cover was generated by *Maple* and depicts a sequence
of damped cosine curves. The *Maple* code used to generate the cover is:

```
> s :={};
> for i from 2 by 2 to 40 do
    a  :=i/10;
    s  :=s union {cos((x^2+a^2) / 4) / (x^2 + a^2 Pi)};
  od:
```

This manual was typeset by the author with Textures by Blue Sky Research, using
LATEX, the document preparation system by Leslie Lamport built atop the TEX
engine of Donald Knuth. Special design macros were provided by ETP Services. The
illustrations were prepared on a Macintosh IIci with *Maple* and MacDraw Pro.

Library of Congress Cataloging-in-Publication Data

Robertson, John S.
    Engineering mathematics with Maple / John S. Robertson.
    p.   cm. — (International series in pure and applied
mathematics)
    Includes bibliographical references and index.
    ISBN 0-07-053120-x
    1. Engineering mathematics—Data processing.   2. Maple (Computer
file) I. Title.   II. Series.
TA345.R58   1996
620'.00285'53—dc20   95-11318

ABOUT THE AUTHOR

John S. Robertson is Professor and Chair of Mathematics and Computer Science at Georgia College. He received his Ph.D. in Mathematics from Rensselaer Polytechnic Institute. He is an active researcher in computational acoustics and computer applications to mathematics education. His work has been supported by the Office of Naval Research, the National Aeronautics and Space Administration, and a number of Army research agencies. He is a member of the Acoustical Society of America, the Society for Industrial and Applied Mathematics, and the Mathematical Association of America.

To my good friends Mike, Gabe, Raphe, Pete, Paul, and John
Omnia in bonum!

CONTENTS

PREFACE

This book is intended for use as a supplemental tool for courses in engineering mathematics, applied ordinary and partial differential equations, vector analysis, applied complex analysis, and other advanced courses in which *Maple*[1] is used. My goal in writing this text was to prepare a supplementary book that could be used to guide students through a series of laboratory exercises that would do the following:

- present cogent applications of the mathematics
- demonstrate the effective uses of the computational tool (in this case, *Maple*) to do the mathematics
- provide discussion of the results obtained by using *Maple*
- stimulate thought about and analysis of additional applications

Each chapter has been written so that the material it contains may be covered in a typical laboratory session of about 1-1/2 to 2 hours. The goals for every laboratory are stated at the beginning of each chapter. Mathematical concepts are then discussed within a framework of abundant engineering applications and problem-solving techniques using *Maple*. I have tried to keep the *Maple* instruction *per se* to a minimum, but have included enough material to get students up and running quickly.

Each chapter is followed by a set of exercises. Many of these are exploratory in nature and are intended to serve as a starting point for a student's mathematical experimentation. In addition, since most of the exercises can be solved

---

[1] *Maple* is a registered trademark of Waterloo Maple Software.

in more than one way, I have not provided an answer key for the student or instructor. Students should be encouraged to develop their own problem-solving skills with *Maple* and not just look for the "correct" answer.

Colleges and universities across the nation have been carefully re-examining the ways in which undergraduate mathematics is taught and done. The advent of computer algebra systems such as *Maple*, which can perform elaborate symbolic calculations, in conjunction with the rapidly expanding power of computers to function as graphic visualization devices have forced a critical re-thinking of how much of what is called higher mathematics ought to be taught and done.

The calculus reform movement has already borne much fruit. As it matures, the same style of innovative thinking must subsequently be brought to bear on virtually all the mathematics courses taken by upperclassmen. While core mathematics has been the object of substantial national attention, less emphasis has been placed on adapting advanced courses to the technology and the student expectations it brings with it.

For these reasons, one of the most promising areas in which to exploit computation is in "engineering mathematics," a rubric which covers applied ordinary and partial differential equations, vector analysis, and applied complex analysis in courses normally taken junior and senior year. One approach to this problem is to write new textbooks with clearly-woven computational threads. I have taken a different approach by presenting discussion that is compatible with a broad range of engineering mathematics texts, as well as smaller, more specialized texts in differential equations and complex variables.

Although it might be desirable to make such a laboratory text independent of any particular software package, this goal is not yet in sight. There are simply too many differences in package front-ends and capabilities. In my view, a laboratory text must deal concretely with the details of a specific package. For a number of reasons, I have selected *Maple* as the computer algebra package for this text. *Maple* possesses a wealth of features which make it an excellent laboratory tool for engineering mathematics. In addition, *Maple* is available on a broad array of platforms—386 PCs, Macintoshes, Sun Sparcstations, IBM RS/6000s, etc.—and is found at many universities.

I would like to thank many, many people for their help while I prepared this book. My bride, Julia, provided all the support while the writing was in progress. Dr. Norbert Carballo, Fr. Bob Brisson, Jim Keenly, Charlie Frank, and Ryan Berry provided good reasons to press on, as did the cadets of the Thayer Circle. Howard Graves and Gerry Galloway played their part too. Mae Carpenter gave me a big boost at the right time. I wish to especially thank Prof. Robert J. Lopez of Rose-Hulman Institute of Technology, who carefully read the manuscript, and offered an abundance of savagely sincere criticisms and suggestions which substantially improved the book. My editor, Maggie Lanzillo, showed more confidence in me than I deserved.

John S. Robertson

ENGINEERING MATHEMATICS
WITH MAPLE

CHAPTER
1

INTRODUCTION

1.1 GOALS

a. To become familiar with the basic syntax of *Maple*.
b. To plot two-dimensional graphs.
c. To plot three-dimensional surfaces.

1.2 ABOUT *Maple*

Maple is a powerful symbolic algebra tool that provides an extraordinarily rich variety of symbolic, graphical, and numerical capabilities to anyone working with engineering mathematics.

MapleFPU

FIGURE 1.1
Clicking on this (or a similar) icon starts *Maple* on the Macintosh. (The FPU at the end of this icon name means that this version of *Maple* requires a special chip for floating point calculations. Your Macintosh probably has one.)

  Maple sessions are started differently on different machines. For example, on the Macintosh, you can click on a *Maple* icon, as shown in Fig. 1.1. This will open a *Maple* worksheet into which you can start typing. On a UNIX-based workstation, such as an IBM RISC System 6000, you would type `maple` at the command prompt. In this case you will see the following text in your window:[1]

```
      |\^/|      Maple V Release 3 (Behemoth State University)
   ._|\|   |/|_. Copyright (c) 1981-1994 by Waterloo Maple Software and the
    \  MAPLE  /  University of Waterloo. All rights reserved. Maple and Maple V
    <____ ____>  are registered trademarks of Waterloo Maple Software.
         |       Type ? for help.
    >
```

Refer to the *Maple Reference Guide*[2] that came with your *Maple* implementation on starting *Maple* on other computer systems.[3]

   Maple syntax, while initially a bit strange, is fairly easy to learn and remarkably consistent. As you work with it, keep the following rules in mind:

- *Maple* is case-sensitive.
- *Maple* expressions must end with either a semi-colon, ;, or a colon, :. Otherwise, the expression will not be evaluated.
- Function arguments are always delineated with parentheses, i.e. (...).
- Sets are always delineated with curly brackets, i.e. { ... }.
- Lists are always delineated with curly brackets, i.e. [...].
- Variable ranges (for integration, plotting, and counting) look like this: x = 0 .. 2, which would mean that $0 \le x \le 2$.
- A question mark ? followed by the *Maple* function name will elicit more information on that function, as well as detailed examples. Even so, there is no substitute for referring to the *Maple* book[4] for definitive guidance on a particular function or operation.

1.3   BASIC ALGEBRA AND CALCULUS OPERATIONS

There are a few fundamental operations which must be mastered early on if the power of *Maple* is to be put to good use in the laboratory exercises. Consider the following expression:

---

[1] As of this writing, worksheets are available for many major UNIX platforms. But if you dial into a big computer from your home, dormitory, or office, the worksheet feature is usually not available.

[2] Bruce W. Char, Keith O. Geddes, Gaston H. Gonnet, Benton L. Leong, Michael B. Monagan, and Stephen M. Watt: *Maple V Language Reference Manual*, Springer Verlag, New York, 1991.

[3] In this and all subsequent chapters, input and output will be confined between the upward- and downward-facing horizontal brackets as shown in the above example.

[4] Darren Redfern, *The Maple Handbook*, Springer Verlag, New York, 1993.

```
> (x + y)^2;
```

$$(x + y)^2$$

In this example, x and y are variables and the ^ operator denotes exponentiation. *Maple* returns the result in display form, not unlike the way we would write the result down on paper.[5] Input lines are always begin with the symbol > and output lines are always centered across the screen.

    Maple can be directed to expand the result with the **expand()** function:

```
> expand(");
```

$$x^2 + 2\,x\,y + y^2$$

The " symbol stands for the output of the immediately previous calculation. In this example, " is equivalent to (x + y)^2. This result of the last command can be further manipulated, say, by subtracting 4 * x * y from it:

```
> " - 4 * x * y;
```

$$x^2 - 2\,x\,y + y^2$$

In output, note that spaces between symbols designate *implied* multiplication.
    In any case, to factor this last result we use the **factor()** function:

```
> factor(");
```

$$(x - y)^2$$

Maple contains a large number of powerful functions for performing basic algebra operations. Many of these will be introduced in subsequent chapters of this book. A complete listing of all the *Maple* operators, functions, and special symbols we use is given in Appendix A.[6]

[5]If you are using a worksheet, the output can be made to appear far more elegant.

[6]The index also contains cross-references to their use in the text.

Maple can also perform a variety of calculus operations. For example, let $f(x) = x/(x^2+1)$. Then the derivative $f'(x)$ can be determined with the `diff()` function, which takes two arguments. The first is the function to be differentiated while the second is the variable of differentiation:[7]

```
> f := x / (x^2 + 1);

                       x
              f  :=  ------
                       2
                      x  + 1

> diff(f, x);

                                     2
              1                     x
           ------  -  2  ---------
              2                 2      2
             x  + 1        (x   + 1)
```

In the previous input line, we assigned to the symbol `f` the expression `x / (x^2 + 1)`.

The indefinite integral is obtained with the `int()` function. The arguments are the same as those of `diff()`:

```
> int(f, x);
                          2
                  1/2 ln(x  + 1)
```

where `ln()` denotes the natural logarithm function.[8]

Definite integrals may also be evaluated with the `int()` function, although the function syntax is slightly different. The second argument is given as the range of the integration variable. For example, suppose we need to calculate the expression $\int_0^4 f(x)\,dx$. We enter:

```
> int(f, x = 0 .. 4);
                  1/2 ln(17)
```

---

[7]`diff()` can take partial derivatives of a function of several variables, since *Maple* normally treats all symbols as independent variables.

[8]*Maple* knows all about the analytical and numerical properties of all the elementary functions, and an impressive menagerie of special functions, too. The nomenclature and syntax of these will be introduced as they appear in later chapters. See Appendix A.

The ellipsis operator .. indicates that the variable x lies in the range from 0 to 4. We emphasize that this is a *symbolic* result: *Maple* has calculated this result *exactly*. When required, *Maple* can also perform numerical integrations with the `evalf` function. This function can be applied to integrals that *Maple* cannot do analytically. For example, to evaluate $\int_0^{10} \exp(-x^3)\,dx$, we first set up the definite integral as follows. We will use the `exp()` to perform exponentiation:

```
> int(exp(-x^3), x = 0 .. 10);

                          10
                          /
                          |          3
                          |    exp(- x ) dx
                          |
                          /
                          0
```

Note that *Maple* returns the result in the form of a symbolic integral when the integration cannot be done exactly. Now we use `evalf()` to force a numerical evaluation of this expression:

```
> evalf(");

                       .8929795122
```

1.4 TWO-DIMENSIONAL GRAPHICS

Two-dimensional plotting is straightforward in *Maple*. The `plot()` function generally takes two arguments. The first is the function to be plotted, while the second is the domain of the independent variable. Thus, to plot the graph of the function $f(x) = \sin x$ on the interval $[0, 2\pi]$, you give the following command to *Maple*:

```
> plot(sin(x), x = 0 .. 2 * Pi);
```

Depending upon your interface, the plot will appear somewhere on your screen. The `sin()` function is used to determine the sine of a real number, and `Pi` is a symbol used by *Maple* to denote the exact value of π.[9] The result of this

---

[9]Other special symbols are `E`, which is e, is the base of the natural logarithm, and `I`, which is $i = \sqrt{-1}$.

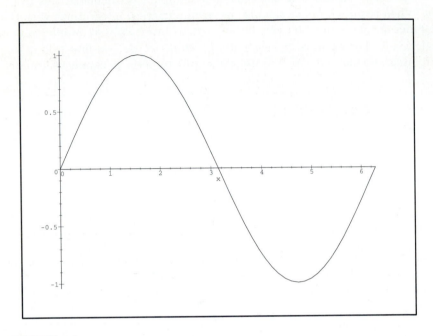

FIGURE 1.2
A plot of the sine function on $[0, 2\pi]$.

command is shown in Fig. 1.2. *Maple* normally scales the x- and y-axes in a natural way, typically to show as much of the plot as possible. Occasionally, the default choices *Maple* makes are inadequate. The scaling can be modified with additional arguments to the `plot()` function.

We now assign the output of this call to `plot()` to the symbol `plot1`:

```
> plot1 := ":
```

Note the use of the colon : to terminate the input line. The colon suppresses the output line, which in this case, is several pages long and whose exact form is unimportant.

As another example, consider the graph of the function $\cos x$ on the interval $\pi/2 \leq x \leq 5\pi/2$. The commands to generate the graph of this function and assign it to the symbol `plot2` are:

```
> plot(cos(x), x = Pi / 2 .. 5 * Pi / 2);
> plot2 := ":
```

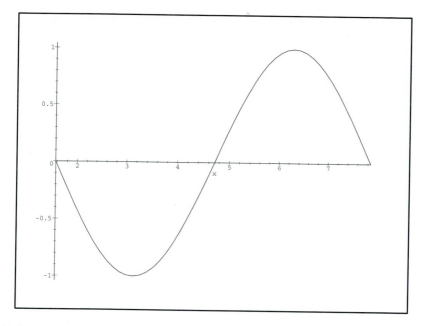

FIGURE 1.3
A plot of the cosine function on $[\pi/2, 5\pi/2]$.

with the result shown in Fig. 1.3. Note how *Maple* shifted the scale on the x-axis to accommodate the domain for this plot.

It is often desirable to combine two or more graphs on the same set of axes. *Maple* has a powerful facility for this kind of operation. The `plot()` function with the `[display]` function option can be used to overlay both graphs with automatic axis scaling:

```
> plot[display]({plot1, plot2});
```

Note that argument consists of a set of symbols, {`plot1`, `plot2`}, which contain information about the two curves we want to see. The result of this command is shown in Fig. 1.4. Note that each curve is displayed only over the domain for which it was defined. In addition, the `plot()` function when used with the `display` option works with the stored graphic, not with the underlying computation that was used by `plot()` to make the graphic. Thus, plot manipulation with `plot[display]()` is very efficient. *Maple* permits an arbitrary number of curves to be combined in this way. To make complicated pictures easier to understand, *Maple* also has the ability to change line patterns and thicknesses and

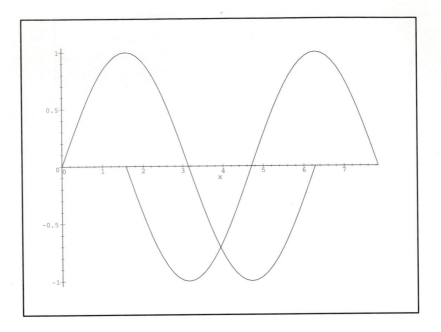

FIGURE 1.4
A plot of both sine and cosine functions on $[0, 5\pi/2]$. Note that the correct domain is shown for each curve.

to add all sorts of other information to the plot. See Appendix B for some hints on how to do this.

1.5   THREE-DIMENSIONAL GRAPHICS

Not all of *Maple*'s three-dimensional functions are available when *Maple* is first started. Several of those we need are loaded from *packages* with the `with()` function. Since the package containing the three-dimensional graphing functions is called `plots`, we load it as follows:

```
> with(plots);

[animate, animate3d, conformal, contourplot, cylinderplot, densityplot,

    display, display3d, fieldplot, fieldplot3d, gradplot, gradplot3d,

    implicitplot, implicitplot3d, loglogplot, logplot, matrixplot, odeplot,

    pointplot, polarplot, polygonplot, polygonplot3d, polyhedraplot,
```

```
replot, setoptions, setoptions3d, spacecurve, sparsematrixplot,

sphereplot, surfdata, textplot, textplot3d, tubeplot]
```

We could have suppressed the output line by using a colon to terminate the call to the `with()` function.[10]

One of *Maple*'s most powerful features is its ability to manipulate three-dimensional information. The surface plot is one way this is done. The appropriate *Maple* function is `plot3d()`, which takes three arguments: a function of two variables, and two variable domains. For example, consider the surface generated by the function $z = \cos x \sin y$, with $x \in [0, 4\pi]$ and $y \in [0, 4\pi]$. This surface is plotted and assigned to the variable `plot3` with the two commands:

```
> plot3d(cos(x) * sin(y), x = 0 .. 4 * Pi, y = 0 .. 4 * Pi, style = PATCH);
> plot3 := ":
```

with the result shown in Fig. 1.5. The option `style = PATCH` causes the surface to be shaded as shown in the figure.[11]

Once this figure is constructed, there are several other simple ways to visualize the characteristic behavior of the surface. For example, a density plot can be generated by the `densityplot()` function:

```
> densityplot(cos(x) * sin(y), x = 0 .. 4 * Pi, y = 0 .. 4 * Pi);
```

with the result shown in Fig. 1.6.[12] Density plots give a more precise way of locating specific surface features with regard to their locations in the coordinated plane. The darkest areas correspond to the smallest value of z while the lightest areas correspond to the largest value of z. We can see that the maximum and minimum values of z in this example are evenly spaced in both the horizontal and vertical directions.

A different way to visualize three-dimensional information is by drawing contour lines with the `contourplot()` function:

---

[10]After you become familiar with this package, you may decide to always load it with the colon.

[11]Other styles are POINT, WIREFRAME, and HIDDEN. Try experimenting with these, and observe the different ways the surface is rendered.

[12]Both the vertical and horizontal lines appear to be bent, but this is only an optical illusion.

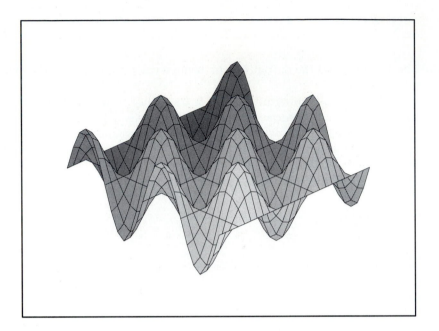

FIGURE 1.5
A surface plot of $z = \cos x \sin y$ on $x \in [0, 4\pi]$ and $y \in [0, 4\pi]$.

```
> contourplot(cos(x) * sin(y), x = 0 .. 4 * Pi, y = 0 .. 4 * Pi);
```

The result of this function call is shown in Fig. 1.7. The slightly jagged appearance of the contour lines is a consequence of the grid size used in the computation. The contours can be further smoothed by refining the grid size by including the **numpoints** option.[13]

It is also possible to overlay multiple surfaces in *Maple* in much the same way as discussed in the previous section. To illustrate the point, we now generate a second surface with $z = \sin(y/2)$, with $x \in [0, 4\pi]$ and $y \in [0, 4\pi]$ and assign it to the symbol **plot4**. This is done with the commands

```
> plot3d(sin(y/2), x = 0 .. 4 * Pi, y = 0 .. 4 * Pi, style = PATCH);
> plot4 := ":
```

[13]The default grid size is 25 by 25. The option **numpoint=n**, where **n** is an integer, will use a square grid of about the size of **sqrt(n)**.

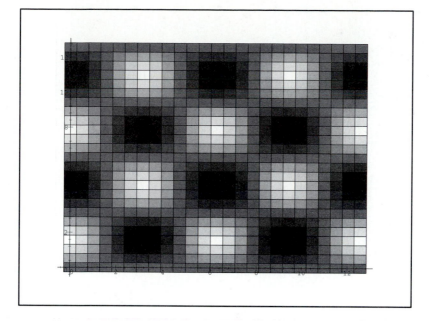

FIGURE 1.6
Density plot of the surface in Fig. 1.5.

and the resulting surface is illustrated in Fig. 1.8. Note that this surface does not vary with x since z depends only on y. Both Fig. 1.5 and Fig. 1.8 can be overlain with the `display3d` function from the `plots` package as follows:

```
> plots[display3d]({plot3, plot4});
```

This new surface may take a few additional moments to generate. When the figure does appear on the screen, it will look like the one shown in Fig. 1.9. As a final note to this section, *Maple* allows you to change your viewpoint of the surface. This can be done by manipulating the three-dimensional graphic window on most machines. Many other options can be altered to produce interesting, even stunning, visual effects. See Appendix B for additional details.

EXERCISES

1.1. Use *Maple* to verify the well-known formulas for factoring the sum and difference of two cubes. Determine all integers $3 < n \le 15$ such that $x^n + 1$ has more than two factors.

FIGURE 1.7
Contour plot of the surface shown in Fig. 1.5

1.2. Let $f(x) = x^x$. Plot $f(x)$ and $f'(x)$ on the interval $(0, 2]$ and graphically estimate the minimum value of $f(x)$. Can you determine an analytical expression for this value?

1.3. Let $g(x) = 1/\ln(x)$. Plot $\int g(x)\, dx$ on $(0, 3)$.

1.4. Let $h(x, y) = x/(x^2 + y^2)$. Plot the surface represented by $z = h(x, y)$ with $-1 \le x \le 1$ and $-1 \le y \le 1$. What is happening at the origin?

1.5. For many gases, viscosity μ is computed with Sutherland's formula:[14]

$$\mu = C_1 \frac{T^{1.5}}{T + C_2},$$

where T is the temperature in degrees Kelvin and both C_1 and C_2 are empirically-determined constants. For hydrogen, $C_1 = 0.649 \times 10^{-6}$ and $C_2 = 70.6$, while for nitrogen, $C_1 = 1.39 \times 10^{-6}$ and $C_2 = 102$. (Units for C_1 and C_2 are kg s^{-1}m^{-1}K$^{-0.5}$ and K respectively.) Plot the viscosity of both gases for the temperature range -20 to 120 degrees Celsius.

1.6. Burger's equation is a nonlinear parabolic partial differential equation which can be used to model certain types of viscous fluid flows. One form of this equation

[14]John J. Bertin, *Engineering Fluid Mechanics*, Prentice-Hall, Englewood Cliffs, 1984, pp. 12–13.

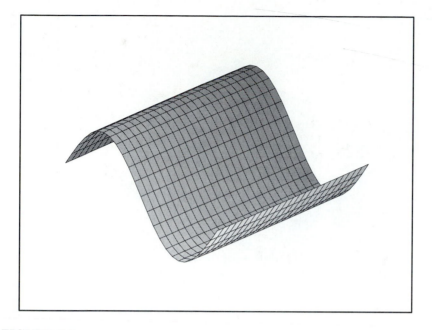

FIGURE 1.8
Plot of the surface $z = \sin(y/2)$ on $x \in [0, 4\pi]$ and $y \in [0, 4\pi]$.

is

$$\frac{\partial u}{\partial t} + (c + bu)\frac{\partial u}{\partial x} = \mu \frac{\partial^2 u}{\partial x^2}.$$

Surprisingly, this equation has the *exact* solution (when the flow is stationary) u given by[15]

$$u = -\frac{c}{b}\left[1 + \tanh \frac{c(x - x_0)}{2\mu}\right].$$

(*a*) Show by direct computation that the given form of u is actually a solution to Burger's equation.

(*b*) Let $c = 1$ and $\mu = 1/4$. Plot the surface corresponding to u as a function of both b and $(x - x_0)$. Experiment with values of b around -1 and a range of $x - x_0$ within three units either side of the origin.

1.7. When plane electromagnetic waves pass through a small circular aperture at an oblique angle, the transmission coefficients for the two states of polarization are given by:

$$T_{\parallel} = \frac{64}{27\pi^2}(ka)^4\left(\frac{4 + \sin^2 \alpha}{4\cos \alpha}\right),$$

[15]Dale A. Anderson, John C. Tannehill, and Richard H. Pletcher, *Computational Fluid Mechanics and Heat Transfer*, Hemisphere Publishing, Washington, 1984, p. 155.

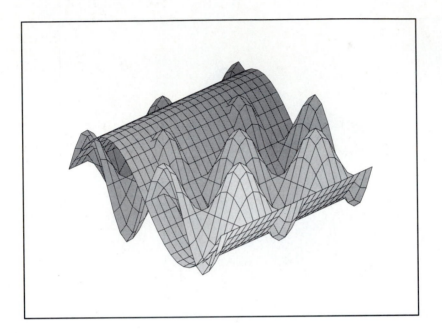

FIGURE 1.9
Intersection of the surfaces shown in Fig. 1.5 and Fig. 1.8. Note that *Maple* correctly hides masked portions of the surfaces.

and

$$T_\perp = \frac{64}{27\pi^2}(ka)^4 \cos\alpha,$$

where $T_\parallel$ and $T_\perp$ are the transmission coefficients for parallel and transverse polarization, a is the radius of the hole, k is the wave number, and α is the angle of incidence. Plot $T_\parallel$ and $T_\perp$ as functions of α and graphically determine values of α, if any, for which they are equal.

1.8. One result from the theory of special relativity is the parallel-velocity addition law:

$$v = \frac{v_1 + v_2}{1 + v_1 v_2/c^2},$$

where c is the speed of light. Plot v as a function of v_1 and v_2 and interpret the figure. [Hint: You may find it easier to use the dimensionless velocities $u_1 = v_1/c$ and $u_2 = v_2/c$.]

CHAPTER
2

VECTOR ALGEBRA

2.1 LABORATORY GOALS

a. To create vectors and perform basic algebraic manipulations with them.

b. To take dot products, cross products, and scalar triple products of vectors.

2.2 BUILDING VECTORS

Before proceeding further, the `linalg` package should be loaded:

```
> with(linalg):

Warning: new definition for    norm
Warning: new definition for    trace
```

Packages are collections of *Maple* functions and routines which must be loaded individually. Several dozen packages come with the *Maple* distribution. They are described in *The Maple Handbook*.[1] The warning messages tell us that the definitions of the `trace()` and `norm()` functions have had their definitions changed.[2]

---

[1] Redfern, *op. cit.*

[2] This presents no problem.

15

   Maple uses the notion of a *list* to build and manipulate vectors. A list is built by placing objects inside a a pair of square brackets, []. The list is then turned into a vector by passing the list to the **array()** function. For example, consider the three-dimensional vector $\mathbf{v}_1 = 3\mathbf{i} + 2\mathbf{j} - \mathbf{k}$.[3] This vector would be represented in *Maple* as:

```
> v1 := array([3, 2, -1]);
```
$$v1 := [\ 3,\ 2,\ -1\ ]$$

This object behaves just like we would expect a vector to behave. For example, scalar multiplication has the obvious effect:

```
> 3 * v1;
```
$$3\ v1$$
```
> evalm(");
```
$$[\ 9,\ 6,\ -3\ ]$$

Note that the multiplication is not actually distributed over the components of the vector until the **evalm()** function is invoked. **evalm()** is called whenever expressions involving matrices, vectors, and several special operators require evaluation.[4]

   Vector addition is also done as expected. Let $\mathbf{v}_2 = 4\mathbf{i} + 5\mathbf{j} + \mathbf{k}$. Then

```
> v2 := array([4, 5, 1]);
```
$$v2 := [\ 4,\ 5,\ 1\ ]$$

and the sum $\mathbf{v}_1 + \mathbf{v}_2$ is found by:

```
> evalm(v1 + v2);
```
$$[\ 7,\ 7,\ 0\ ]$$

---

[3]$\mathbf{i}$, $\mathbf{j}$, and $\mathbf{k}$ represent the three coordinate unit vectors in cartesian coordinates.

[4]We will see some of these special operators in later chapters.

To access a component of a vector, we use the name of the vector together with the [] construct. This operator gives us a way of grabbing on to the components of a vector.[5] Thus to extract the second element of $\mathbf{v}_1$, we give the following command:

```
> v1[2];

                              2
```

To replace any component of a vector, the same construct is used. For example, to change the third component of $\mathbf{v}_2$ from $\mathbf{k}$ to $-3\mathbf{k}$, we do the following:

```
> v2[3] := -3;

                        v2[3] := -3

> print(v2);

                     [ 4, 5, -3 ]
```

Note the use of the **print()** function to print the value of the expression **v2**.

The number of components, or length, of a vector is obtained with the **vectdim()** function:

```
> vectdim(v2);

                              3
```

Maple contains many other functions for manipulating the contents of lists, vectors, and as we will see later, matrices.

2.3   VECTOR PRODUCTS

Maple contains functions for computing the dot product and the cross product. For example, to compute $\mathbf{v}_1 \cdot \mathbf{v}_2$, we use the **dotprod()** function:[6]

---

[5]Think of it as a form of subscripting.

[6]The dot product here assumes that the vector is expressed in cartesian coordinates.

```
> dotprod(v1, v2);

                              25
```

The norm of a vector is easily determined using the `norm()` function.[7] `norm()` takes two arguments: the first is the name of the vector whose norm is needed, and the second is the type of norm.[8] The usual Euclidean norm is invoked when this argument is set to 2. Thus:

```
> norm(v1, 2);

                             1/2
                           14
```

Recalling that $\mathbf{v}_1 \cdot \mathbf{v}_2 = |\mathbf{v}_1||\mathbf{v}_2|\cos\theta$ where θ is the angle between the two vectors, we can find that angle as follows:

```
> arccos(dotprod(v1, v2) /
         (norm(v1, 2) * norm(v2, 2)));

                          1/2   1/2
             arccos(5/28 14    2    )
```

The result in degrees is obtained with:

```
> evalf(180 * " / Pi);

                    19.10660535
```

Another way to obtain this result is with the `angle()` function, which is part of the `linalg` package. This function takes two vectors as arguments and returns the angle between them:

---

[7]If you need this function and you have not loaded the `linalg` package, you can invoke it with by calling `linalg[norm](v1, 2)`.

[8]Other norms sometimes encountered are the one norm and the infinity norm. They are encountered in certain computer and signal processing applications.

```
> angle(v1, v2);

                                1/2    1/2
                     arccos(1/28 14     50    )

> evalf(convert(", degrees));

                       19.10660537 degrees
```

We then used the `convert()` and `evalf()` functions to convert the value returned by `angle()` into degrees.

Cross products are easily computed with the `crossprod()` function:[9]

```
> v3 := crossprod(v1, v2);

                       v3 := [ -1, 5, 7 ]
```

Note the result obtained for $\mathbf{v}_1 \cdot \mathbf{v}_2$:

```
> dotprod(v1, v3);

                                0
```

This is the well-known result that the cross product is orthogonal to both its factors.

The scalar triple product is given by the formula $\mathbf{v}_1 \cdot (\mathbf{v}_2 \times \mathbf{v}_3)$. Although *Maple* does not have a built-in function to compute scalar triple products, we can *define* a function with does so, as shown in the following command:

```
> tripprod := (a, b, c) -> dotprod(a, crossprod(b, c));

           tripprod := (a,b,c) -> dotprod(a, crossprod(b, c))
```

This command has the following effect: it defines `tripprod()` to be function of three variables, `(a, b, c)`, and returns the value of the expression `dotprod(a, crossprod(b, c))`.[10] It is invoked like any other *Maple* function:

---

[9] Also assuming cartesian coordinates for now.

[10] a, b, and c are dummy variables.

```
> tripprod(v1, v2, v3);

                                    75
```

2.4   DETERMINING DIRECTION COSINES

As an application of these vector abilities of *Maple* we will now develop expressions for the direction cosines of a vector. The direction cosines are the cosines of the angles a given vector makes with the three unit vectors each of which are parallel to the cartesian coordinate axes. If α is the direction cosine from $\mathbf{v}$ to $\mathbf{i}$, then $\cos \alpha = (\mathbf{v} \cdot \mathbf{i})/(|\mathbf{v}||\mathbf{i}|)$. But $\mathbf{v} \cdot \mathbf{i}$ is just the first component of $\mathbf{v}$ and $|\mathbf{i}| = 1$. Using similar arguments for the other two direction cosines, we can determine the three direction cosines for $\mathbf{v}_1$:

```
> dcosalpha := v1[1] / norm(v1, 2);

                                            1/2
                        dcosalpha := 3/14 14

> dcosbeta := v1[2] / norm(v1, 2);

                                          1/2
                        dcosbeta := 1/7 14

> dcosgamma := v1[3] / norm(v1, 2);

                                             1/2
                        dcosgamma := - 1/14 14
```

Note that the sum of the squares of the three direction cosines is one:

```
> dcosalpha^2 + dcosbeta^2 + dcosgamma^2;

                                    1
```

2.5   APPLICATIONS

Consider the situation as depicted in Fig. 2.1. Three cables are attached to a fastening as indicated. The tensions on the wires are $F_1 = 500$ N, $F_2 = 400$

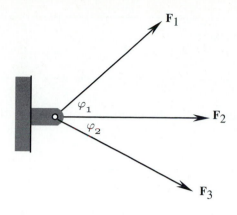

FIGURE 2.1
Three wires under tension pull on a hook attached to a wall. The net force on the hook is sought.

N, and $F_3 = 700$ N. The angles are $\varphi_1 = 30°$ and $\varphi_2 = -50°$. We need to determine the magnitude and direction of the resultant force. First, we write each force as a vector:

```
> f1 := 500 * array([cos(30 * Pi / 180), sin(30 * Pi / 180)]);

                            1/2
                f1 := 500 [ 1/2 3    , 1/2 ]

> f2 := 400 * array([1, 0]);

                    f2 := 400 [ 1, 0 ]

> f3 := 700 * array([cos(-50 * Pi / 180), sin(-50 * Pi / 180)]);

            f3 := 700 [ cos(5/18 Pi), - sin(5/18 Pi) ]
```

The resultant is obtained by adding the three forces:

```
> fr := evalm(f1 + f2 + f3);

              1/2
    fr := [ 250 3    + 400 + 700 cos(5/18 Pi), 250 - 700 sin(5/18 Pi) ]
```

The magnitude of the resultant is given by the norm of `fr`:

```
> evalf(norm(fr, 2));

                              1.
```

To determine the direction of the resultant, we compute the angle between its two components:

```
> arctan(fr[2]/fr[1]);

                        250 - 700 sin(5/18 Pi)
              arctan(-------------------------------)
                              1/2
                        250 3    + 400 + 700 cos(5/18 Pi)
```

We can express this as a result in degrees with the following operation:

```
> evalf(" * 180 / Pi);

                          -12.57680310
```

Therefore the resultant force direction is about $12.6°$ *below* the horizontal reference line.

Now consider the bracket shown in Fig. 2.2. A force of magnitude 10 N is applied at angle of $\varphi = 40°$ at the indicated point. The two sides of the bracket are $a = 4$ cm and $b = 3$ cm respectively. We seek the magnitude of the moment generated by the force about the point O.

First, we write the force as a vector. Since we will take cross products, we include the z-component of the force:

```
> f := 10 * array([cos(40 * Pi / 180), sin(40 * Pi / 180), 0]);

              f := 10 [ cos(2/9 Pi), sin(2/9 Pi), 0 ]
```

The moment arm length is 5 cm (by inspection), and the cosine moment arm angle is 4/5 while the sine is 3/5. Thus the moment arm is written in vector form as

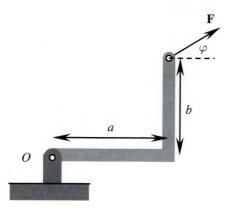

FIGURE 2.2
A force **F** produces a moment about the point O.

```
> r := 5 * array([4/5, 3/5, 0]) / 100;

              r := 1/20 [ 4/5, 3/5, 0 ]
```

where we have divided by 100 in order to convert the result to meters. The moment is given by $\mathbf{M} = \mathbf{r} \times \mathbf{F}$, which is expressed in *Maple* as

```
> m := crossprod(r, f);

        m := [ 0, 0, 2/5 sin(2/9 Pi) - 3/10 cos(2/9 Pi) ]
```

The magnitude of the moment is then found to be

```
> evalf(norm(m));

                    .0273017110
```

Thus, $|M| = 2.73 \times 10^{-2}$ N-m.

EXERCISES

2.1. Write a sequence of *Maple* statements which reverses the components of a given three-dimensional vector.

2.2. Determine the angle between the vectors $(3, 7, 1)$ and $(9, -3, -3)$. [With this notation, $(3, 7, 1) = 3\mathbf{i} + 7\mathbf{j} + \mathbf{k}$.]

2.3. Determine the direction cosines of the following vectors:
(a) $(2, 3, 1)$
(b) $(-1, -1, -2)$

2.4. Evaluate the cross products:
(a) $(3, 2, 1)$ with $(1, 2, 3)$
(b) $(2, 2, 1)$ with $(-4, -4, -2)$

2.5. A block of weight 10 lbs is placed on a plane inclined at an angle of θ as shown in Fig. 2.3. The coefficient of friction is $\mu = 0.32$. What is the largest inclination

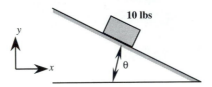

FIGURE 2.3
The block is at rest on the inclined plane.

angle θ by which the plane can be inclined without slippage?

2.6. A mass weighing 5 N is suspended from two cables as shown in Fig. 2.4.

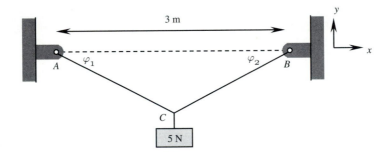

FIGURE 2.4
The weight is at rest.

(a) Determine the tension in the cables if $\varphi_1 = \varphi_2 = 20°$.
(b) Determine the tension in the cables if $\varphi_1 = \varphi_2 = 10°$.

2.7. A force with magnitude 11 kN is applied to the links pinned together at C as shown in Fig. 2.5. The length of each link is 2.5 m. Determine the moments $\mathbf{M}_A$ and $\mathbf{M}_B$.

2.8. Evaluate the scalar triple product of $(2, 0, 1)$, $(3, 2, 1)$, and $(a, -2, -1)$. For what value of a does the triple product vanish?

2.9. A pick-up truck has been stranded in a ditch, but the driver has a coil of rope in the back of the vehicle. He ties one end of the rope to the front of the truck and the other end tightly to a telephone pole about 12 meters from the truck. He then pushes on the middle of the rope with a force of about 500 N, displacing the center of the rope 1 meter from its equilibrium position. What force is exerted

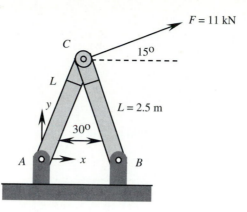

FIGURE 2.5
The force is applied in the indicated direction to a pair of identical pinned links.

on the truck? Assuming this force were sufficient to move the truck and that the driver pushed the midpoint of the rope an additional 1 meter, how far would the truck move? Would you conclude that this is a practical method for getting a vehicle out of a ditch?

CHAPTER
3

MANIPULATING DISCRETE DATA

3.1 LABORATORY GOALS

a. To perform basic manipulations on arrays of numbers.

b. To read discrete data from a file into a *Maple* list.

c. To construct interpolating functions to discrete data sets.

d. To plot discrete data sets.

3.2 ARRAYS

Maple provides a variety of useful functions for the manipulation of discrete sets of data. The most basic form used is that of the array. Arrays are built from lists of objects separated by commas and delineated by square brackets that are then passed to the `array()` function. Thus[1]

```
> a := array([-1, 2, 1, 1/2]);

                a := [ -1, 2, 1, 1/2 ]
```

[1] In character mode *Maple* displays arrays and lists in the same way, although they will behave differently when passed as arguments to certain functions or used with certain operators. If you are using a worksheet with true-math notation, then the array will not contain commas; elements will be delineated by spaces only. A list in true-math notation will still have commas.

a is an array containing four numbers. The elements of a array can be anything: numbers, variables, functions, and even other arrays or lists. In this laboratory we are concerned primarily with arrays of numbers.

There are many ways to manipulate arrays. For example, each element of the array a can be incremented by 1 by just adding 1 to the array. Thus,

```
> a + 1;

                            a + 1
> evalm(");

                    [ 0, 3, 2, 3/2 ]
```

The `evalm()` function causes expressions passed to it that involve arrays to be evaluated. Arrays can also be scaled by multiplying them by a scaling factor. For example,

```
> b := evalm(2 * a);

                b := [ -2, 4, 2, 1 ]
```

Arrays can also be used as arguments to many functions. This is done through the use of the `map()` function. The result obtained is that the function is *mapped* or applied to each element of the array which, of course, produces a new array:

```
> map(abs, map(sqrt, b));

              1/2        1/2
          [ 2    , 2, 2    , 1 ]
```

In this example, `map()` was first used to apply the `sqrt()` function to b, and then used again to take the modulus of each term in that result with the `abs()` function. An equivalent result can be obtained with the composition operator @ which permits `map()` to work directly with the composition of the two functions `sqrt()` and `abs()`:

```
> map(abs@sqrt, b);
              1/2        1/2
          [ 2    , 2, 2    , 1 ]
```

Two arrays of the same dimensions may be added, subtracted, multiplied, or divided, and the result is a new array whose components are obtained by applying the operation term-by-term to the elements of the two arrays. Arrays are added or subtracted as in this example:

```
> evalm(a + b);

              [ -3, 6, 3, 3/2 ]
```

To multiply or divide array elements, we first need to define a function which we can pass to the `zip()` for application. For example, we can define a divide function with the following construct:

```
> div := (x, y) -> x / y;

              div := (x,y) -> x/y
```

This defines a function named `div()` that takes two variables, and returns the ratio of those variables.[2] To apply this function to the two arrays, we use it in a call to `zip()`:

```
> zip(div, a, b);

              [ 1/2, 1/2, 1/2, 1/2 ]
```

This call to `zip()` returns a list whose nth element is obtained by using the nth arguments of a and b as arguments to `div()`.[3]

Attempts to operate on two lists with different numbers of elements will generate an error message:

```
> c := array([2, 1, 2, 1, -2]);

              c := [ 2, 1, 2, 1, -2 ]

> evalm(a + c);

Error, (in linalg[add]) vector dimensions incompatible
```

---

[2]In defining functions this way, the two arguments x and y are *local* variables. They function as place-holders only—we might just as well have used a and b or any other pair of symbols.

[3]Note that `zip()` returns a list, not an array.

3.3   READING LISTS OF DATA

TABLE 3.1
Rotary Pump Speed Reduction

Fluid Viscosity	Percentage Reduction of Pump Speed
600	2
800	6
1000	10
1500	12
2000	14
4000	20
6000	30
8000	40
10000	50
20000	55
30000	57
40000	60

Maple has the ability to read data into a list structure. This is useful when discrete data are available from, say, an experiment or data table. For example, consider the data in Table 3.1, which indicate the reduction in percent of rated pump speed for different liquid viscosities. Suppose these data are contained in the file with name `PumpData`, with each viscosity and reduction entry on a separate line. The first three lines in this file might look like this:

```
600    2
800    6
1000   10
```

We can use the `readdata()` function to read the contents of this file into a *Maple* list. `readdata()` takes three arguments. The first is the name of the file to be read, entered as string, and the second tells *Maple* what kind of data types to expect. These can be either `integer` of `float` In this instance, all the data are of type `float`. After we tell *Maple* about `readdata()` with the `readlib()` function, the file is read in as follows:

```
> readlib(readdata):
> pumpdata := readdata('PumpData.Maple', float, 2);

 pumpdata := [[600., 2.], [800., 6.], [1000., 10.], [1500., 12.],

     [2000., 14.], [4000., 20.], [6000., 30.], [8000., 40.], [10000., 50.],
```

```
        [20000., 55.], [30000., 57.], [40000., 60.]]
```

We can no convert this list into a matrix with the `convert()` function:

```
> pumpdata := convert(pumpdata, matrix);
```

$$
pumpdata := \begin{bmatrix}
600. & 2. \\
800. & 6. \\
1000. & 10. \\
1500. & 12. \\
2000. & 14. \\
4000. & 20. \\
6000. & 30. \\
8000. & 40. \\
10000. & 50. \\
20000. & 55. \\
30000. & 57. \\
40000. & 60.
\end{bmatrix}
$$

We can now plot these data with the `plot()` function:

```
> plot(pumpdata, style=POINT);
```

with the result shown in Fig. 3.1.   Note that *Maple* has automatically scaled the two axes to conform to the range of data corresponding to each axis. The style option `POINT` tells *Maple* to plot the data as discrete points.

In this example, it may be more natural to think of the pump reduction percentage as a function of fluid viscosity. This involves transposing the two coordinate axes. In order to do this in *Maple* we will have to switch the data in each pair of coordinates contained in `pumpdata`. The first step involves determining the transpose of the `pumpdata` data set. This is done with the `transpose()` function. Since this function is part of the `linalg` package which we have not loaded during this session, we must tell *Maple* where to find `transpose()`:

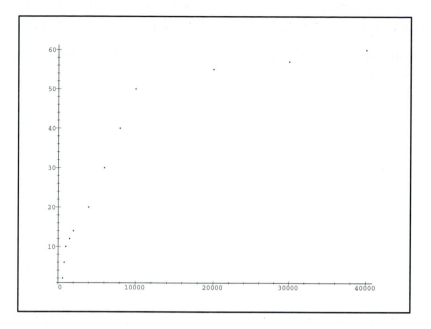

FIGURE 3.1
Discrete plot of the data contained in Table 3.1.

```
> t1 := linalg[transpose](pumpdata);

t1 :=

    [600, 800, 1000, 1500, 2000, 4000, 6000, 8000, 10000, 20000, 30000, 40000]

              [2, 6, 10, 12, 14, 20, 30, 40, 50, 55, 57, 60]
```

The result of this calculation is now a 2x12 matrix. The first row corresponds to the viscosities, while the second represents the pump reduction rates. Next we interchange these two rows of data with the **swaprow()** function:[4]

```
> t2 := linalg[swaprow](t1, 1, 2);

t2 :=
```

[4]**swaprow()** is also in the **linalg** package.

$$[2, \; 6, \; 10, \; 12, \; 14, \; 20, \; 30, \; 40, \; 50, \; 55, \; 57, \; 60]$$

$$[600, \; 800, \; 1000, \; 1500, \; 2000, \; 4000, \; 6000, \; 8000, \; 10000, \; 20000, \; 30000, \; 40000]$$

Finally, we transpose this back to the original form of the data set with another call to **transpose()**:

```
> t3 := linalg[transpose](t2);
```

$$
t3 := \begin{bmatrix}
2 & 600 \\
6 & 800 \\
10 & 1000 \\
12 & 1500 \\
14 & 2000 \\
20 & 4000 \\
30 & 6000 \\
40 & 8000 \\
50 & 10000 \\
55 & 20000 \\
57 & 30000 \\
60 & 40000
\end{bmatrix}
$$

We can see from this *Maple* expression that the data has the desired form, i.e. an array of lists each of which contains two numbers. To verify our work, we plot this last array again with **plot()**:

```
> plot(t3, style=POINT);
```

The result is shown in Fig. 3.2.

We can also use *Maple* to construct functions which approximate discrete data sets. One way this is done with the **spline()** function. First, we make this function available with the following call to **readlib()**:[5]

---

[5]Be sure to terminate this command with a colon!

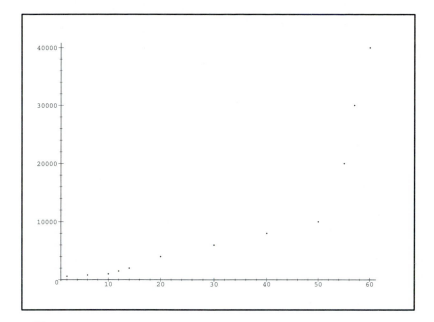

FIGURE 3.2
Discrete transposed plot of the data contained in Table 3.1.

```
> readlib(spline):
```

The `spline()` takes four arguments: two arrays which contain the independent and dependent variable data respectively, the name of the independent variable we wish to use, and the type of spline desired. In the following example, we use the `col()` function to extract the first and second columns from `t3` for passing to `spline()`, we choose x as our independent variable, and we request a cubic spline:[6]

```
> s :=  spline(linalg[col](t3, 1), linalg[col](t3, 2), x, cubic):
```

Be sure to use a colon after the call to `spline()`! Otherwise, *Maple* will return the detailed structure of the spline function, something we don't need to worry about

---

[6]For a more complete discussion of how this and other interpolating functions work, see *The Maple Handbook*.

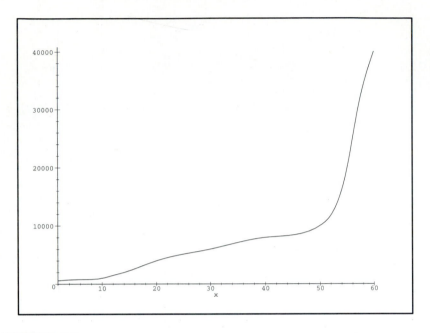

FIGURE 3.3
Continuous approximation to the discrete transposed plot of the data contained in Table 3.1.

right now. Before we can use this spline for plots and other computations, we must turn it into a *Maple* procedure. This is done with a call to the `makeproc()` function:

```
> pumpf := 'spline/makeproc'(s,x):
```

`pumpf()` is our desired spline function.

We are now ready to use this spline for plotting. Note that we must force *Maple* to postpone immediate evaluation of the by enclosing it in single quotes ' as it is passed `plot()`. Failure to do so will produce an error.[7]

```
> plot('pumpf(x)', x = 2 .. 60);
```

---

[7]By omitting the single quotes, the call to `pumpf()` with argument x will fail, since x does not yet have a value. In other words, passing `pumpf(x)` to `plot` without quotes causes the immediate (and undesired) evaluation of the spline.

The result is shown in Fig. 3.3. Compare this result to that shown in Fig. 3.2. The approximation is excellent. This function could now be used to provide estimates of the reduction rate for different viscosities, to obtain mean values of selected ranges, and for other purposes as well.

3.4 PLOTTING MULTIDIMENSIONAL DATA

Discrete data are also frequently available for cases in which there are more than one independent variable. *Maple* can also plot this type of data, although it has no interpolating functions in its standard load of packages with a multidimensional ability. For example, consider the data given in the following *Maple* expression:

```
> surf := array([[1, 2, 3, 4], [1, 2, 1, 2], [2, 2, 3, 3],
        [4, 3, 2, 1]]);

                        [ 1  2  3  4 ]
                        [            ]
                        [ 1  2  1  2 ]
             surf :=  [            ]
                        [ 2  2  3  3 ]
                        [            ]
                        [ 4  3  2  1 ]
```

The array `surf` contains four lists each containing four data values. To generate a surface with these data function, we must construct a list containing coordinates for each of the data points. One way to do this is with the `seq()` function. We will assume that the coordinate values run from 1 through 4 for both independent variables. The following rather ponderous expression constructs a table of three-element lists. The first and second element of each list correspond to the variables `i` and `j`. The third element corresponds to the appropriate data point for that set of coordinates, and is obtained by picking the right value from the set of data in `surf`.[8]

```
> A := [seq([seq([i,j,surf[i,j]], i=1..4) ], j=1..4)];

    A := [[[1, 1, 1], [2, 1, 1], [3, 1, 2], [4, 1, 4]],

          [[1, 2, 2], [2, 2, 2], [3, 2, 2], [4, 2, 3]],

          [[1, 3, 3], [2, 3, 1], [3, 3, 3], [4, 3, 2]],

          [[1, 4, 4], [2, 4, 2], [3, 4, 3], [4, 4, 1]]]
```

[8]Facility with multidimensional data sets requires a great deal of practice!

We can use `surfdata()`[9] to visualize the surface corresponding to these data:

```
> plots[surfdata](A, style=PATCH);
```

The resulting surface is displayed in Fig. 3.4.

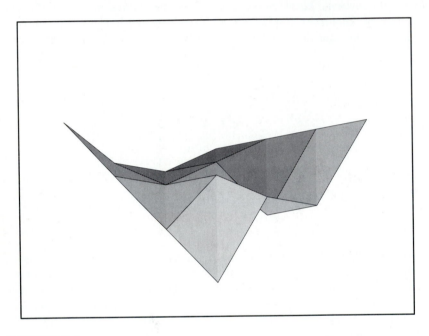

FIGURE 3.4
Approximation of example three-dimensional data set.

EXERCISES

3.1. Use the `seq()` function to build a list containing the function $f(x) = (\sin x)/x$ evaluated at the points $x = n\pi/10$, with $n = 1, 2, \ldots, 10$. Build an interpolating function using different values for `InterpolatingOrder`. Which choice gives the best approximation? Which choices give poorer approximations? Can you think of some reasons why?

3.2. The required minimum fire flow rates for municipalities with indicated populations are listed in Table 3.2. Plot the flow rates as a function of population. Determine an interpolating polynomial for the flow rate and estimate the required rate for a city of population 115,000.

[9]`surfdata()` is part of the `plots` package.

TABLE 3.2
Required Fire Flow Rates

Population Thousands	Flow Rate liter/(second)
22	284
28	315
40	379
60	442
80	505
100	568
125	631
150	694
200	757

3.3. In a certain North American City, the average monthly percentages of sunshine and total insolation (the total amount of energy arriving in that city from the sun) is given in Table 3.3.

(a) Plot the percentage of sunshine and total insolation as a function of the month.

(b) If a certain solar collector has a total surface area of $1.2 m^2$, and operates with an efficiency of 41%, determine the average monthly energy output of the collector.

(c) Determine the average annual energy output of the collector.

TABLE 3.3
Solar Energy Availability

Month	Mean Sunshine Percent	Total Insolation $W/(m^2 day)$
Jan	49	4662.9
Feb	54	6220.1
Mar	55	7025.5
Apr	57	7150.1
May	60	7044.4
Jun	64	6955.7
Jul	72	6939.5
Aug	69	6940.4
Sep	60	6675.7
Oct	54	5870.6
Nov	40	4565.5
Dec	40	3941.2

3.4. The cross-sectional temperature distribution (in relative degrees) of a rectangular plate is given in Table 3.4. The plate dimensions are 4 cm and 5 cm respectively. Temperatures are provided at equi-spaced nodes as indicated in the table.

(a) Plot the temperature distribution as a function of both dimensions.

(*b*) Can you think of a way to determine the average value of the temperature distribution?

TABLE 3.4
Temperature Distribution of Plate.

	0	1	2	3	4
0	0	0	0	0	0
1	0	0.07	0	−0.2	−0.38
2	0	0.083	0	−0.25	−0.47
3	0	−0.12	0	0.37	0.71
4	0	−0.27	0	0.81	1.52
5	0.1	0	−0.11	0	0.09

MATRICES

4.1 LABORATORY GOALS

a. To learn the syntax of matrix manipulation with *Maple*.

b. To compute eigenvalues and eigenvectors of square matrices.

c. To use matrices to compute n-step transition probabilities.

d. To become familiar with writing *Maple* procedures.

e. To use matrices to encrypt and decrypt messages.

4.2 PRODUCTS, TRANSPOSES, AND INVERSES

Matrices and matrix manipulation methods are used extensively throughout engineering mathematics. Models of many systems and approximations to many models can assume the form of a matrix. Before proceeding, we need to load the `linalg` into *Maple*:

```
> with(linalg):

Warning: new definition for    norm
Warning: new definition for    trace
```

Consider the matrix A with

$$A = \begin{bmatrix} 1 & 2 \\ 3 & 4 \end{bmatrix}. \tag{4.1}$$

This matrix can be entered into *Maple* by converting a list of lists into an array. Thus each row of the matrix is in the form of a list. For example,

```
> a := array([[1, 2], [3, 4]]);

                    [ 1   2 ]
              a := [        ]
                    [ 3   4 ]
```

Maple contains a number of functions for manipulating matrices, especially square matrices. For example, let $B = A^{-1}$. To determine the inverse B, we can use the `inverse()` function:

```
> b := inverse(a);

                    [ -2    1  ]
              b := [           ]
                    [ 3/2  -1/2 ]
```

Note that *Maple* uses exact arithmetic in calculating the inverse of this matrix.[1] To demonstrate that B is in fact the inverse of A, we can multiply the two together with the `&*` operator and evaluating the subsequent expression with a call to the `evalm()` function:

```
> evalm(a &* b);

                    [ 1   0 ]
                    [       ]
                    [ 0   1 ]
```

You may recognize this as the identity matrix. Matrix multiplication can be done with matrices of any size, provided the dimensions are compatible.

It is also straightforward to determine A^T, the transpose of A, and $|A|$, the determinant of A. Each is returned by the `transpose()` and `det()` functions respectively:

---

[1] Whenever *Maple* encounters expressions containing symbols (such as `Pi`), variables, integers and rational numbers (explicit ratios of integers), the arithmetic is done exactly.

```
> transpose(a);
                                [ 1   3 ]
                                [       ]
                                [ 2   4 ]


> det(a);
                                  -2
```

For example, consider the matrix A with

$$A = \begin{bmatrix} 1 & 2 & 1 \\ 1 & -1 & 5 \\ d & 2 & -1 \end{bmatrix} \qquad (4.2)$$

For what values of d is this matrix singular? First, enter A into *Maple*:

```
> A := array([[1, 2, 1], [1, -1, 5], [d, 2, 1]]);
                                [ 1    2   1 ]
                                [            ]
                          A := [ 1   -1   5 ]
                                [            ]
                                [ d    2   1 ]
```

Now, compute A^{-1}:

```
> B := inverse(A);
              [            1                            1          ]
              [        - -------          0          -------       ]
              [          - 1 + d                     - 1 + d       ]
              [                                                    ]
              [        - 1 + 5 d                        4          ]
        B := [ 1/11  ---------      -1/11    -   -------------     ]
              [        - 1 + d                    11 (- 1 + d)     ]
              [                                                    ]
              [          2 + d                         3           ]
              [ 1/11   -------        2/11    -   -------------     ]
              [        - 1 + d                    11 (- 1 + d)     ]
```

from which we see that the inverse exists if and only if $d \neq 1$. A specific value of d can be used to get a particular result. Suppose we want to let $d = 2$. This substitution is made with the **subs()** function. This function takes two arguments. The first is the substituted variable, while the second is the expression into which the substitution will be made.

```
> subs(d = 2, evalm(B));

                    [  -1     0     1  ]
                    [                  ]
                    [ 9/11  -1/11  -4/11 ]
                    [                  ]
                    [ 4/11   2/11  -3/11 ]
```

4.3   POWERS, EIGENVALUES, AND EIGENVECTORS

Additional *Maple* functions allow you to compute matrix powers, eigenvalues, and eigenvectors. For example, the eigenvalues of A can be found with the `eigenvals()` function:

```
> eigA := eigenvals(A);

              1/3    - 40/9 - 1/3 d
    eigA := %1     - -------------- + 1/3,
                          1/3
                        %1


          1/3        - 40/9 - 1/3 d               1/2 /  1/3    - 40/9 - 1/3 d\
  - 1/2 %1    + 1/2 -------------- + 1/3 + 1/2 I 3    |%1     + --------------|
                          1/3                        |             1/3      |
                        %1                           \            %1        /


      ,

          1/3        - 40/9 - 1/3 d               1/2 /  1/3    - 40/9 - 1/3 d\
  - 1/2 %1    + 1/2 -------------- + 1/3 - 1/2 I 3    |%1     + --------------|
                          1/3                        |             1/3      |
                        %1                           \            %1        /


            89                                    2      3 1/2
    %1 :=  - ---- + 17/3 d + 1/9 (- 6231 - 4626 d + 2481 d  - 3 d )
            27
```

an exact sequence containing the eigenvalues. In order to shorten the expression, note that *Maple* generates the symbol %1 to be used in the eigenvalues, and then lists the definition for that symbol in the last line of the output.

We can access the individual eigenvalues by using the selection operator []. Thus, the first eigenvalue in the sequence can be obtained with the the symbol `eigA[1]`:

```
> eigA[1];

  /   89                                        2       3 1/2\1/3
  |- ---- + 17/3 d + 1/9 (- 6231 - 4626 d + 2481 d   - 3 d )   |
  \   27                                                       /

                                    - 40/9 - 1/3 d
  -  --------------------------------------------------------------
      /   89                                        2       3 1/2\1/3
      |- ---- + 17/3 d + 1/9 (- 6231 - 4626 d + 2481 d   - 3 d )   |
      \   27                                                       /

  + 1/3
```

Note that *Maple* made the substitution for %1 automatically.

One benefit to symbolic manipulation of matrices is apparent from this example. The eigenvalue list above provides one simple and direct way to study how that eigenvalue depends upon the parameter d. There is, in general, no simple and direct way to do this.

Eigenvectors are computed with the **eigenvects()** function. We use this function to obtain the following (formidable) result:

```
> eigvA := eigenvects(A);

eigvA := [

                    2                              2       2
              %1 d + 11 - %1          2 %1 + 2 %1 d - d %1  + 9 d + d  - 2
  %1, 1, {[ ---------------, - 1/2 ------------------------------------, 1 ]}
                2                                    2
              d  - 2 d - 2                         d  - 2 d - 2

  ]

                          3    2
  %1 :=        RootOf(_Z  - _Z  + (- 13 - d) _Z + 11 - 11 d)
```

The **eigenvects()** function returns a list of three items. The first element of the list is the eigenvalue, the second is the multiplicity of that eigenvalue, and the third is a set containing the corresponding eigenvalues. Note that *Maple* again simplifies the output through the use of the expression %1. The **RootOf()** function used in %1 represents the roots of the given polynomial with respect to the variable _Z.[2]

---

[2] The command **eigenvects(A, radical)** would produced expressions for the eigenvectors in radicals, without the appearance of the **RootOf()** function.

Calculating eigenvectors for such a matrix by hand would be unthinkable, yet *Maple* makes this kind of computation effortlessly.[3] Even more, the tedious additional work sometimes required for eigenvectors corresponding to eigenvalues of multiplicity greater than one is obviated.

Suppose we want the eigenvectors evaluated when $d = 3$. We can obtain this with the `subs()` function and the selection operator:

```
> subs(d = 3, eigvA);

                              2               2
        [%1, 1, {[ 3 %1 + 11 - %1 , - 17 + 3/2 %1  - 4 %1, 1 ]}]

                              3   2
%1 :=                RootOf(_Z  - _Z  - 16 _Z - 22)
\end{mathemtica}
This symbolic result can be converted into a numerical expression with the
{\tt allvalues()}\indf{allvalues} and {\tt evalf()}\indf{evalf} functions:
\begin{mathematica}
> tmp1 := evalf(allvalues(", 'd'));

tmp1 := [5.040349812, 1., {[ .71592321, .946290104, 1. ]}],

[ - 2.020174906 + .5326065770 I, 1.,

    {[ 1.142038397 + 3.749736614 I,  - 3.223145042 - 5.358301633 I, 1. ]}],

[ - 2.020174906 - .5326065770 I, 1.,

    {[ 1.142038397 - 3.749736614 I,  - 3.223145042 + 5.358301633 I, 1. ]}]
```

The `allvalues()` function causes the roots of the expression in `RootOf()` to be evaluated. The optional parameter `'d'` ensures that the evaluation of `RootsOf()` is done only once for each evaluation of `eigvA`. Finally, `evalf()` forces numerical evaluations of the subsequent expressions. In this case, we can see that there are three distinct eigenvalues, each of multiplicity one. Individual eigenvectors can be picked with the appropriate selection operator. For example,

```
> tmp1[1][3];

                {[ .71592321, .946290104, 1. ]}
```

returns the eigenvector associated with the first eigenvalue.

---

[3]Effortless in the sense that the machine does all the work. The actual determination of these eigenvalues can take some time. The eigenvectors of A took many minutes to find on the author's Macintosh IIci.

It is also possible to generate the powers of a matrix using the `evalm()` function. For example, let

$$B = \begin{bmatrix} -1 & 1 & 0 & 0 \\ 2 & 0 & 0 & 1 \\ 0 & 1 & 0 & 0 \\ 0 & -1 & 0 & -3 \end{bmatrix}, \tag{4.3}$$

and suppose we require B^5. First, enter B into *Maple*. Then we use the exponentiation operator to raise B to the fifth power and pass this result to `evalm()`:

```
> B := array([[-1,1,0,0], [2,0,0,1], [0,1,0,0], [0,-1,0,-3]]);

            [ -1    1   0    0 ]
            [                  ]
            [  2    0   0    1 ]
       B := [                  ]
            [  0    1   0    0 ]
            [                  ]
            [  0   -1   0   -3 ]

> evalm(B^5);

            [ -11   -5   0   -43 ]
            [                    ]
            [ -10   27   0    81 ]
            [                    ]
            [  -2   -6   0   -29 ]
            [                    ]
            [  86  -81   0  -130 ]
```

As you can see, the ability of *Maple* to manipulate matrices is extraordinary, making the exploration of matrix applications in engineering mathematics an exciting possibility.

4.4 TRANSITION PROBABILITIES

Consider a two-player game in which each player starts with $2. A coin is flipped and player A calls it. If the call is correct, player A wins $1 from B, else he loses $1 to B. Assuming that the coin is fair, the probability of gaining or losing a dollar on each turn is $1/2$, unless either player is bankrupt. This situation is modeled mathematically by saying that there are five possible states for player A (and thus for player B), S_{i+1}, $i = 0, \ldots, 4$ where i represents the amount of money in the possession of A. If A has one, two, or three dollars, the probability of gaining or losing a dollar is $1/2$, i.e. the probability $p_{i(i \pm 1)}$ of moving from state S_i to S_{i+1} is $1/2$ if $i = 1, 2, 3$. If A is bankrupt, the probability of remaining so is 1 and of changing to any other state is 0. Thus $p_{11} = 1$ and $p_{1j} = 0$ if $j > 1$. Similarly if B is bankrupt, the probability that A gains or loses any money is 0 while the probability that A remains with all the money is 1. Thus $p_{55} = 1$ and $p_{5j} = 0$ if $j < 5$. This set of probabilities can be described by the probability transition matrix P:

$$P = \begin{bmatrix} 1 & 0 & 0 & 0 & 0 \\ 1/2 & 0 & 1/2 & 0 & 0 \\ 0 & 1/2 & 0 & 1/2 & 0 \\ 0 & 0 & 1/2 & 0 & 1/2 \\ 0 & 0 & 0 & 0 & 1 \end{bmatrix}, \tag{4.4}$$

This matrix is entered in *Maple* as follows:

```
>  P := array([[1, 0, 0, 0, 0],
             [1/2, 0, 1/2, 0, 0],
             [0, 1/2, 0, 1/2, 0],
             [0, 0, 1/2, 0, 1/2],
             [0, 0, 0, 0, 1]]);

              [ 1    0    0    0    0 ]
              [                       ]
              [ 1/2  0   1/2   0    0 ]
              [                       ]
        P := [  0   1/2   0   1/2   0 ]
              [                       ]
              [  0    0   1/2   0   1/2 ]
              [                       ]
              [  0    0    0    0    1 ]
```

The probabilities of two-step transitions are merely components of the square of this matrix, and the n-step transition probabilities are given in P^n. For example, what is the probability that A is bankrupt after 4 turns? First, we calculate P^4:

```
> evalm(P^4);

              [ 1    0    0    0    0 ]
              [                       ]
              [ 5/8  1/8   0   1/8  1/8 ]
              [                       ]
              [ 3/8   0   1/4   0   3/8 ]
              [                       ]
              [ 1/8  1/8   0   1/8  5/8 ]
              [                       ]
              [  0    0    0    0    1 ]
```

This probability corresponds to the transition from S_3 (that A has two dollars) to S_1 (A has nothing), or $p_{31}^{(4)}$. Note that the superscript $^{(4)}$ denotes that the element is taken from P^4. From the *Maple* result, we see that $p_{31}^{(4)} = 3/8$.

4.5 APPLICATION TO CRYPTOGRAPHY

Another interesting application of matrices is to the encoding and decoding of information. There are many ways to attack this problem, but we will use one based on an interesting property of matrices with integer elements. If a matrix A has integer elements, then its inverse A^{-1} will have integer coefficients if and only if $|A| = \pm 1$. Suppose we have such a pair of matrices. Let **b** be an n-component vector with all integer entries. **b** is called the *plaintext*. The product $A\mathbf{b}$ is called the *ciphertext*. The ciphertext is decode by multiplying it by A^{-1}. The reason for insisting on integer coefficients for both A and its inverse is straightforward: integer arithmetic is exact, that is, it can be performed by machines without introducing any round-off errors. This guarantees that the ciphertext will produce an exact copy of the plain text when the matrix multiplication is performed.

Suppose we want to encipher the message "Meet noon" using this method. Our approach will be to take the plaintext and convert it into nine integers using the standard ASCII codes.[4] Then we construct a 3x3 array containing these nine integers. We produce the ciphertext by multiplying the plaintext by the *key* matrix, and demonstrate how the process is reversed.

The first requirement is a key matrix, a 3x3 array of integers whose inverse also consists of all integers. We begin by guessing a matrix A as follows:

$$A = \begin{bmatrix} 1 & b & 6 \\ 4 & 9 & 11 \\ a & -4 & 3 \end{bmatrix} \tag{4.5}$$

where a and b are two integers to be determined. In *Maple*, we represent this as

```
> key := array([[1, b, 6], [4, 9, 11], [a, -4, 3]]);

              [ 1    b    6 ]
              [             ]
      key := [ 4    9   11 ]
              [             ]
              [ a   -4    3 ]
```

Now we compute the determinant of A:

```
> detkey := det(key);

      detkey := - 25 - 12 b + 11 a b - 54 a
```

---

[4]Each upper and lower case letter of the alphabet, as well as all common punctuation, is represented as an integer between 32 and 127. It is the most common scheme in use for representing English text in computers and other digital devices.

Next, we set this equal to 1 and use the `solve()` function to solve for a in terms of b:

```
> a1 := solve(detkey = 1, a);

                          - 26 - 12 b
              a1 :=  -  -----------
                          11 b - 54
```

It is not immediately clear what values (if any) for b yield integer results for this expression. We therefore use the time-honored engineering approach of trying a few guesses. In particular we try values of b from 1 to 10 and see what happens. This is done with the `seq()` function:

```
seq(a1, b = 1..10);

     38       25       62                        110    61    134   73
  - ----, - ----, - ----, -37/5, 86, 49/6, ---, ----, ---, ----
     43       16       21                         23    17    45    28
```

and we can see that $b = 5$ works. We will use this value now to determine a:

```
> subs(b = 5, a1);

                              86
```

We can now obtain the matrix A by substituting these values for a and b into the expression we had for `key`:

```
> b := 'b';

                              b := b
> key := subs(a = 86, b = 5, evalm(key));

                          [  1    5    6 ]
                          [              ]
              key :=  [  4    9   11 ]
                          [              ]
                          [ 86   -4    3 ]
```

To verify that A has the desired property, we compute its inverse:

```
> keyinv := inverse(key);
                            [  71    -39     1  ]
                            [                   ]
                  keyinv := [  934   -513    13 ]
                            [                   ]
                            [ -790    434   -11 ]
```

We now need to construct procedures that will translate a string into an array of integers and vice-versa. Since *Maple* does not come with a built-in function to either of these tasks, we must develop them here.

First we enter the plaintext as a character string:

```
> mess := 'Meet at Noon';

                        mess := Meet at Noon
```

The following procedure will go through this string and convert each letter into an integer:

```
> tointeger := proc(message)
               local i, result;
               result := [];
               for i from 1 to length(message)
               do
                  result := [op(result), Codes[substring(message, i..i)]];
               od;
               RETURN(array(result));
       end:
```

The `tointeger()` function takes a string, and successively converts each character into an integer from a table called `Codes`. Each of the integers is added to a list. The function returns this list to *Maple* for further processing. The table `Codes` is defined as follows:

```
> Codes := table(['M' = 1, '1' = 'M', 'e' = 2, '2' = 'e',
              't' = 3, '3' = 't', 'a' = 4, '4' = 'a',
              'N' = 5, '5' = 'N', 'o' = 6, '6' = 'o',
              'n' = 7, '7' = 'n', ' ' = 99, '99' = ' ']);

                     Codes := table([
                                 M = 1
                                 t = 3
                                 1 = M
```

```
                                          2 = e
                                          3 = t
                                          4 = a
                                          5 = N
                                          6 = o
                                            = 99
                                          7 = n
                                          o = 6
                                          n = 7
                                         99 =
                                          a = 4
                                          N = 5
                                          e = 2
                              ])
```

Note that there is nothing special about the way we assigned integers to characters. It is only necessary that each character corresponds to one and only one integer.

Here is the result of applying **tointeger()** to our string:

```
> abg := tointeger(mess);

          abg := [ 1, 2, 2, 3, 99, 4, 3, 99, 5, 6, 6, 7 ]
```

To convert this list back into a character string, we define the function **tostring()** as follows:

```
> tostring   := proc(codedmessage)
                local i, result;
                result := ' ';
                for i from 1 to nops(convert(codedmessage, list))
                do
                   result := cat(result, Codes[codedmessage[i]]);

                od;
                RETURN(result);
      end:
```

Here is the result of applying our list of integers to this function:

```
> answer := tostring(abg);

                    answer := Meet at Noon
```

We need two more procedures. It is not practical to construct a 12x12 matrix to encrypt a 12-element list. Therefore, we want to be able to take the list and pack it into a size that conforms to the dimensions of the key matrix we are using. This is done with the `pack()` procedure:

```
> pack := proc(codedmessage, rows, columns)
          local elements, size, i, scratch;
          elements := rows * columns;
          size := linalg[vectdim](codedmessage);
          if size > elements then
             RETURN(codedmessage);
          else
             scratch := convert(codedmessage, list);
             for i from size + 1 to elements
             do
               scratch := [op(scratch), 32];
             od;
             RETURN(linalg[matrix](rows, columns, scratch));
          fi;
     end:
```

`pack()` takes three arguments: the list of integers to be encoded, and the dimensions of the desired two-dimensional array. For example, to pack our list `abg` into a 3x4 matrix, we would invoke `pack()` as follows:

```
> packex1 := pack(abg, 3, 4);

                              [  1   2   2    3 ]
                              [                 ]
                  packex1 :=  [ 99   4   3   99 ]
                              [                 ]
                              [  5   6   6    7 ]
```

The reverse process is performed by the procedure `unpack()`:

```
> unpack := proc(packedmessage)
            local rows, i, scratch;
            rows := linalg[rowdim](packedmessage);
            scratch := [];
            for i from 1 to rows
               do
               scratch := [op(scratch),
                          op(convert(linalg[row](packedmessage,i), list))];
            od;
            RETURN(array(scratch));
     end:
```

And here is an example of this function at work:

```
> unpack(packex1);

              [1, 2, 2, 3, 99, 4, 3, 99, 5, 6, 6, 7]
```

We now illustrate the use of these procedures to encrypt and decrypt the message 'Meet at noon':

```
> cryptlist := evalm(key &* packex1);

                            [  526    58    53    540 ]
                            [                         ]
              cryptlist := [  950   110   101    980 ]
                            [                         ]
                            [ -295   174   178   -117 ]

> tmp := evalm(keyinv &* cryptlist);

                            [  1   2   2    3 ]
                            [                 ]
                   tmp := [ 99   4   3   99 ]
                            [                 ]
                            [  5   6   6    7 ]

> tostring(unpack(tmp));

                            Meet at Noon
```

EXERCISES

4.1. What *Maple* expression would you use to extract a single element from a matrix? A whole row? An entire column?

4.2. Consider the matrix A with

$$A = \begin{bmatrix} 1 & 2 & 1 \\ 1 & -1 & 0 \\ 0 & 2 & -1 \end{bmatrix} \tag{4.6}$$

- (*a*) Determine the eigenvalues of A.
- (*b*) Determine the eigenvectors of A.
- (*c*) Determine the characteristic polynomial of A. Use the `solve()` function[5] to find the roots of this polynomial and show that they are the eigenvalues of A.

[5]You may peek ahead to the next chapter.

(*d*) Show that *A* itself satisfies its characteristic polynomial.

(*e*) Show by direct computation that the eigenvectors of *A* are orthogonal.

4.3. Regarding Section 4.4, what is the probability that *A* will be bankrupted at the fourth turn but not at the third turn?

4.4. Regarding Section 4.4, what is the probability that *A* will bankrupt *B* at the twentieth turn?

4.5. Construct a 3x3 key matrix of your own. Make your initial guess different from the one in the text, and apply the procedure described there. Verify that the inverse has the correct property.

4.6. Describe a strategy for using a 3x3 key matrix to encrypt a message consisting of more than nine characters. For example, encrypt the message "Attack at dawn".

4.7. How should you construct a table to encode the letters from *any* message? Build such a table and test that your idea really works.[6]

4.8. Suppose you had both the plaintext and the ciphertext, but not the key. Could you deduce the key? What does this imply about security requirements for the key and the ciphertext?

[6]Two such tables are in widespread use: ASCII and EBCDIC.

CHAPTER
5

LINEAR AND NONLINEAR EQUATIONS

5.1 LABORATORY GOALS

a. To solve simultaneous linear equations.

b. To obtain numerical solutions to transcendental equations.

c. To become familiar with the `solve()` and `fsolve()` functions.

5.2 LINEAR EQUATIONS

The solution of simultaneous linear equations occurs frequently in applications of engineering mathematics. Consider the pair of equations given by

$$x + 3y = 1 \qquad\qquad (5.1)$$

$$2x - 4y = 3. \qquad\qquad (5.2)$$

In *Maple* this system is represented by

```
> eq1 := x + 3*y = 1;

                        eq1 := x + 3 y = 1

> eq2 := 2*x - 4*y = 3;
                        eq2 := 2 x - 4 y = 3
```

In this context the symbol = is used to construct a symbolic equation rather than as an assignment operator. Symbolic equations are passed as arguments to functions which determine analytical as well as numerical solutions. The `solve()` function determines the solution to this system:

```
> sol1 := solve({eq1, eq2}, {x, y});

                                              13
                    sol1 := {y = -1/10, x = ----}
                                              10
```

Note that the equations to be solved are given as a set, i.e. they are enclosed in curly brackets {}. The variables to be determined, x and y, are also specified as a set. The result as given above by *Maple* is set in a form which permits substitution of the solutions into general expressions involving either x or y. For example, suppose that $f(x, y) = x^3 - y^3$, so that

```
> f := (x, y) -> x^3 - y^3;

                              3    3
                 f := (x,y) -> x  - y
```

In order to evaluate this function at the values specified by `sol1`, we use the `subs()` function which causes the substitutions $x = 13/10$ and $y = -1/10$ contained in that set to be made for `f(x, y)`:

```
> subs(sol1, f(x, y));

                            1099
                            ----
                            500
```

There is in principal no limit to the size of systems that can be solved in this way.

If the system is underdetermined, we would normally expect to obtain infinitely many solutions. Consider the system

$$x + y = 2 \tag{5.3}$$

$$2x + 2y = 4. \tag{5.4}$$

This system is solved with the following sequence of *Maple* statements:

```
> eq3 := x + y = 2;
                        eq3 := x + y = 2

> eq4 := 2*x + 2*y = 4;
                        eq4 := 2 x + 2 y = 4

> sol2 := solve({eq3, eq4}, {x, y});
                        sol2 := {y = - x + 2, x = x}
```

Note that *Maple* has correctly characterized the infinite family of solutions in this case, i.e. for all y such that $y = -x + 2$. If, on the other hand, the system is overdetermined or inconsistent, there may or may not be solutions. Consider this obviously inconsistent system:

```
> eq5 := x + y = 1;
                        eq5 := x + y = 1

> eq6 := x + y = -1;
                        eq6 := x + y = -1

> sol3 := solve({eq5, eq6}, {x, y});
                        sol3 :=
```

Note that *Maple* produced nothing in this instance, meaning that it could find no solution.[1]

5.3   NONLINEAR EQUATIONS

Nonlinear equations arise in a number of instances: optimization, equilibrium determination, eigenvalue calculations, etc. Let us begin with an easy example. Let $g(x) = x^2 - 5x - 6$ be a quadratic polynomial. *Maple* can determine the roots of this polynomial using the `solve()` function:

```
> quad := x^2 - 5*x - 6;
                                    2
                        quad := x  - 5 x - 6

> quadsol := solve(quad, {x});
                        quadsol := {x = 6}, {x = -1}
```

[1]The claim that no solution was found *may* mean that no solution exists. Some sort of double-check should be performed to be sure that such an answer makes sense. This *caveat* is particularly apropos when working with nonlinear equations.

Maple correctly determines both roots. Either of them[2] can be gotten for further manipulation by using single brackets [] to access the individual members of the solution list. For example, the second root is obtained with

```
> quadsol[2];
                          {x = -1}
```

while the first can be obtained with `quadsol[1]`.

A more challenging problem is to seek solutions to a pair of nonlinear equations. Consider the pair of quadratic polynomials $y_1 = (x-2)^2/2$ and $y_2 = -(x+3)^2/4 + 9$. We represent both polynomials in *Maple* as follows:

```
> y1 := (x - 1)^2 / 2;
                                        2
                          y1 := 1/2 (x - 1)

> y2 := -(x + 3)^2 / 4 + 9;
                                        2
                          y2 := - 1/4 (x + 3)  + 9
```

The `solve()` function is now invoked like this:

```
> sols := solve({y1 = y2}, {x});
                          1/2                        1/2
        sols := {x = - 1/3 + 2/3 19   }, {x = - 1/3 - 2/3 19   }
```

Numerical approximations of this list is obtained with the `evalf()` function, which renders all exact constants into floating point form:[3]

```
> evalf(sols);
             {x = 2.572599296}, {x = -3.239265962}
```

---

[2]In the call to `solve()`, if there is only one solution variable, it need not be enclosed in curly brackets; however, if it is not so enclosed, the form of the result changes slightly. Try it for yourself.

[3]Elaborate symbolic expressions are often simplified considerably this way.

To visualize the location of these solutions, we can have *Maple* plot both y_1 and y_2:

```
> plot({y1, y2}, x = -5 .. 5);
```

The two polynomials are seen to intersect twice in Fig. 5.1. The value of the

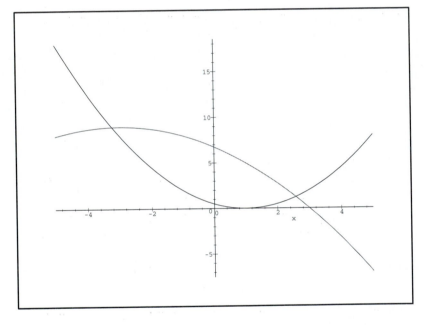

FIGURE 5.1
Plot of $y_1 = (x-1)^2/2$ and $y_2 = -(x+3)^2/4 + 9$

polynomials at the intersection points is obtained by substituting the solution list **sols** into one of the polynomials:

```
> evalf(subs(sols[2], y1));
                        8.985687950

> evalf(subs(sols[1], y1));
                        1.236534273
```

These results represent the numerical values of the y-coordinate of the left and right points of intersection respectively.

5.4 GRAPHICAL AND NUMERICAL SOLUTIONS

In many instances, exact solutions to nonlinear equations may be simply unobtainable. For example, a problem which often arises when solving boundary value problems involving homogeneous boundary conditions of the third kind[4] is to determine all solutions to equations of this form:

$$\tan \lambda = \lambda \qquad\qquad (5.5)$$

The roots of this equation are related to the eigenvalues of the underlying problem. Equations such as Eq. (5.5) are called transcendental equations. Their solutions can usually only be obtained numerically. The first step in such problems is to estimate the location of solutions using graphical means, and then to use that information to calculate precise numerical approximations.

In this case, we first plot the function $f(\lambda) = \tan \lambda - \lambda$:

```
> g := tan(lambda) - lambda;

                    g := tan(lambda) - lambda

> plot(g, lambda = 0 .. 15, -5 .. 5);
```

As seen in Fig. 5.2, there are roots immediately to the left of each vertical asymptote (except the first at $x = \pi/2$). Note that the third argument to the `plot()` function forces *Maple* to scale the plot to those specified vertical values. By examining the graph, we can estimate the approximate location of the the desired roots. The `fsolve()` can then be used to give an accurate computation of the root. To use this function we must provide an initial guess "sufficiently close" to the root. How close is sufficiently close? It depends very much on the function involved, but in general, the better the guess, the more likely `fsolve()` will converge *quickly* to the *desired* root.

As seen in Fig. 5.2, the first root is $\lambda_1 \approx 4.4$. Then we give the following *Maple* command:

```
> fsolve(g, lambda, 4 .. 5);

                    4.493409457
```

---

[4]They take the form $y(\alpha) + \beta y'(\alpha)$, and are also called mixed or Robin conditions.

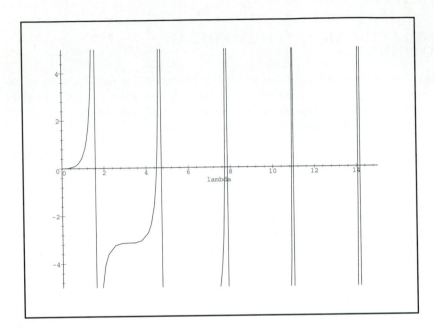

FIGURE 5.2
Plot of $f(\lambda) = \tan\lambda - \lambda$.

`fsolve()` takes as arguments a set of equations (in this case one), and set of variables to be solved for, and a range which bounds the desired root. The solution returned by `fsolve()` is correct to the indicated number of decimal places. More accuracy can be obtained (at a sometimes serious performance cost) by raising the value of the `Digits` variable. Thus

```
> Digits := 20;
                            Digits := 20

> fsolve(g, lambda, 4 .. 5);

              4.4934094579090641753
```

Our result is accurate to 20 decimal places![5]

---

[5] *Maple* can generate arbitrarily accurate answers but be warned: Anything beyond the default value of `Digits` on most systems forces *Maple* to do floating point calculations in software rather than in hardware. Software floating point manipulations are relatively slow. Moreover, in engineering computations, accuracy beyond machine hardware limits is not often needed. Demand this kind of accuracy only when the nature of the problem warrants it.

EXERCISES

5.1. Determine all solutions to the following linear system:

$$x + 2y + 4z = 3$$
$$3x + 4y + 5z = 7$$
$$x + 3y + 4z = 4$$

5.2. Determine all solutions to the following linear system:

$$x - y + z - 2w = -1$$
$$-3x + y - z + 2z = 3$$
$$x + y + z - w = 1$$
$$x - y - z - w = -2$$

5.3. Determine the points of intersection of the ellipse $x^2/4 + y^2/9 = 1$ and the parabola $y = x^2 - 4$.

5.4. Let $f(x) = 2\sin x - x/2$. Compute all real zeroes of $f(x)$.

5.5. Determine the first five positive roots of $\cot x = 2x$. [Hint: Some of your initial guesses must be very good!]

5.6. Consider a small sphere of radius ρ moving with speed v through air. The resistive force on the sphere is given by

$$f = 3.1 \times 10^{-4}\rho v + 0.87\rho^2 v^2. \tag{5.6}$$

(All units are MKS). What is the terminal velocity of a raindrop with $\rho = 3$ mm falling under its own weight?

5.7. Show that[6]

$$\phi(\xi) = \alpha + \beta \operatorname{sech}^2 \sqrt{\frac{\beta\xi}{12k}}$$

is a solution to the Korteweg-deVries equation

$$\frac{\partial\psi}{\partial t} = \psi\frac{\partial\psi}{\partial x} + \nu\frac{\partial^3\psi}{\partial x^3},$$

provided $\xi = x - ct$ and $c = \alpha + \beta/3$. (This equation models the propagation of waves in dispersive, nonlinear media.) Plot the solution ϕ function of x and t. This type of wave is known as a soliton.

---

[6]$\operatorname{sech}(x) = \sinh(x)/\cosh(x)$ is called the *hyperbolic secant* function. The corresponding *Maple* expression is `sech()`.

CHAPTER
6

FIRST-
ORDER ODES

6.1 LABORATORY GOALS

a. To determine the general solutions to first order linear and non-linear ordinary differential equations.

b. To manipulate the form of certain types of first-order equations.

6.2 FIRST-ORDER LINEAR ODES

Consider the first-order linear ODE[1].

$$y'(x) + p(x)y(x) = f(x). \tag{6.1}$$

This differential equation can always be solved, and, in fact, there is a formula for the solution. *Maple* uses this formula to construct solutions. For example, let $p(x) = 1/x$ and $f(x) = 1$. The differential equation is solved with the `dsolve()` function:

---

[1]ODE means *ordinary differential equation*

```
> sol1 := dsolve(diff(y(x), x) +  y(x) / x = 1, y(x));
```

$$sol1 := y(x) = \frac{1}{2} \frac{x^2 + 2\_C1}{x}$$

The `dsolve()` function determines a symbolic solution to a differential equation. As arguments, it takes the differential equation and the name of the dependent variable. Note that the explicit functional dependence of `y` on `x` is given. Also note that the derivative is expressed with the `diff()` function. The solution shown here uses _C1 for the arbitrary constant. This symbol is the standard one for representing all arbitrary constants in symbolic solutions to differential equations in *Maple*.

The general solution to our ODE is therefore

$$y = x/2 + c_1/x \tag{6.2}$$

where c_1 is an arbitrary constant _C1. There are two ways to apply an initial condition to these kinds of equations. The first way is to use the `solve()` function to determine the constant. Suppose, for example, that we require $y(1) = -1$. Then, using the result we just obtained, we set $y(x) = 1$, demand that $x = 1$ and solve for c_1:

```
> solve(subs({x = 1, y(x) = -1}, sol1), {_C1});
```

$$\{\_C1 = -3/2\}$$

Thus $c_1 = -3/2$. Note our embedded use of the `subs()` function here. A second approach is to specify the initial condition within the `dsolve()` function. Suppose again that $y(1) = -1$. Then

```
> dsolve({diff(y(x), x) +  y(x) / x = 1, y(1) = -1}, y(x));
```

$$y(x) = \frac{1}{2} x - \frac{3}{2x}$$

Note that the initial condition was expressed as the symbolic equation `y(1) = -1`, and included with the differential equation as the element of a set. This set, i.e. the differential equation along with the initial condition, becomes the first argument to `dsolve()`.

Even though a formula exists for the solutions to first-order linear ODEs, *Maple* may not always evaluate the subsequent integral explicitly. Consider the innocent-looking equation

$$y' + x^2 y = x. \tag{6.3}$$

```
> dsolve(diff(y(x), x) +  x^2 * y(x) = x, y(x));


                            /
                    3       |          3                    3
        y(x) = exp(- 1/3 x )  |   exp(1/3 x ) x dx + exp(- 1/3 x ) _C1
                            |
                            /
```

The best that *Maple* can do[2] is to present the solution in the form

$$y = \exp(-x^3/3) \left[c_1 + \int x \exp(-x^3/3) \, dx \right]. \tag{6.4}$$

6.3   SEPARABLE EQUATIONS

Another class of first-order differential equations that can be attacked with *Maple* has (or can be put into) the following form:

$$y'(x) = p(x)/q(y). \tag{6.5}$$

Such a differential equation is said to be separable. For example, let $p(x) = 8x^3$ and $q(y) = 1/y^2$. Again we use `dsolve()` to determine the general solution:

```
> dsolve(diff(y(x), x) = 8 * x^3 * y(x)^2, y(x));

                    1           4
                   ---- = - 2 x    + _C1
                   y(x)
```

Note that this result is given as an implicit function of y. *Maple* will attempt to return an explicit representation of the solution by passing the equation `explicit=true` as a third argument to `dsolve()`:

---

[2]Sometimes (but not always), *Maple* can evaluate certain difficult integrals in terms of special functions. This example allows for no such representation.

```
> dsolve(diff(y(x), x) = 8 * x^3 * y(x)^2, y(x), explicit=true);
                              1
             y(x) = - ----------
                          4
                       2 x  - _C1
```

Thus $y = -1/(2x^4 + c_1)$. Another example is the differential equation

$$y' = (x + y - 3)^2 - 2(x + y - 3). \qquad (6.6)$$

Maple easily handles this equation as follows:

```
> dsolve(diff(y(x), x) = (x + y(x) - 3)^2 - 2 * (x + y(x) - 3), y(x));
                            1
             y(x) = - x + 4 + -------
                            _C1 - x
```

6.4   HOMOGENEOUS EQUATIONS

Let $y' = f(x, y)$. If $f(\lambda x, \lambda y) = \lambda^n f(x, y)$, the differential equation is said to be *homogeneous*. *Maple* can find the general solution to most homogeneous equations. For example, let $y' = (x - y)^2$. The `dsolve()` function produces the following result:

```
> dsolve(diff(y(x), x) = (x - y)^2, y(x));
                              exp(- 2 x)
             y(x) = x - 1 + ---------------------
                            _C1 + 1/2 exp(- 2 x)
```

A more complicated example is given by the equation

$$xy' - y = \sqrt{x^2 - y^2}, \qquad (6.7)$$

which is solved by *Maple* as:

```
> dsolve(x * diff(y(x), x) - y = sqrt(x^2 - y^2), y(x));

                                        /    x    \
                                        |---------|
                                        |    2 1/2|
             2 1/2          2       2 1/2 \(- x )  /
```

```
        _C1 ((- x )      y(x) + (x  - y(x) )      x)
    x = ---------------------------------------------------------
                                  /   x   \
                                  |---------|
                                  |    2 1/2|
                                  \(- x )  /
                                       x
```

Maple cannot provide an explicit represetnation of the solution for this example. If `dsolve()` is called with the optional equation `explicit=true`, an empty result is returned.

6.5   SPECIAL FIRST-ORDER EQUATIONS

Consider the differential equation

$$3xy' + y + x^2 y^4 = 0, \tag{6.8}$$

which is an example of Bernoulli's equation, whose general form is $y' + P(x)y = Q(x)y^n$. The `dsolve()` function can handle this equation:

```
> dsolve(3 * x * diff(y(x), x) + y(x) + x^2 * (y(x))^4 = 0, y(x),
    explicit=true);

              /    1      \1/3          1/2 /    1      \1/3
  y(x) = - 1/2 |-----------|    + 1/2 I 3   |-----------|    ,
              \x (x + _C1)/               \x (x + _C1)/

              /    1      \1/3          1/2 /    1      \1/3
     y(x) = - 1/2 |-----------|    - 1/2 I 3   |-----------|    ,
                 \x (x + _C1)/               \x (x + _C1)/

              /    1      \1/3
     y(x) = |-----------|
                 \x (x + _C1)/
```

Note that *Maple* returns *three* forms of the solution. Which of the three is appropriate depends upon the initial value selected in a particular problem. A multiplicity of solution forms (nonuniqueness of solutions) is often seen when working with non-linear differential equations.

Another type of special equation is called the Ricatti equation, with form $y' = P(x)y^2 + Q(x)y + R(x)$. For example consider

$$y' = y^2 + (1 - 2x)y + (x^2 - x + 1). \tag{6.9}$$

The general solution can also be found with the `dsolve()` function:

```
> ricc := diff(y(x), x) =
              (y(x))^2 + (1 - 2 * x) * y(x) + (x^2 - x + 1);

              d              2                    2
    ricc := ---- y(x) = y(x)  + (1 - 2 x) y(x) + x  - x + 1
              dx

> riccsol := dsolve(ricc, y(x));

                                        exp(x)
              riccsol := y(x) = x + ------------
                                     _C1 - exp(x)
```

In order to verify that this is indeed the solution, we can substitute `riccsol` into `ricc` with the `subs()` function:

```
> subs(riccsol, ricc);
      d /       exp(x)   \
     ---- |x + ------------| =
      dx \   _C1 - exp(x)/

      /       exp(x)   \2          /       exp(x)   \    2
      |x + ------------|  + (1 - 2 x) |x + ------------| + x  - x + 1
      \   _C1 - exp(x)/          \   _C1 - exp(x)/
```

This result can be simplified with the `simplify()` function:

```
> simplify(");
        2                              2
     _C1  - _C1 exp(x) + exp(2 x)   _C1  - _C1 exp(x) + exp(2 x)
     ---------------------------- = ----------------------------
                    2                             2
          (_C1 - exp(x))                 (_C1 - exp(x))
```

This result is evidently an identity.

EXERCISES

6.1. Determine the general solution to the equation $y' = 2y/(x+1) + (x+1)^3$.

6.2. Solve the initial value problem $y' = \sec(y/x) + (y/x)$, with $y(2) = \pi$.

6.3. Determine the general solution to the equation $y' = (x+y-3)^2 - 2(x+y-3)$.

6.4. Determine the general solution to the Ricatti equation $y' = (y-1)(y+1/x)$.

6.5. Determine the general solution to the Ricatti equation $y' = x^3(y-x)^2 + y/x$.

6.6. Water evaporates from most porous substances at a rate proportional to the moisture content of the substance. Suppose a towel hung on a clothesline on a mild, windy day loses 1/3 its moisture in a half hour. How long will it take for the towel to be dry? (You will have to decide what "dry" means.)

6.7. The police are called to the scene of a homicide, and the investigating detective determines that the temperature of the corpse is 75 degrees Farenheit. After one hour, the temperature of the body was measured at 73 degrees. He also notes that the ambient room temperature is 65 degrees. How long ago was the murder committed? (Use Newton's Law of Cooling.)

6.8. The population $p(t)$ of a small city is governed by the logistics equation

$$dp/dt = p(0.2 - 0.0000005p), \tag{6.10}$$

where t is measured in months.

(*a*) If the initial population is 5,000, what will be the limiting population?

(*b*) How many years will it take for the population to achieve one-half of the limiting value?

7

SECOND-ORDER CONSTANT-COEFFICIENT ODES

7.1 LABORATORY GOALS

a. To determine the general solution to second-order linear homogeneous and nonhomogeneous constant coefficient ordinary differential equations.

b. To apply initial conditions to determine particular solutions.

c. To manipulate parts of expressions with *Maple* functions.

d. To analyze solutions to spring-mass problems.

7.2 GENERAL SOLUTIONS

Consider the second-order ODE

$$y''(x) + y(x) = 0. \tag{7.1}$$

This equation has constant coefficients, and is both linear and homogeneous. It is represented in *Maple* as a symbolic equation:

```
> eq1 := diff(y(x), x$2) + y(x) = 0;

              /  2      \
              |  d      |
       eq1 := |----- y(x)| + y(x) = 0
              |   2      |
              \ dx      /
```

Note the form of the second argument to the `diff()` function. In order to indicate a second derivative, the symbol `$2` is appended to the independent variable `x`. The general solution to this equation can be obtained with the `dsolve()` function:

```
> sol1 := dsolve(eq1, y(x));

       sol1 := y(x) = _C1 cos(x) + _C2 sin(x)
```

Note that the general solution is provided with two arbitrary constants, `_C1` and `_C2`.

The `dsolve()` function can also be used to solve second-order equations with nonhomogeneous right-hand sides, for example

$$y'' + y = x. \tag{7.2}$$

The setup and solution of this equation in *Maple* proceeds just as it did above:

```
> eq2 := diff(y(x), x$2) + y(x) = x;

              /  2      \
              |  d      |
       eq2 := |----- y(x)| + y(x) = x
              |   2      |
              \ dx      /

> sol2 := dsolve(eq2, y(x));

       sol2 := y(x) = x + _C1 cos(x) + _C2 sin(x)
```

More complicated nonhomogeneous terms are equally straightforward to handle. For example, the following ODE arises in the study of an undamped spring-mass system being driven by a sinusoidal driving force:

$$y''(t) + \omega_0^2 y(t) = \sin(\omega t), \tag{7.3}$$

where ω_0 is the natural frequency of the sprig-mass system and ω is the frequency of the driving force. In *Maple* we have

```
> sol3 := dsolve(diff(y(t), t$2) + w0^2 * y(t) = sin(w * t), y(t));

sol3 := y(t) = - 1/2 (cos(w0 t) sin(w t - w0 t) w

     + cos(w0 t) sin(w t - w0 t) w0 - cos(w0 t) sin(w t + w0 t) w

     + cos(w0 t) sin(w t + w0 t) w0 + sin(w0 t) cos(w t + w0 t) w

     - sin(w0 t) cos(w t + w0 t) w0 + sin(w0 t) cos(w t - w0 t) w

                                        /       2      2
     + sin(w0 t) cos(w t - w0 t) w0)   /  (w0 (w  - w0 )) + _C1 cos(w0 t)
                                        /

     + _C2 sin(w0 t)
```

Note that *Maple* assumed that $\omega \neq \omega_0$. In order to explicitly account for the case in which $\omega = \omega_0$, we must solve the differential equation again, but with the appropriate change made:

```
> sol4 := dsolve(diff(y(t), t$2) + w0^2 * y(t) = sin(w0 * t), y(t),
          laplace);

sol4 := y(t) =

           t cos(w0 t)        sin(w0 t)                        D(y)(0) sin(w0 t)
    - 1/2 -----------  + 1/2 ---------  + y(0) cos(w0 t) +  -----------------
               w0                 2                                   w0
                                w0
```

Note the use of an optional third argument, `laplace` to `dsolve()`. The use of this argument substantially simplifies the form of certain solution expressions.[1] Also note that instead of two arbitrary constants, the unspecified values of the initial conditions appear as `y(0)` and `D(y)(0)`.

Recall that the general solution to a nonhomogeneous ODE consists of two parts: the complementary solution, which is the solution to the homogeneous problem, and a particular solution, which solves the nonhomogeneous problem. The particular solution represents the principal effect of the nonhomogeneous term of the solution to the differential equation. In order to examine the form of the particular solution we obtained above, we can set the initial conditions to zero with the `subs()` function:

---

[1] The `laplace` argument actually tells *Maple* to use Laplace transforms when solving the differential equation. (We will have more to say about Laplace transforms in Chapter 8.) You might want to try the call to `dsolve()` without the `laplace` option. With this release of *Maple*, the resulting expression for the solution, while correct, is extremely convoluted, and looks nothing like the solution you would obtain if you solved the differential equation by hand.

```
> sol4a := subs({y(0) = 0, D(y)(0) = 0}, sol4);

                              t cos(w0 t)         sin(w0 t)
             sol4a := y(t) = - 1/2 -----------  + 1/2 ---------
                                       w0                 2
                                                        w0
```

We can now discern more clearly the form of the particular solution. Especially important is the term proportional to $t \cos(\omega_0 t)$. This amplitude of this term grows linearly with time, a characteristic feature of resonance occurring in undamped spring-mass systems.

7.3   USING INITIAL CONDITIONS

Consider now the equation

$$y'' + y = \sin t, \tag{7.4}$$

along with the initial conditions $y(0) = 0$ and $y'(0) = 1$. These conditions are added as components of the list which is the first argument of `dsolve()`:

```
> eq5 := dsolve({diff(y(t), t$2) + y(t) = sin(t), y(0) = 0,
              D(y)(0) = 1}, y(t), laplace);

    eq5 := y(t) = - 1/2 t cos(t) + 3/2 sin(t)
```

Since there are no arbitrary constants, this solution can be plotted directly with the `plot()` function:

```
> plot(rhs(eq5)), t = 0 .. 4 * Pi);
```

Note the use of the `rhs()` function to obtain the right-hand side of `eq5`. The linear growth in amplitude observable in Fig. 7.1 is directly attributable to the term $t \cos t$ which appears in the solution found by *Maple*.

7.4   DAMPED MOTION

The dynamical behavior of spring-mass systems in the presence of damping as well as forcing can lead to a variety of interesting results. As shown in Fig. 7.2, we consider a mass suspended from a vertical support to which a driving force is imparted. The motion of the mass is damped by a device called a dashpot, shown in the figure. When properly constructed, the damping force is proportional to

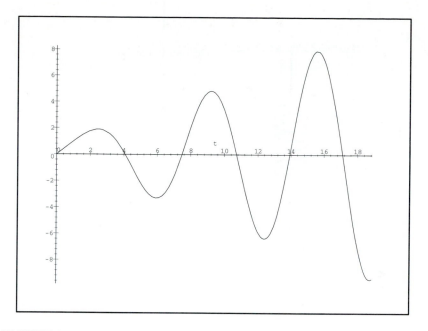

FIGURE 7.1
Solution to Eq. 7.4 over the interval $t \in [0, 6\pi]$. Note the growth in amplitude.

the instantaneous speed of the mass. The most general differential equation that
describes such a system is

$$my'' + \gamma y' + ky = F(t), \tag{7.5}$$

where m is the mass, k is the spring constant, and γ is the damping coefficient.
This equation can also be written as

$$y'' + \beta y' + \omega_0^2 y = G(t). \tag{7.6}$$

where $\beta = \gamma/m$ and $\omega_0 = \sqrt{k/m}$.

We first examine the behavior of this system in the absence of forcing,
i.e. when $F(t) = 0$. We set up the differential equation and then apply initial
conditions $y(0) = 1$ and $y'(0) = 0$. This is equivalent to releasing the system
from rest. These initial conditions are passed to `dsolve()` as elements `y(0)` =
0 and `D(y)(0)` = 0 of the first argument:

```
> spring1 := diff(y(t), t$2) + b * diff(y(t), t) + w0^2 * y(t) = 0;
```

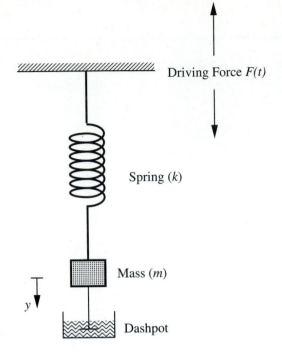

FIGURE 7.2
Spring-mass system with damping and subject to a driving force.

$$\text{spring1} := \left(\dfrac{d^2}{dt^2}\, y(t)\right) + b \left(\dfrac{d}{dt}\, y(t)\right) + w0^2\, y(t) = 0$$

```
> sys1 := dsolve({spring1, y(0) = 1, D(y)(0) = 0}, y(t), laplace);
```

$$\text{sys1} := y(t) = \dfrac{b \exp(-\tfrac{1}{2} b\, t)\, \sin(\tfrac{1}{2}(4\, w0^2 - b^2)^{1/2}\, t)}{(4\, w0^2 - b^2)^{1/2}}$$

$$+ \exp(-\tfrac{1}{2} b\, t)\, \cos(\tfrac{1}{2}(4\, w0^2 - b^2)^{1/2}\, t)$$

Suppose we fix $\omega_0 = 1$ and wish to examine changes in the system response for different values of β. We are especially interested in values slightly above and below $\beta = 2$, the value for which the system is critically damped. To do this in *Maple*, we can use the `seq()` and `subs()` functions together with the `plot()`

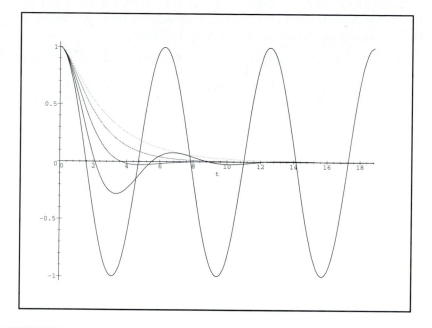

FIGURE 7.3
Solution to Eq. 7.6 for five values of β and $\omega_0 = 1$ over the interval $t \in [0, 6\pi]$. (The different shades of gray used to draw the curves in this figure are usually drawn as different colors on your computer's monitor.)

function to generate a series of plots with a single command. The `seq()` function takes as arguments a list of expressions, and a variable whose domain is (in this case) given by an explicit list.[2] The `seq()` function is combined with a call to `subs()` in order to generate a set of five expressions to be plotted:

```
>  bb := [0, .75, 1.5, 2.25, 3];

                     bb := [0, .75, 1.5, 2.25, 3]

>  plot({seq(subs({w0 = 1, b = bb}, rhs(sys1)), b = bb)}, t = 0 .. 6 * Pi);
```

The result of this command is shown in Fig. 7.3.

---

[2]The `seq()` function behaves somewhat like a `for` loop in programming languages.

7.5 FORCED MOTION

We now consider the motion of a damped spring-mass system subject to a periodic driving force as shown in Fig. 7.2. In this instance, $F(t) = \cos(\omega t)/2$. The system is described by the following initial-value problem:

$$y'' + \beta y' + y = \cos(\omega t)/2, \quad y(0) = 0, \quad y'(0) = 0. \tag{7.7}$$

In Eq. 7.7, we set $\beta = 2$ (the system's critical damping value) and we let the driving force be periodic with circular frequency ω. First, we obtain the solution to the initial value problem:

```
> spring2 := diff(y(t), t$2) + 2 * diff(y(t), t) + y(t) = cos(w * t);

                 /  2      \
                 |  d      |     /  d      \
     spring2 :=  |----- y(t)| + 2 |---- y(t)| + y(t) = cos(w t)
                 |   2     |     \  dt     /
                 \  dt     /

> sys2 := dsolve({spring2, y(0) = 0, D(y)(0) = 0}, y(t), laplace);

              2
             w  exp(- t)        exp(- t)      t exp(- t)       w sin(w t)
sys2 := y(t) = -------------- - -------------- - ---------- + 2 -------------
              4     2          4     2             2          4     2
             w  + 2 w  + 1    w  + 2 w  + 1     1 + w        w  + 2 w  + 1


        2
       w  cos(w t)        cos(w t)
     - -------------- + --------------
        4     2          4     2
       w  + 2 w  + 1    w  + 2 w  + 1
```

and then we examine the system response for five values of ω, again using the `seq()` and `plot()` functions:

```
> ww := [0, .5, 1, 1.5, 2];

                    ww := [0, .5, 1, 1.5, 2]

> plot({seq(rhs(sys2), w = ww)}, t = 0 .. 6 * Pi);
```

The result is illustrated in Fig. 7.4.

One interesting question to ask is this: What are the amplitude and phase of the steady-state solution to this problem? The desired information is contained in the solution found for us by *Maple*. To extract it, we first make a copy of the solution for further manipulation:

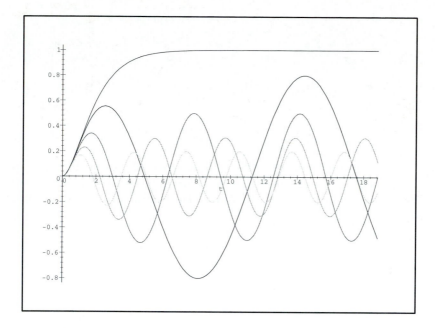

FIGURE 7.4

Solution to Eq. 7.7 for five values of $\omega_0 = 1$ over the interval $t \in [0, 6\pi]$.

```
s2 := rhs(sys2);
```

$$s2 := \frac{w^2 \exp(-t)}{w^4 + 2w^2 + 1} - \frac{\exp(-t)}{w^4 + 2w^2 + 1} - \frac{t\, \exp(-t)}{1 + w^2} + 2\,\frac{w\,\sin(w\,t)}{w^4 + 2w^2 + 1}$$

$$- \frac{w^2 \cos(w\,t)}{w^4 + 2w^2 + 1} + \frac{\cos(w\,t)}{w^4 + 2w^2 + 1}$$

In order to determine the steady-state portion of the solution, we rearrange terms based on the presence of the factor e^{-t}. The `collect()` function will do this for us:

```
> collect(s2, exp(-t));
```

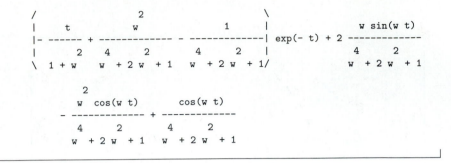

The steady-state solution is the second term in this result.[3] This can be extracted with calls to the op() function, which grabs the indicated part of the expression given as its first argument. In this case we want the fourth, fifth and sixth terms in the expression for s2:

```
> ss := op((4, s2)) + op((5, s2)) + op((6, s2));

                              2
             w sin(w t)      w  cos(w t)      cos(w t)
   ss := 2 -------------  - -------------  + -------------
             4                4                4
            w  + 2 w  + 1     w  + 2 w  + 1    w  + 2 w  + 1
```

We further rearrange this result by separating the $\cos(\omega t)$ and $\sin(\omega t)$ terms, again using the collect() function for the necessary algebra:

```
> collect(ss, cos(w * t));

    /       2                    \
    |      w             1       |               w sin(w t)
    |- ------------- + ----------| cos(w t) + 2 -------------
    |   4              4         |               4
    \  w  + 2 w  + 1   w + 2 w + 1/              w  + 2 w  + 1
```

If the steady-state solution to a spring-mass problem is given by

$$y = a_1 \cos(\omega t) + a_2 \sin(\omega t), \tag{7.8}$$

then this can be re-written as

$$y = A \cos(\omega t + \phi), \tag{7.9}$$

---

[3]The transient is the portion that decays exponentially in time.

where $A = \sqrt{a_1^2 + a_2^2}$ and $\phi = \tan^{-1}(a_2/a_1)$. A is called the amplitude and ϕ is called the phase.

In order to compute the amplitude, we use the `coeff()` function to extract the appropriate coefficients:

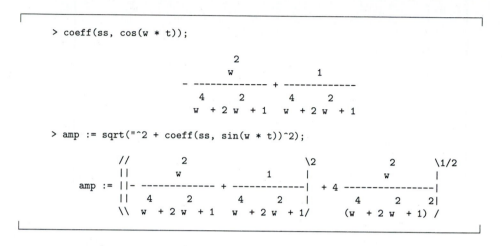

```
> coeff(ss, cos(w * t));
```

Before simplifying this last expression, we need to tell *Maple* that w is a real variable. We can do this with the `assume()` function:

```
> assume(w > 0);

> amp := simplify(amp);
```

$$amp := \frac{1}{w^{\sim 2} + 1}$$

The tilde ˜ after the w indicates that *Maple* has made an assumption about that particular symbol.

We can plot A with this call to `plot()`:

```
> plot(amp, w = 0 .. 10);
```

We note that the maximum amplitude occurs at $\omega = 0$.[4]

The phase ϕ can be just as simply computed:

_____
[4]Can you think of a physical interpretation for this result?

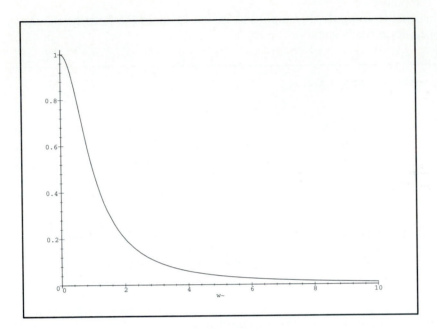

FIGURE 7.5
Amplitude of the steady-state solution to Eq. 7.7.

```
> phi := simplify(arctan(coeff(ss, cos(w * t)) / coeff(ss, sin(w * t))));
```

$$phi := - \arctan(1/2 \; \frac{w\text{\textasciitilde}^2 - 1}{w\text{\textasciitilde}})$$

We can plot the phase in degrees with the following command:

```
> plot((180 / Pi) * phi, w = 0.1 ... 3);
```

From Fig. 7.6 it can be seen that the solution is in phase with the driving force only when $\omega = 1$, i.e. when the driving force is tuned to the natural frequency of the system.

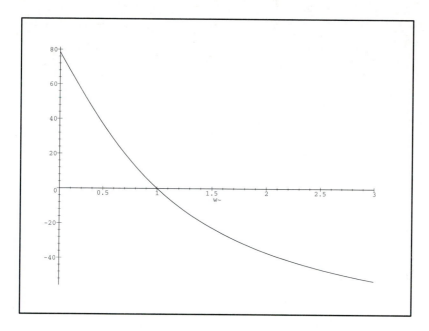

FIGURE 7.6
Phase of the steady-state solution to Eq. 7.7.

EXERCISES

7.1. Find the general solution to $y'' - y = 0$.

7.2. Find the particular solution to $y'' + \omega^2 y = e^{-t}$ with $y(0) = 1$ and $y'(0) = 0$.

7.3. Consider the damped spring-mass system modeled by $y'' + \beta y + y = \sin(2t)$, $y(0) = 0$ and $y'(0) = 0$. What value of β maximizes the amplitude of the steady-state response?

7.4. Consider the damped spring-mass system of the previous problem, but with a forcing function of $\sin(2t) + \sin(4t)$. Discuss the behavior of the steady-state phase as a function of β.

7.5. Consider the RLC circuit shown in Fig. 7.7.

    (a) Determine the current in this circuit assuming that the initial current and capacitor charge are both zero, and $R = 100$ ohms, $L = 1$ henry, $C = 0.005$ farad, and $E(t) = 12\sin(20t)$ volts.

    (b) Suppose instead that the applied voltage is $E(t) = 12\sin(\omega t)$ volts, and that the values of R, L, and C, as well as the initial conditions are as above. What value of ω will produce the largest current amplitude?

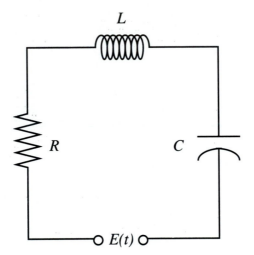

FIGURE 7.7
RLC circuit.

CHAPTER 8

LAPLACE TRANSFORMS

8.1 LABORATORY GOALS

a. To determine the Laplace and inverse Laplace transforms of given functions.

b. To solve linear ODEs with Laplace transforms.

8.2 SIMPLE TRANSFORMS

Maple can evaluate a large variety of Laplace transforms. Direct transforms are calculated with the `laplace()` function. For example, let $f(t) = e^{-2t} \sin 3t$. Then the Laplace transform $\mathcal{L}\{f(t)\}$ is found with the following call:

```
> laplace(exp(-2 * t) * sin(3 * t), t, s);

                    3
              -------------
                     2
              (s + 2)  + 9
```

The `laplace()` takes three arguments. The first is the function or expression to be transformed, the second is the name of the independent variable, and the third is the name of the transform variable.

Maple can also determine the transforms of a variety of exotic functions. For example, suppose $f(t) = J_0(t)$ where J_0 is the Bessel function of the first kind of order zero. The calculation is set up in the following way:

```
> laplace(BesselJ(0, t), t, s);

               1
          ------------
           2       1/2
          (s  + 1)
```

In this example, `BesselJ()` takes two arguments. The first is the order of the Bessel function, and the second is the independent variable.

Inverse Laplace transforms are found with the `invlaplace()` function. For example, suppose $F(s) = s/(s^2 + 25)$.[1] Then $\mathcal{L}^{-1}\{F(s)\}$ is found by:

```
> invlaplace(s/(s^2 + 25), s, t);

               cos(5 t)
```

The syntax for the `invlaplace()` function is similar to that of the `laplace()` function. A wide variety of inverse transforms can be handled as well. Let $F(s) = \tan^{-1}(1/s)/s$. Then the inverse transform is found with the following command:

```
> invlaplace(arctan(1/s) / s, s, t);

               Si(t)
```

This result, sometimes called the *sine integral*, is the integral $\int_0^t (\sin t)/t \, dt$, a special function built into *Maple*.

Maple contains the definition for the Dirac delta function. Thus

```
> laplace(Dirac(t - 3), t, s);

               exp(- 3 s)
```

---

[1] If $f(t)$ is the function in the time domain, then $F(s)$ is a typical representation of the transformed function.

and the `Dirac()` function will often appear in inverse transforms. The Heaviside step function is also available in *Maple*. For example, suppose we seek the transform of $f(t) = \mathcal{U}(t - \pi)\cos(t)$ where $\mathcal{U}$ is the Heaviside step function. *Maple* performs this transform in a straightforward way:

```
> laplace(Heaviside(t - Pi) * cos(t), t, s);

              exp(- Pi s) s
          - -------------
                 2
              s  + 1
```

The inverse Laplace transform can produce Heaviside step functions as part of the returned expression:

```
> invlaplace(exp(-s) / s, s, t);

              Heaviside(t - 1)
```

which is typically written as $\mathcal{U}(t - 1)$. As another example, consider the inverse transform of $F(s) = e^{-2s}/(s + 1)$.:

```
> result1 := invlaplace(exp(-2 * s) / (s + 1), s, t);

        result1 := Heaviside(t - 2) exp(- t + 2)
```

This kind of result can be plotted in a straightforward way with the `plot()` function:

```
> plot(result1, t = 0 .. 4);
```

The result is shown in Fig. 8.1.

8.3 APPLICATION TO DIFFERENTIAL EQUATIONS

Consider the second-order differential equation

$$y'' + y = 0, \tag{8.1}$$

with $y(0) = 1$ and $y'(0) = -1$. To solve this problem with Laplace transforms, we first enter the differential equation and then apply the `laplace()` function:

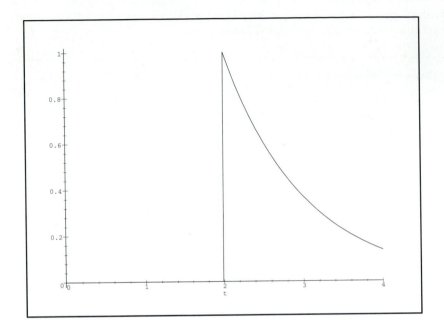

FIGURE 8.1
Plot of the function $f(t) = \mathcal{U}(t-2)\exp[-(t-2)]$ for $0 \le t \le 3$.

```
> eq1 := diff(y(t), t$2) + y(t) = 0;
```

$$eq1 := \left(\frac{d^2}{dt^2} y(t) \right) + y(t) = 0$$

```
> teq1 := laplace(eq1, t, s);

  teq1 := (laplace(y(t), t, s) s - y(0)) s - D(y)(0) + laplace(y(t), t, s) = 0
```

Note that *Maple* correctly applies the rules for taking the Laplace transform of ordinary derivatives.[2] Now, we solve this equation with the solve() function for $Y(s)$, the transform of $y(t)$ which *Maple* calls laplace(y(t), t, s):

---

[2] *Maple* can handle the usual *operational* properties of the Laplace and inverse Laplace transform.

```
> solve(teq1, laplace(y(t), t, s));
```

$$- \frac{-s\, y(0) - D(y)(0)}{s^2 + 1}$$

We apply the initial conditions with the **subs()** function:

```
> subs({y(0) = 1, D(y)(0) = -1}, ");
```

$$- \frac{-s + 1}{s^2 + 1}$$

Finally we take the inverse transform of this result:

```
>  invlaplace(", s, t);
```

$$\cos(t) - \sin(t)$$

Thus the solution to Eq. (8.1) satisfying the initial conditions is $y = \cos t - \sin t$.

8.4   A CIRCUIT ANALYSIS PROBLEM

Consider the electrical circuit shown in Fig. 8.2   The input voltage is a transient

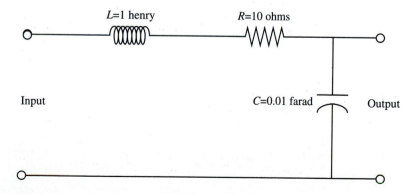

FIGURE 8.2
Sample electric circuit. The input voltage is $f(t) = \delta(t)$.

of unit magnitude, and this is modeled by $f(t) = \delta(t)$. The inductance is 1 henry, the resistance is 10 ohms, and the capacitance is 0.01 farads. We assume that at $t = 0$, there is no voltage or current present in the circuit. The differential equation which models this problem is

$$q'' + 10q' + 100q = \delta(t), \quad q(0) = q'(0) = 0, \tag{8.2}$$

where the output voltage is q/C and C is the capacitance in farads. First, we set up the differential equation in *Maple*:

```
> circuit := diff(q(t), t$2) + 10 * diff(q(t), t) + 100 * q(t) = Dirac(t);

                    /  2      \
                    |  d      |     / d      \
          circuit := |----- q(t)| + 10 |---- q(t)| + 100 q(t) = Dirac(t)
                    |  2      |     \ dt     /
                    \ dt      /
```

Now we take the Laplace transform of this equation:

```
> laplace(circuit, t, s);

     (laplace(q(t), t, s) s - q(0)) s - D(q)(0) + 10 laplace(q(t), t, s) s

        - 10 q(0) + 100 laplace(q(t), t, s) = 1
```

Next, we solve for the Laplace transform itself:

```
> solve(", laplace(q(t), t, s));

               - s q(0) - D(q)(0) - 10 q(0) - 1
          -    --------------------------------
                            2
                          s   + 10 s + 100
```

Then, apply the initial conditions and take the inverse Laplace transform:

```
> subs({q(0) = 0, D(q)(0) = 0}, ");
```

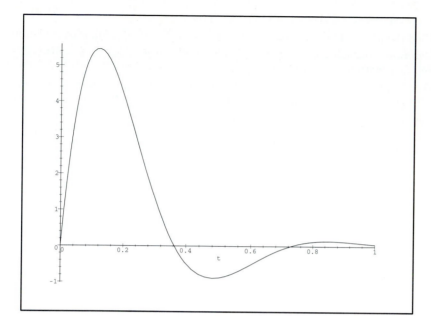

FIGURE 8.3
Output voltage of sample electric circuit.

```
> exsol := invlaplace(", s, t);
```

$$exsol := 1/15 \; exp(-\;5\;t)\;sin(5\;3^{1/2}\;t)\;3^{1/2}$$

The output voltage can then be plotted with the `plot()` function. Recalling that since $V = q/C$, we can visualize the voltage with this command:

```
> plot(exsol / 0.01, t = 0 .. 1);
```

The result is shown in Fig. 8.3.

We note here that the `dsolve()` function can directly solve differential equations with Laplace transforms. This is forced with the use of the `laplace` option, discussed in Chapter 7. This method may not always work, and in any case, can obscure intermediate results that are sometimes useful.

EXERCISES

8.1. Derive Eq. (8.2).

8.2. Find the Laplace transform of $f(t) = e^{-t}(1 - \cos t)/t$.

8.3. Find the inverse Laplace transform of $F(s) = 2e^{-3s}/[s^3(s^2 + 5)]$. Plot the result.

8.4. Determine the solution to the initial value problem $y'' + 5y' + 5y = \delta(t - 2) - 3\delta(t - 5)$ with $y(0) = y'(0) = 0$.

8.5. Determine the solution to the initial value problem $y'' + y' + 15y = 1 - \mathcal{U}(t - 2)$ with $y(0) = y'(0) = 0$. [Hint: Take the transform of the right-hand side by hand.]

8.6. Suppose a 1 kg mass stretches a spring 0.25 m. If the spring-mass system is at its equilibrium position, determine the motion of the mass if a sinusoidal driving force of $F(t) = 0.5 \sin(6\pi t)$ newtons is applied for $0 \le t \le \pi$ seconds.

CHAPTER
9

SYSTEMS OF ODES

9.1 LABORATORY GOALS

a. To use the `dsolve()` function to determine solutions to systems of ordinary differential equations.

b. To use matrix methods to determine the solutions to homogeneous and non-homogeneous systems.

9.2 HOMOGENEOUS LINEAR SYSTEMS

We treat here systems of first-order linear ordinary differential equations with constant coefficients. For example, consider the system:

$$x_1' = 4x_1 + 2x_2, \tag{9.1}$$

$$x_2' = 3x_1 + 3x_2. \tag{9.2}$$

There are several ways to attack this system in *Maple*. First, we write this system as a set containing two symbolic equations, to which we give the name `ex1`:

```
> ex1 := {diff(x1(t), t) = 4 * x1(t) + 2 * x2(t),
          diff(x2(t), t) = 3 * x1(t) + 3 * x2(t)};

              d                            d
    ex1 := {---- x2(t) = 3 x1(t) + 3 x2(t), ---- x1(t) = 4 x1(t) + 2 x2(t)}
              dt                           dt
```

Now we call `dsolve()` to generate the general solution:

```
> dsolve(ex1, {x1(t), x2(t)});

    {x2(t) = _C2 exp(6 t) - 3/2 _C1 exp(t), x1(t) = _C2 exp(6 t) + _C1 exp(t)}
```

In this result, _C1 and _C2 are arbitrary constants.

Initial conditions can also be prescribed. Suppose that $x_1(0) = 1$ and $x_2(0) = -1$. We modify the *Maple* set `ex1` by appending the initial conditions to it. We do this by using the `union` operator, which returns the union of two sets:

```
> ex2 := ex1 union {x1(0) = 1, x2(0) = -1};

              d                            d
    ex2 := {---- x2(t) = 3 x1(t) + 3 x2(t), ---- x1(t) = 4 x1(t) + 2 x2(t),
              dt                           dt

           x2(0) = -1, x1(0) = 1}
```

We again use `dsolve()`, but this time the call will produce the specific solution to the system:

```
> dsolve(ex2, {x1(t), x2(t)});

    {x2(t) = 1/5 exp(6 t) - 6/5 exp(t), x1(t) = 1/5 exp(6 t) + 4/5 exp(t)}
```

An alternate solution method involves the matrix exponential form of the solution. For constant coefficient homogeneous systems of the form $X' = AX$, the solution can be written as $X = \exp(At)C$ where A is the coefficient matrix and C is a vector containing the initial conditions. In the example given in Eqs. (9.2) and (9.2), the coefficient matrix A is constructed with the `matrix()` function (here called from the `linalg` package):

```
> A := linalg[matrix](2, 2, [[4, 2], [3, 3]]);

                        [ 4  2 ]
                A := [        ]
                        [ 3  3 ]
```

The matrix exponential is determined with the `exponential()` function:

```
> gs := linalg[exponential](A*t);

          [ 2/5 exp(t) + 3/5 exp(6 t)   2/5 exp(6 t) - 2/5 exp(t) ]
    gs := [                                                        ]
          [ 3/5 exp(6 t) - 3/5 exp(t)   3/5 exp(t) + 2/5 exp(6 t) ]
```

Now we multiply this by a vector composed of the two initial conditions using the special operator **&*** for matrix multiplication:

```
> ps := evalm(gs &* array([1, -1]));

    ps := [ 1/5 exp(6 t) + 4/5 exp(t), 1/5 exp(6 t) - 6/5 exp(t) ]
```

This result (except for the order of the terms) is identical to that obtained using the `dsolve()` function. Note that use of the `exponential()` does not involve the vexing problem of determining the canonical form of the matrix. The underlying linear algebraic manipulations of eigenvalues and eigenvectors is performed automatically by *Maple*. Either method is straightforward to apply. The matrix approach does permit easy evaluation of the eigenvalues in the event that stability questions arise. The `dsolve()` approach makes it easier to go back and compute numerical solutions by slightly modifying the argument list (see Chapter 10).

9.3 NONHOMOGENEOUS LINEAR SYSTEMS

To illustrate the solution of nonhomogeneous systems, we modify the system used in the previous section by adding a nonhomogeneous term to each equation:

$$x_1' = 4x_1 + 2x_2 + \sin t, \tag{9.3}$$

$$x_2' = 3x_1 + 3x_2 - \cos t. \tag{9.4}$$

and utilize the same initial conditions, viz. $x_1(0) = 1$ and $x_2(0) = -1$. We use the symbol `ex3` and specifically add to it the two initial conditions as symbolic equations:

```
> ex3 := {diff(x1(t), t) = 4 * x1(t) + 2 * x2(t) + sin(t),
          diff(x2(t), t) = 3 * x1(t) + 3 * x2(t) + cos(t),
          x1(0) = 1, x2(0) = -1};

                            d
   ex3 := {x2(0) = -1, x1(0) = 1, ---- x1(t) = 4 x1(t) + 2 x2(t) + sin(t),
                            dt

       d
      ---- x2(t) = 3 x1(t) + 3 x2(t) + cos(t)}
       dt
```

As before, `dsolve()` generates the specific solution:

```
> dsolve(ex3, {x1(t), x2(t)});
                       18            52
   {x1(t) = - 3/37 cos(t) - ---- sin(t) + --- exp(6 t) + 4/5 exp(t),
                       37            185

                          19            52
       x2(t) = - 3/37 cos(t) + ---- sin(t) + --- exp(6 t) - 6/5 exp(t)}
                          37            185
```

The method of variation of parameters can also be used to determine the solution in this case. If a nonhomogeneous system is written as $X' = AX + G$, then the general solution is given by $X = \Phi C + \Phi \int \Phi^{-1} G \, dt$ where Φ is a fundamental matrix of the system. Since $\exp(At)$ is a fundamental matrix, we see the way clear for applying this formula to obtain the general solution to our nonhomogeneous problem. First we compute the fundamental matrix with the `exponential()` function:

```
> phi := linalg[exponential](A * t);
                [ 2/5 exp(t) + 3/5 exp(6 t)   2/5 exp(6 t) - 2/5 exp(t) ]
        phi := [                                                        ]
                [ 3/5 exp(6 t) - 3/5 exp(t)   3/5 exp(t) + 2/5 exp(6 t) ]
```

Now we can apply the variation of parameters formula using the functions `inverse()` and `int()`.[1]

---

[1] Note the use of the `map()` function to distribute the integrations over each component of the matrix.

```
> gsol := evalm(
              phi &* array([_C1, _C2])  + phi &*
               map(int, evalm(linalg[inverse](phi) &*
                   array([sin(t), -cos(t)]))), t)
                 );

gsol := [

     2/5 _C1 exp(t) + 3/5 _C1 exp(6 t) + 2/5 _C2 exp(6 t) - 2/5 _C2 exp(t)

          - 2/5 exp(t) exp(- t) cos(t) + 9/185 exp(6 t) exp(- 6 t) cos(t)

          - 4/37 exp(6 t) exp(- 6 t) sin(t),

     3/5 _C1 exp(6 t) - 3/5 _C1 exp(t) + 3/5 _C2 exp(t) + 2/5 _C2 exp(6 t)

          + 9/185 exp(6 t) exp(- 6 t) cos(t) - 4/37 exp(6 t) exp(- 6 t) sin(t)

          + 3/5 exp(t) exp(- t) cos(t)

     ]
```

We now apply the initial conditions and build a set of two equations for our unknown constants _C1 and _C2, using the subs() function:

```
> res1 := {subs(t = 0, gsol[1]) = 1, subs(t = 0, gsol[2]) = -1};

                        24         2                    2
   res1 := {_C2 exp(0) + ---- exp(0)  cos(0) - 4/37 exp(0)  sin(0) = -1,
                        37

                    13         2                    2
       _C1 exp(0) - ---- exp(0)  cos(0) - 4/37 exp(0)  sin(0) = 1}
                    37
```

Now we solve this set of equations for the constants with a call to solve():

```
> res2 := solve(res1, {_C1, _C2});

                        50            61
             res2 := {_C1 = ----, _C2 = - ----}
                        37            37
```

Finally, we substitute this back into the general solution:

```
> psol := subs(res2, evalm(gsol));

psol := [

                28
   6/5 exp(t) + --- exp(6 t) - 2/5 exp(t) exp(- t) cos(t)
                185

        + 9/185 exp(6 t) exp(- 6 t) cos(t) - 4/37 exp(6 t) exp(- 6 t) sin(t),

    28
   --- exp(6 t) - 9/5 exp(t) + 9/185 exp(6 t) exp(- 6 t) cos(t)
   185

        - 4/37 exp(6 t) exp(- 6 t) sin(t) + 3/5 exp(t) exp(- t) cos(t) ]
```

This result can be simplified by using `map()` to distribute `simplify()` over the components of `psol`:

```
> map(simplify, evalm(psol));

                     28            13
        [ 6/5 exp(t) + --- exp(6 t) - ---- cos(t) - 4/37 sin(t),
                     185           37

         28                   24
        --- exp(6 t) - 9/5 exp(t) + ---- cos(t) - 4/37 sin(t) ]
        185                  37
```

This, apart from the form of the list, is the same as that obtained with `dsolve()`. In the nonhomogeneous case, using `dsolve()` involves decidedly less manipulation of intermediate results. On the other hand, `dsolve()` can be painfully slow, especially if there are unassigned constants in the problem. Both approaches have their place.

9.4   CHEMICAL MIXING

Consider the chemical mixing problem depicted in Fig. 9.1. Tank A and Tank B are connected by a series of pipes. Initially, Tank A contains 20 liters of water and 1000 grams of salt, while Tank B contains 40 liters of water and no salt. At the start of the mixing operation ($t = 0$), fresh water is pumped into Tank A at the rate of 3 liters per minute. Salt water is exchanged between the tanks at the indicated rates. We wish to determine the amount of salt in both tanks for $t > 0$.

Note from Fig. 9.1 that the amount of solution flowing into and out of each tank is the same. Therefore, the quantity of salt solution in each tank never

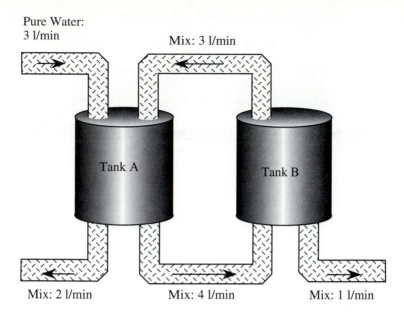

Pure Water:
3 l/min

Mix: 3 l/min

Tank A

Tank B

Mix: 2 l/min   Mix: 4 l/min   Mix: 1 l/min

FIGURE 9.1
Each tank starts with a different concentration and the amount of salt water.

changes (although the concentration does). Let x_1 represent the mass of salt in Tank A and x_2 represent the mass in Tank B. The pure water inlet adds no salt to Tank A. Since 6 l/min of solution are leaving Tank A and Tank A has a volume of 20 l, the salt mass in Tank A is being decreased by 6/20 times the instantaneous amount of salt in Tank A, namely x_1. Tank A is also gaining salt from Tank B and the rate of 3/40 times the instantaneous amount of salt in Tank B, namely x_2. The total rate of change of salt in Tank A is therefore $x_1' = -(6/20)x_1 + (3/40)x_2$. A similar argument can be used to establish the rate of change of salt in Tank B (see Exercise 2). The system of differential equations which governs this problem is :

$$x_1' = -\frac{6}{20}x_1 + \frac{3}{40}x_2, \tag{9.5}$$

$$x_2' = \frac{4}{20}x_1 - \frac{4}{40}x_2. \tag{9.6}$$

along with the initial conditions $x_1(0) = 1000$ and $x_2(0) = 0$. This system is entered into *Maple* as follows:

```
> tanks := {diff(x1(t), t) = (-6/20) * x1(t) + (3/40) * x2(t),
            diff(x2(t), t) = (4/20) * x1(t) + (-4/40) * x2(t),
            x1(0) = 20, x2(0) = 0};
```

d

```
    tanks := {---- x2(t) = 1/5 x1(t) - 1/10 x2(t),
              dt


           d
           ---- x1(t) = - 3/10 x1(t) + 3/40 x2(t), x1(0) = 20, x2(0) = 0}
           dt
```

As before, `dsolve()` generates the specific solution:

```
    > sol := dsolve(tanks, {x1(t), x2(t)});
    sol := {

    x2(t) =

                   1/2                1/2   1/2                       1/2
        (40/3 - 8/3 10   + 2/3 (10 - 2 10   ) 10   ) exp(1/20 (- 4 + 10   ) t)

                   1/2                1/2   1/2                     1/2
      + (40/3 + 8/3 10   - 2/3 (10 + 2 10   ) 10   ) exp(- 1/20 (4 + 10   ) t)


        ,

                  1/2                       1/2
    x1(t) = (10 - 2 10   ) exp(1/20 (- 4 + 10   ) t)

                  1/2                     1/2
        + (10 + 2 10   ) exp(- 1/20 (4 + 10   ) t) }
```

We plot the two solutions together with the following call to `plot()`:

```
    > plot({subs(sol, x1(t)), subs(sol, x2(t))}, t = 0 .. 40);
```

Intuition tells us that the salt in Tank B ought to rise as the solution in Tank A is mixed with that in Tank B. We would also expect to see both salt amounts eventually go to zero, owing to the influx of fresh water into the system. The resulting illustration of both solutions is shown in Fig. 9.2, and our conjectures are confirmed. The amount of salt in Tank A continuously decreases, but the salt in Tank B rises rapidly at first, achieving a maximum value of about 400 grams at about 7 seconds after mixing begins. After that the amount of salt in Tank B also decreases continuously. To confirm our suspicion we evaluate both solutions in the limit as $t \to \infty$ with calls to the `limit()` function. We use []
and the function `rhs()` to pick off the right-hand sides of the expressions for `x1` and `x2` and pass these to `limit()`:

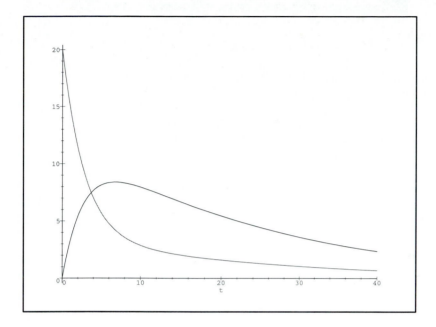

FIGURE 9.2
Solutions to the tank mixing problem. Both solutions approach 0 as $t \to \infty$.

```
> limit(rhs(sol[1]), t = infinity);

                              0

> limit(rhs(sol[2]), t = infinity);

                              0
```

The steady state masses in both tanks is zero.

EXERCISES

9.1. Determine the general solution to the following system:

$$x_1'' + x_2' + 3x_1 = \sin t, \qquad (9.7)$$

$$x_1' + x_2' - x_2 = t. \qquad (9.8)$$

9.2. Complete the derivation of the differential system [Eq. (9.6)] that governs the mixing tank problem.

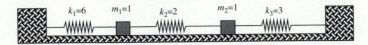

FIGURE 9.3
System of springs and masses used in Exercise 4.

9.3. Determine the precise time at which both salt masses are equal in the mixing problem. What is the mass in each tank at this time?

9.4. Consider the system of springs and masses shown in Fig. 9.3. Assume that both masses start from their equilibrium positions. The first mass (m_1) has an initial speed of $1/2$ while the second mass (m_2) is motionless. Derive a system of first-order equations for this compound spring-mass problem and determine the mass positions as functions of time. Plot the results for $0 \le t \le 10$.

9.5. Suppose both masses are at rest and that a driving force $F(t) = \sin \omega t$ is applied to the first mass. For what value of ω will the two masses collide? You may treat the masses as points and assume that the springs are infinitely compressible.

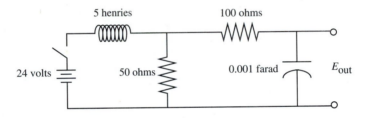

FIGURE 9.4
Electric circuit used in Exercise 6.

9.6. An electric circuit as shown in Fig. 9.4 initially has no current flowing through it and there is no charge on the capacitor. At $t = 0$, the switch is closed, and a constant 24 volts is applied to the system. Determine the output voltage E_{out}.

CHAPTER
10

NUMERICAL SOLUTIONS OF ODES

10.1 LABORATORY GOALS

a. To determine the numerical solution of second order ordinary differential equations.

b. To determine the numerical solutions to systems of first order differential equations.

c. To use the results of the `dsolve()`, `odeplot()`, and `plot()` functions to generate various solution portraits.

10.2 SECOND-ORDER EQUATIONS

Many important problems involving second-order initial value problems are non-linear and cannot be solved in closed-form. Numerical methods often present the best way of getting at the solutions to these problems.

Maple can solve differential equations numerically, while sparing the user from the need to select and implement a particular algorithm or library call. For example consider the motion of a simple pendulum with unit natural frequency:

$$y'' + \sin y = 0. \tag{10.1}$$

If we try to solve this differential equation in Maple, we obtain the following result:

```
> pend := diff(y(x), x$2) +    sin(y(x)) = 0;

                      /  2      \
                      |  d      |
           pend :=    |----- y(x)| + sin(y(x)) = 0
                      |   2      |
                      \ dx      /


> dsolve(pend, y(x));

              y(x)
              /
              |                    1
        x =   |    --------------------------- dy1 - _C2,
              |                          1/2
              /       (2 cos(y1) + _C1)
             0


                y(x)
                /
                |                      1
          x =   |    - --------------------------- dy2 - _C2
                |                            1/2
                /         (2 cos(y2) + _C1)
               0
```

Maple found two implict solutions, expressing x as a function of y in terms of elliptic integrals. Unfortunately, *Maple* has no built-in facility to deal with elliptic integrals.[1]

In instances like this, numerical solutions to such equations are appropriate. These can be obtained `dsolve()` function, with a special third argument. Suppose that $y(0) = 0$ and $y'(0) = 1$. The numerical solution to the pendulum equations is determined with:

```
> sol := dsolve({pend, y(0) = 0, D(y)(0) = 1}, y(x), type=numeric);

  sol := proc(rkf45_x) ... end
```

The solution is returned as a procedure, displayed in abbreviated form. It is usually not necessary to examine the detailed structure of such a procedure. To see a sketch of the result, the `odeplot()` function, part of the `plots` package, can be used. This function is given here with three arguments: the name of the procedure returned by `dsolve()`, a list with the names of the independent and dependent variables, and a range for the independent variable.

---

[1]With an appropriate change of variables, certain elliptic integrals can be evaluated in terms of *Maple*'s family of special functions. Alas, such is not the case in this example.

```
plots[odeplot](sol, [x, y(x)], 0 .. 4 * Pi);
```

The result of this call to `odeplot()` is shown in Fig. 10.1.

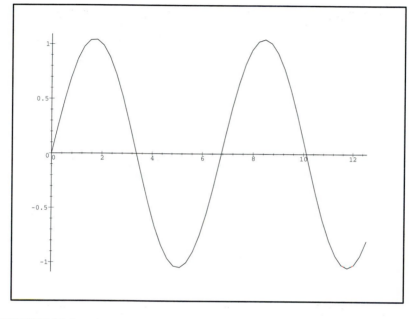

FIGURE 10.1
Numerical solution to the simple pendulum problem obtained by *Maple*.

10.3 MANIPULATING MULTIPLE SOLUTIONS

Suppose we want to compare the motion of the simple pendulum for a variety of initial angular positions. We can combine the `dsolve()` function with the `seq()` function for this purpose:

```
> sol2 := [seq(
            dsolve({pend, y(0) = 0.2 + 3 * (i - 1) / 5, D(y)(0) = 0},
                    y(x), type=numeric),          i = 1 .. 6)];

    sol2 := [proc(rkf45_x) ... end, proc(rkf45_x) ... end,
```

```
        proc(rkf45_x) ... end, proc(rkf45_x) ... end, proc(rkf45_x) ... end,

        proc(rkf45_x) ... end]
```

In this example we started with an initial angle of 0.2 radians and incremented that quantity by 0.5 radians until the value of 3.2 (a little bigger than π radians) was achieved. Next we build a set of the plots of each of these results:

```
> plotset :=
        {seq(plots[odeplot](sol2[i], [x, y(x)], 0 .. 2 * Pi), i = 1 .. 6)}:
```

This set of plots can now be viewed with the `display()` function:

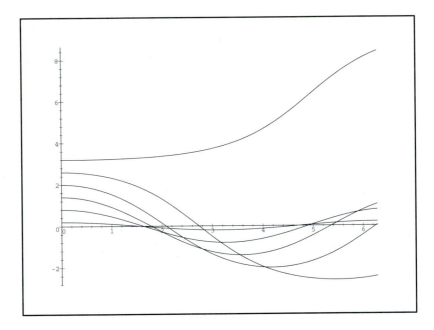

FIGURE 10.2
Numerical solution to the simple pendulum problem for six values of the starting angle.

```
> plots[display](plotset);
```

Figure 10.2 shows the result of this multiple solution evaluation. Note that for the solution with the largest initial angular displacement, $y(0) = 3.2$, the solution *increases* with increasing t. In this case, the pendulum has been started from the *other* side of its unstable equilibrium position $y = \pi$. If that calculation is run out sufficiently far, you will be able to see periodic solutions, but around a different equilibrium position. Also note that the periods of the other solutions change with increasing amplitude. This is a characteristic behavior of nonlinear vibrations.

10.4   SYSTEMS OF ODES

Maple can also handle the numerical solution of systems of ordinary differential equations. Consider the Van der Pol equation:

$$y'' + \epsilon y'(y^2 - 1) + y = 0. \tag{10.2}$$

This equation models the behavior of certain types of nonlinear oscillators which contain positive feedback. First, we re-write this equation as a system of two first-order differential equations:[2]

$$y' = x, \tag{10.3}$$

and

$$x' = -y - \epsilon x(y^2 - 1). \tag{10.4}$$

Consider first the solution for $y(0) = 1/2$, $x(0) = 0$, with $\epsilon = 0.1$:

```
> VDP1 := {diff(y(t), t) = x(t),
           diff(x(t), t) = -y(t) - 0.1 * (y(t)^2 - 1) * x(t),
           y(0) = 1/2, x(0) = 0};

                       d
     VDP1 := {y(0) = 1/2, ---- y(t) = x(t), x(0) = 0,
                       dt

           d                       2
        ---- x(t) = - y(t) - .1 (y(t)  - 1) x(t)}
           dt
```

We first build a set of plots and then plot both components of the solution with the `odeplot()` function:

---

[2]We could have used `dsolve()` directly on the Van der Pol equation. Writing it as a system facilitates the construction of a phase-plane portrait.

```
> sol3 := dsolve(VDP1, {x(t), y(t)}, type = numeric);

sol3 := proc(rkf45_x) ... end

> plots[odeplot](sol3, [[t, x(t)], [t, y(t)]], 0 .. 20);
```

The result is shown in Fig. 10.3. Note that solution $y(t)$, though oscillatory,

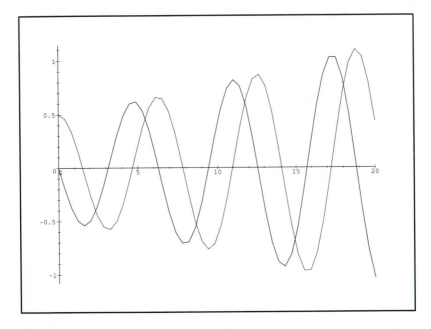

FIGURE 10.3
Numerical solution to the Van der Pol equation with $y(0) = 0.5$, $y'(0) = 0$, and $\epsilon = 0.1$.

grows with time. The behavior of solutions to the Van der Pol equation can also be studied in the phase plane. First, we re-solve the differential equation, and cause the output to be listed in a different format.[3] This enables us to obtain separate expressions for $x(t)$ and $y(t)$:

```
> sol4 := dsolve(VDP1, {x(t), y(t)}, type = numeric,
                       output = listprocedure);
```

[3] At this release of *Maple*, odeplot() improperly scales phase plane plots.

Now we extract our expressions from sol4:

```
> fx := subs(sol4, x(t));
fx := proc(t) ... end

> fy := subs(sol4, y(t));
fy := proc(t) ... end
```

We then generate the phase-plane portrait using these two results and the plot() function. A list consisting of the two functions and the independent variable range is passed as the argument:

```
> plot(['fx(t)', 'fy(t)', t = 0 .. 20]);
```

The phase-plane portrait is shown in Fig. 10.4. Note that $x = 0$ and $y = 0$ is a stationary point of the Van der Pol equation. The stability of this point can be graphically determined from the phase-plane portrait. Note that the solution curve spirals away from the origin, indicating that the origin is an *unstable* equilibrium point.

EXERCISES

10.1. Determine the solution to the simple pendulum equation when $y(0) = 0$ for values above and below and at $y'(0) = 2$.

10.2. The Duffing equation is given by $y'' + \beta y + (y + \epsilon y^3) = 0$. Compare the solutions to the Duffing equation when $\beta = 1$, $y(0) = 0.1$, $y'(0) = 0$, and for several values in the range $-1 \le \epsilon \le 1$.[4]

10.3. Consider the motion of a heavily-damped pendulum with sinusoidal forcing, governed by the equation $y'' + y' + \sin y = \cos \omega t$. Experiment with different values of ω and examine the response of the pendulum. Does it possess a resonant frequency? Generate some phase-plane portraits.[5]

10.4. Examine the solution to the Lorenz equations, given by

$$x' = -3(x - y), \tag{10.5}$$

$$y' = -xz + 26.5x - y, \tag{10.6}$$

$$z' = xy - z, \tag{10.7}$$

$$\tag{10.8}$$

---

[4]Duffing's equation models the motion of a damped, nonlinear spring. If $0 < \epsilon$ the spring is stiffer than the companion linear spring. For $\epsilon < 0$, the spring is softer. If you're up for a challenge, try solving Duffing's equation with $\beta = 0$ using elliptic functions.

[5]Chaos anyone?

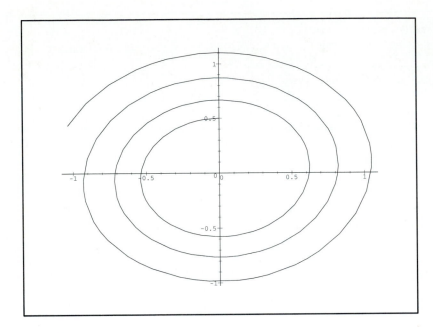

FIGURE 10.4
Phase-plane portrait of the solution to the Van der Pol equation with $y(0) = 0.5$, $y'(0) = 0$, and $\epsilon = 0.1$. The solution curve spirals outward from the origin, indicating that $(0,0)$ is an *unstable* equilibrium point.

with $x(0) = z(0) = 0$, and $y(0) = 1$. Use the interval $0 \leq t \leq 20$, and the **spacecurve**() function. The figure you should get is a picture of the famous Lorenz attractor..

11.1 LABORATORY GOALS

a. To determine solutions to the Cauchy-Euler equation.

b. To determine solutions to other special second-order ODEs.

c. To determine eigenvalues and eigenfunctions of Sturm-Liouville problems.

11.2 CAUCHY-EULER EQUATIONS

A second-order ODE with non-constant coefficients that sometimes arises in boundary value problems is the Cauchy-Euler or *equidimensional* equation:

$$x^2 y'' + bxy' + cy = 0. \tag{11.1}$$

Solutions to this equation can take on three different forms, depending upon the relative magnitudes and signs of b and c. For example, consider the differential equation and boundary values:

$$x^2 y'' + xy' + y = 0, \quad y(1) = 1, \ y(10) = 2. \tag{11.2}$$

We can use the `dsolve()` function directly on this problem:

```
> ex1 := dsolve({x^2 * diff(y(x), x$2) + x * diff(y(x), x) +  y(x) = 0,
              y(1) = 1, y(10) = 2 }, y(x));

                                      (cos(ln(10)) - 2) sin(ln(x))
             ex1 := y(x) = cos(ln(x)) - ----------------------------
                                             sin(ln(10))
```

In this expression, the *Maple* function `ln()` is the natural logatithm function. We plot this result with the `plot()` function:

```
> plot(rhs(ex1), x = 1 .. 10);
```

In Fig. 11.1 we see that indeed the solution satisfies the boundary conditions at each end.

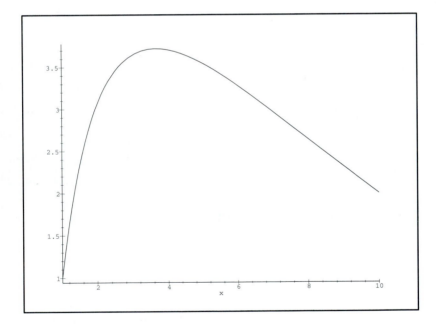

FIGURE 11.1
Solution to Eq. 11.2.

As another example, we solve

$$x^2 y'' - xy' + y = 0, \quad y(1) = 1, y(5) = -1. \tag{11.3}$$

This equation has the characteristic equation $(r-1)^2$, which yields repeated roots and a different solution form given here:

```
> ex2 := dsolve({x^2 * diff(y(x), x$2) - x * diff(y(x), x) +  y(x) = 0,
                y(1) = 1, y(5) = -1 }, y(x));

                                   x ln(x)
                ex2 := y(x) = x - 6/5 -------
                                    ln(5)
> plot(rhs(ex2), x = 1 .. 5);
```

The result shown in Fig. 11.2 satisfies the boundary conditions at each end.

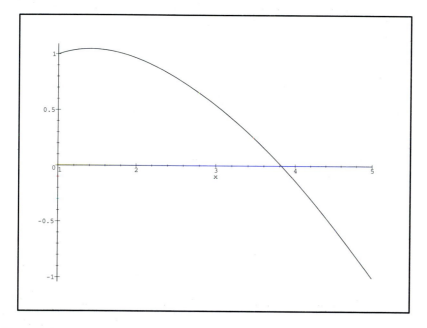

FIGURE 11.2
Solution to Eq. 11.3.

Maple can also solve Cauchy-Euler equations of higher order (see Exercise 2).

11.3   OTHER SPECIAL EQUATIONS

Many other second-order differential equations turn up in engineering mathematics. *Maple* also recognizes a good number of these, and it can present the general solutions in many cases.[1]

Consider first Airy's equation:

$$y'' - ty = 0, \tag{11.4}$$

This ODE occurs in certain wave propagation problems in which the square of the refractive index is a linear function. Here is what `dsolve()` does with it:

```
> dsolve(diff(y(x), x$2) - x * y(x) = 0, y(x));

              1/2                3/2       1/2                3/2
    y(x) = _C1 x    BesselI(1/3, 2/3 x   ) + _C2 x    BesselK(1/3, 2/3 x   )
```

The general solution is given by *Maple* in terms of the Beesel functions `BesselI()` and `BesselK()`. (The standard notation for these functions is $I_n(x)$ and $K_n(x)$ where n is the order of the Bessel function.)[2] *Maple* understands the numerical and analytical properties of these functions, and this ability will be demonstrated in the next section.

Next we consider Bessel's equation:

$$x^2 y'' + xy' + (x^2 - \nu^2)y = 0. \tag{11.5}$$

Suppose first that $\nu = 2$. Here is what `dsolve()` finds:

```
> bessel :=
    x^2 * diff(y(x), x$2) + x * diff(y(x), x) + (x^2 - 4) * y(x) = 0;

                  /  2      \
              2 |  d      |   / d    \   2
    bessel := x  |----- y(x)| + x |---- y(x)| + (x  - 4) y(x) = 0
                  |   2      |   \ dx     /
                  \ dx      /

> dsolve(bessel, y(x));

              y(x) = _C1 BesselJ(2, x) + _C2 BesselY(2, x)
```

---

[1] Particular solutions are another matter. Sometimes, the boundary conditions to be imposed are something like $\lim_{x \to \infty} y(x) = 0$ or $y(x)$ is bounded as $x \to 0$. *Maple* is not yet able to handle conditions like this, so some degree of human intervention is required in order to obtain a particular solution.

[2] These Bessel functions, when they appear in the particular form given here, are also called Airy functions of the first and second kind.

The two linearly-independent solutions are expressed by the functions `BesselY()` and `BesselJ()`. The usual mathematical notation is $Y_\nu(x)$ and $J_\nu(x)$ where ν is the order of the Bessel functions.

The next equation we consider is Legendre's equation:

$$(1 - x^2)y'' - 2xy' + n(n+1)y = 0, \tag{11.6}$$

where n is an integer. In this example, let $n = 1$. Here is what `dsolve()` does in this case:

```
> leg :=
    (1 - x^2) * diff(y(x), x$2) - 2 *  x * diff(y(x), x) + 2 * y(x) = 0;

                        /   2       \
                    2  |   d        |       / d       \
        leg := (1 - x ) |----- y(x)| - 2 x |---- y(x)| + 2 y(x) = 0
                        |    2      |       \ dx      /
                        \  dx       /

> dsolve(leg, y(x));

        y(x) = _C1 x + _C2 (1/2 ln(- 1 + x) x - 1/2 ln(x + 1) x + 1)
```

The standard notations for the linearly independent solutions to Legendre's equation are $P_n(x)$ and $Q_n(x)$. $P_n(x)$ are called Legendre polynomials, and $Q_n(x)$ are called the associated Legendre functions. *Maple* has Legendre polynomials as built-in functions `P()` with the **orthopoly** package. Note, though, that this form is not used in the presentation of the solution by `dsolve()`.

Another well-known equation from mathematical physics is Hermite's equation:

$$y'' - 2xy + 2ny = 0, \tag{11.7}$$

where n is an integer. This equation arises in the solution of the quantum harmonic oscillator. Suppose for example that $n = 2$. Then

```
> hermite :=  diff(y(x), x$2) - 2 *  x * diff(y(x), x) + 2 * y(x) = 0;

                       /   2       \
                      |   d        |       / d       \
        hermite := |----- y(x)| - 2 x |---- y(x)| + 2 y(x) = 0
                      |    2      |       \ dx      /
                       \  dx       /

> dsolve(hermite, y(x));
```

```
                             1/2      2
                    I _C2 (- I Pi    exp(x ) + x erf(I x) Pi)
      y(x) = _C1 x - ---------------------------------------------
                                       1/2
                                     Pi
```

The *Maple* function `erf()` is the error function.[3] One form solutions to this equation takes involves the Hermite polynomial. In *Maple* these are given by the function `H()`, part of the `orthopoly` package. These forms are not part of the solution presented by `dsolve()`.

11.4 APPLICATIONS

We will need the `linalg` package in this section. It is loaded with the following command:

```
> with(linalg):
Warning: new definition for    norm
Warning: new definition for    trace
```

Consider the modified Airy's equation:

$$y'' - (x - \lambda)y = 0, \tag{11.8}$$

together with boundary conditions $y(0) = y(1) = 0$. This type of differential equation is called a Sturm-Liouville equation. The constant λ is an eigenvalue and we seek values of this constant such that the modified Airy equation has nontrivial solutions.

```
> dsolve(diff(y(x), x$2) - (x - lam) * y(x) = 0, y(x));

                  /  2        \
                  |  d        |
      y(x) = DESol({|----- _Y(x)| + (- x + lam) _Y(x)}, {_Y(x)})
                  |    2      |
                  \ dx        /
```

Unfortunately, *Maple* was unable to find an analytical solution to the Airy equation when given in this form. One approach is to change the independent variable. If we let $w = \lambda - x$, Airy's equation can be rewritten as

$$y'' + wy = 0. \tag{11.9}$$

Maple can solve this equation:

---

[3]Recall that `I` is *Maple*'s way of representing the imaginary unit.

```
> dsolve(diff(y(w), w$2) + w * y(w) = 0, y(w));
```

$$y(w) = \_C1\ w^{1/2}\ BesselJ(1/3,\ 2/3\ w^{3/2}) + \_C2\ w^{1/2}\ BesselY(1/3,\ 2/3\ w^{3/2})$$

We now use the **subs()** function to change variables from w back to x, and assign the result to a new symbol:

```
> airy := subs(w = lam - x, rhs("));
```

$$airy := \_C1\ (-\ x + lam)^{1/2}\ BesselJ(1/3,\ 2/3\ (-\ x + lam)^{3/2})$$

$$+ \_C2\ (-\ x + lam)^{1/2}\ BesselY(1/3,\ 2/3\ (-\ x + lam)^{3/2})$$

To find nontrivial solutions, i.e. non-zero values for λ such that both _C1 and _C2 are not both zero, we apply the boundary conditions at both ends. This yields a pair of simultaneous equations for the two constants. Since these equations form a homogeneous system, the coefficient matrix must be singular. We construct the coefficient matrix by selecting the coefficients of _C1 and _C2 and evaluating those coefficients at the appropriate boundary point:

```
> t1 := coeff(airy, _C1);
```

$$t1 := (-\ x + lam)^{1/2}\ BesselJ(1/3,\ 2/3\ (-\ x + lam)^{3/2})$$

```
> t2 := coeff(airy, _C2);
```

$$t2 := (-\ x + lam)^{1/2}\ BesselY(1/3,\ 2/3\ (-\ x + lam)^{3/2})$$

```
> coeffmat := array([[subs(x = 0, t1), subs(x = 0, t2)],
                     [subs(x = 1, t1), subs(x = 1, t2)]]);
   coeffmat :=
```

$$[lam^{1/2}\ BesselJ(1/3,\ 2/3\ lam^{3/2}),\ lam^{1/2}\ BesselY(1/3,\ 2/3\ lam^{3/2})]$$

$$[(-\ 1 + lam)^{1/2}\ BesselJ(1/3,\ 2/3\ (-\ 1 + lam)^{3/2}),$$

$$(-\ 1 + lam)^{1/2}\ BesselY(1/3,\ 2/3\ (-\ 1 + lam)^{3/2})]$$

Values of λ that make this matrix singular will permit the existence of nontrivial solutions Eq. (11.8). We will need to find them numerically with the `fsolve()` function. Before doing that, however, we must estimate the location of the first root. We do this graphically by plotting the determinant of our coefficient matrix:

```
> detcoeffmat := det(coeffmat);
                        1/2                    3/2                1/2
    detcoeffmat := lam     BesselJ(1/3, 2/3 lam    ) (- 1 + lam)

                                    3/2        1/2                        3/2
        BesselY(1/3, 2/3 (- 1 + lam)    ) - lam     BesselY(1/3, 2/3 lam    )

                    1/2                        3/2
        (- 1 + lam)     BesselJ(1/3, 2/3 (- 1 + lam)    )

> plot(detcoeffmat, lam = 1.1 .. 20);
```

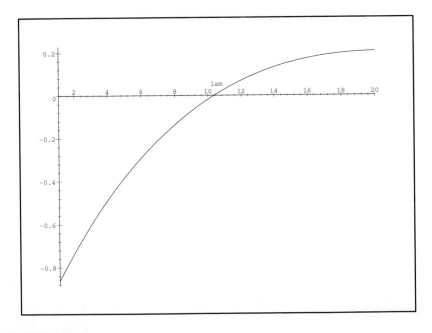

FIGURE 11.3
The determinant of the coefficient matrix plotted as a function of λ.

As shown in Fig. 11.3, the first zero occurs just beyond $\lambda = 10$. We will tell `fsolve()` to search the interval $8 \leq \lambda \leq 12$:

```
> eigen := fsolve(detcoeffmat, lam, 8 .. 12);

                        eigen := 10.36850716
```

We now substitute this back into our expression for the solution and solve for `C[2]` in terms of `C[1]` at the boundary $x = 0$:[4]

```
> airy1 := subs(lam = eigen, airy);
                                   1/2                                          3/2
airy1 := _C1 (- x + 10.36850716)      BesselJ(1/3, 2/3 (- x + 10.36850716)      )

                                     1/2                                          3/2
      + _C2 (- x + 10.36850716)      BesselY(1/3, 2/3 (- x + 10.36850716)      )

> solve(subs(x = 0, airy1), _C1);

                        1.724956778 _C2
```

Now we substitute this back into our expression for the solution and obtain:

```
> airy1 := subs(_C1 = ", airy1);

  airy1 := 1.724956778

                                 1/2                                          3/2
    _C2 (- x + 10.36850716)      BesselJ(1/3, 2/3 (- x + 10.36850716)      )

                                   1/2                                          3/2
      + _C2 (- x + 10.36850716)      BesselY(1/3, 2/3 (- x + 10.36850716)      )
```

Recall that eigenfunctions of homogeneous boundary-value problems are unique up to a multiplicative constant. So, in order to plot the result, we set the arbitrary constant `C[1]` to unity:

```
>  plot(subs(_C2 = 1, airy1), x = 0 .. 1);
```

The eigenfunction is sketched in Fig. 11.4.

---

[4]Note that the same result would be obtained at the other boundary.

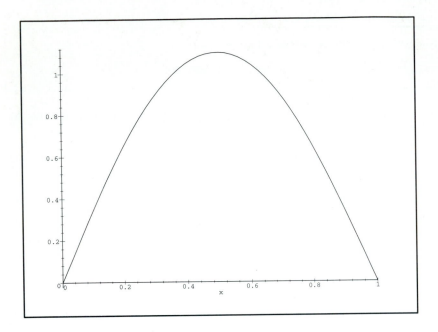

FIGURE 11.4
Solution to Eq. 11.8 for the eigenvalue $\lambda = 10.3685$.

EXERCISES

11.1. Determine the general solution to $x^2y'' - xy' + y = x^2$.

11.2. Determine the general solution to $x^3y''' - 3x^2y'' + 7xy' - 8y = 0$.

11.3. Determine the general solution to Laguerre's equation:

$$xy'' + (\alpha + 1 - x)y' + ny = 0, \tag{11.10}$$

where n is an integer. [Hint: Pick explicit values for α and n.]

11.4. Determine the general solution to Chebyshev's equation:

$$(1 - x^2)y'' - xy' + n^2y = 0, \tag{11.11}$$

where n is an integer.

11.5. Determine the general solution to the parametric Bessel's equation of order three:

$$x^2y'' + xy' + (\lambda^2x^2 - 9)y = 0. \tag{11.12}$$

Suppose that $y(0)$ is bounded and $y(2) = 0$. Determine the smallest positive eigenvalue and its corresponding eigenfunction.

11.6. Consider the Cauchy-Euler equation

$$x^2y'' + xy' - \lambda^2y = 0 \tag{11.13}$$

with $y(1) = y(2) = 0$. Determine the lowest eigenvalue and plot the corresponding eigenfunction.

11.7. Verify that second eigenfunction of the Airy equation describe in Section 11.3 is orthogonal to the first eigenfunction. [Hints: Use numerical integration and consider what the weighting function should be.]

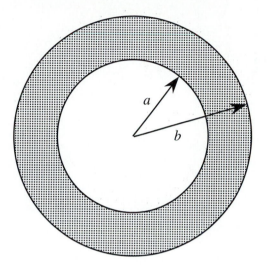

FIGURE 11.5
Cross-section of pipe insulation.

11.8. Suppose a long pipe containing steam is wrapped with a layer of insulation as suggested in Fig. 11.5. The pipe radius is $a = 3$ cm, and the insulation is 2.5 cm thick, so that the outer radius of the insulated pipe is $b = 5.5$ cm. Assuming no angular variations in the insulation jacket, the temperature in the insulation is described by the one-dimensional Laplace equation in polar coordinates:

$$\frac{d^2u}{dr^2} + \frac{1}{r}\frac{du}{dr} = 0,$$

with $u(a)$ and $u(b)$ prescribed.

(a) If the steam temperature is 110 degrees Centigrade, and the insulated pipe is in a duct whose nominal ambient temperature is 25 degrees Centigrade, determine the temperature distribution inside the insulation.

(b) What is the average temperature of the insulation?

CHAPTER
12

FOURIER
SERIES

12.1 LABORATORY GOALS

a. To determine Fourier trigonometric series coefficients symbolically and numerically.

b. To plot and compare Fourier series and the functions they approximate.

12.2 FOURIER SINE SERIES

Consider the function $f(x) = 1$, $1/3 < x < 2/3$, and 0 otherwise in the interval $[0, 1]$ with $f(x + 1) = f(x)$.

Before defining this function, we need to build a separate function that can compute the modulus of two real numbers.[1] This is done with the following definition:

```
> amod := (x, y) -> x - floor(x / y) * y;

              amod := (x,y) -> x - floor(x/y) y
```

---

[1] *Maple* lacks such a function.

amod() will return x mod y. The floor() function returns the greatest integer less than or equal to x. Our periodic function $f(x)$ can now be defined in *Maple* as

```
> f := x -> if (amod(x, 1) > 1/3) and (amod(x, 1) < 2/3) then
                 1 else 0 fi;
f := proc(x)
        options operator,arrow;
            if 1/3 < amod(x,1) and amod(x,1) < 2/3 then 1 else 0 fi
        end
```

The amod() function returns the remainder after dividing x by 1, thus causing the if construction to always return a value of 1 when x is in the middle third of any unit interval. The graph of this function in the interval $[0, 3]$ is produced with the *Maple* commands:[2]

```
> plot1:= plot('f(x)', x = 0 .. 3):

> plot[display](plot1);
```

and shown in Fig. 12.1.

We seek expressions for the Fourier sine and cosine coefficients of $f(x)$. First we determine expressions for the Fourier sine terms. These are given by the following:

$$b_n = \frac{2}{L} \int_0^L f(x) \sin\left(\frac{n\pi x}{L}\right)\, dx, \tag{12.1}$$

In our example, $L = 1$. An expression for the Fourier coefficients can be built up within *Maple* in the following way:

```
> b:=  n -> 2 * int(sin(n * Pi * x), x = 1/3 .. 2/3);

                                2/3
                                 /
                                 |
              b := n -> 2        |    sin(n Pi x) dx
                                 |
                                 /
                                1/3
```

We can now have *Maple* determine as many coefficients as we require. In this case, we shall use the seq() function to list the first ten Fourier sine coefficients for $f(x)$:

---

[2]We are using plot[display]() because we will be overlaying graphs later in this section.

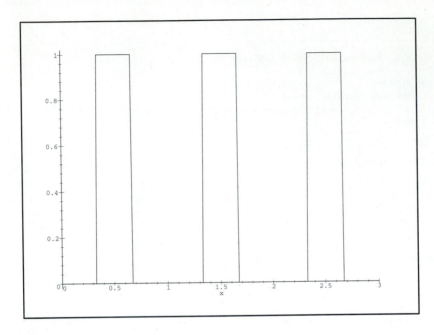

FIGURE 12.1
The square-wave function. The vertical lines are artifacts from the graphics process, not part
of the function.

```
> col := seq(b(n), n = 1 .. 10);

              2          4         2        2         4
    col := ----, 0, - ----, 0, ----, 0, ----, 0, - ----, 0
            Pi         3 Pi      5 Pi     7 Pi      9 Pi
```

Note that all coefficients with even subscripts are zero (why?).
    The partial sums of the Fourier sine series for $f(x)$ can be constructed with
the sum() function:

```
> g := (x, n) -> sum(col[j] * sin(j * Pi * x), j = 1 .. n);
                          n
                        -----
                         \
    g := (x,n) ->         )    col[j] sin(j Pi x)
                         /
                        -----
                        j = 1
```

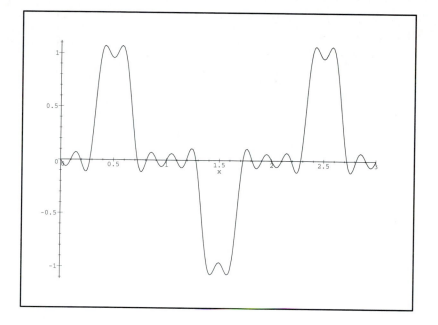

FIGURE 12.2
Tenth partial sum of the Fourier sine series for $f(x)$.

sum() takes as arguments an expression and a variable range. The partial sum of the first ten terms of the Fourier sine series look like this when sketched:

```
> plot2 := plot('g(x, 9)', x = 0 .. 3):

> plot[display](plot2);
```

This result is shown in Fig. 12.2. The function and its Fourier sine series can be viewed together with the display() command:

```
> plot[display]({plot1, plot2});
```

with the result shown in Fig. 12.3.

Convergence of the partial sums to $f(x)$ within the interval $[0, 1]$ is evident in this figure. Note the disparity between the partial sum and $f(x)$ within $[1, 2]$.

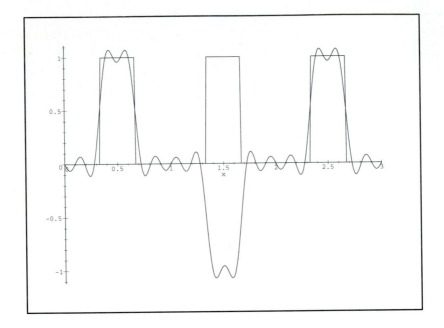

FIGURE 12.3
Composite Figure created with `plot[display]`(). The graph of the square wave $f(x)$ is shown together with the graph of the tenth partial sum of the Fourier sine series for $f(x)$ on the interval $[0, 3]$.

This occurs because the Fourier sine series is an odd periodic function. Agreement with $f(x)$ is guaranteed only within $[0, 1]$, the interval in which the coefficients are calculated. The Fourier series also shows evidence of Gibb's phenomenon, in the vicinity of the corners of the square wave.[3]

12.3   FOURIER COSINE SERIES

The Fourier cosine series for $f(x)$ discussed in the preceding section is also straightforward to compute. These coefficients are given as

$$a_0 = \frac{1}{L} \int_0^L f(x)\, dx \qquad (12.2)$$

[3]Gibb's phenomenon states that the partial sums of a Fourier series will always overshoot in the vicinity of a discontinuity of the function, a consequence of the non-uniform convergence of the series.

and

$$a_n = \frac{2}{L} \int_0^L f(x) \cos\left(\frac{n\pi x}{L}\right) \, dx, \tag{12.3}$$

where, in our example, $L = 1$.

These coefficients can be represented in *Maple* as follows:

```
> a:=  n -> if (n = 0) then int(1, x = 1/3 .. 2/3)
              else
                2 * int(sin(n * Pi * x), x = 1/3 .. 2/3)
              fi;

a := proc(n)
       options operator,arrow;
           if n = 0 then int(1,x = 1/3 .. 2/3)
           else 2*int(sin(n*Pi*x),x = 1/3 .. 2/3)
           fi
     end
```

As before, we construct a table of the first eleven terms of the Fourier cosine coefficients:

```
> co2 := seq(a(n), n = 0 .. 10);

                    1/2            1/2                1/2          1/2
                   3              3                  3            3
       co2 := 1/3, 0, - ----, 0, 1/2 ----, 0, 0, 0, - 1/4 ----, 0, 1/5 ----
                   Pi             Pi                 Pi           Pi
```

Note that all the odd-numbered coefficients are zero (why?).[4]

Partial sums are set up and plotted just as they were before with `plot()` and `sum()`:

```
> h := (x, n) -> sum(co2[j] * cos(j * Pi * x), j = 0 .. n);

                             n
                           -----
                            \
       h := (x,n) ->       )    co2[j] cos(j Pi x)
                            /
                           -----
                           j = 0
```

---

[4]Also note that $a_6 = 0$. Can you think of a symmetry argument that would account for this? Would you expect any other even coefficients to be zero?

```
> plot3 := plot('h(x, 10)', x = 0 .. 3):

> plot[display](plot3);
```

as shown in Fig. 12.4.   This figure and the illustration of $f(x)$ can also be

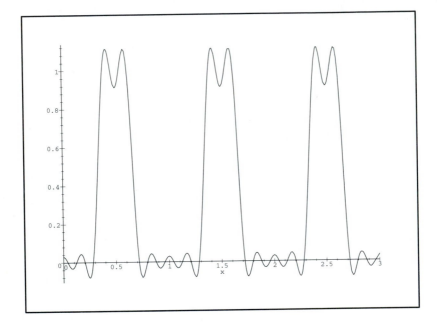

FIGURE 12.4
Eleventh Partial Sum of the Fourier cosine series for $f(x)$.

overlain with the plot[display]() command:

```
> plot[display]({plot1, plot3});
```

with the result shown in Fig. 12.5.   The partial sum and the function $f(x)$ are in much better agreement on $[1, 2]$ because the Fourier cosine series (and its partial sums) are even, as is $f(x)$.

A word of caution is in order. Note that in the previous two sections we never used the explicit form of f(x) in our integrations; instead we integrated

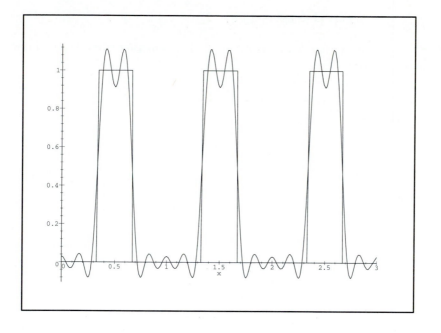

FIGURE 12.5
Composite figure created with `plot[display]()`. The graph of the square wave $f(x)$ is shown together with the graph of the eleventh partial sum of the Fourier cosine series for $f(x)$ on the interval $[0, 3]$.

over a restricted interval in which $f(x) \neq 0$. The *form* of `f(x)` does not lend itself to a clean symbolic integration. Moreover, the use of numerical integration (the `int()` called from within `evalf()` function) is also fraught with difficulty. The discontinuities in $f(x)$, together with the oscillatory factor `sin(N * Pi * x)` can result in unacceptable performance of the integration routines.[5] The lesson here is quite clear: in many cases, symbolic expressions really need to be thought about by a human being before asking *Maple* to perform a computation. Sometimes, a step done by hand, as we did in the previous sections, is absolutely essential to *Maple*'s success.

---

[5]Try the following command: `evalf(Int('f(x)' , x = 0 .. 1));` Be sure and capitalize the I in `Int()`! The answer returned by *Maple*, .2500000000, is obviously wrong. The integrand is presents serious problems to the integration routines. If you are in an adventuresome mood, give the following command: `infolevel['evalf/int'] := 1;` and re-run the integration. The detailed informational messages give some idea of the difficulties which *Maple* is encountering.

12.4 FOURIER SERIES

Consider the function

$$h(x) = (1 - x)(x + 1)(x - 2), \quad -1 \le x \le 1, \tag{12.4}$$

with $h(x + 2) = h(x)$ so that $h(x)$ has period 2. This function is represented and plotted in *Maple* as follows:

```
> hh := (1 - x) * (x + 1) * (x - 2);

                    hh := (1 - x) (x + 1) (x - 2)

> plot4 := plot(hh, x = -1 .. 1):

> plot[display](plot4);
```

Note that this function is *asymmetric* with respect to the origin and the *y*-axis as shown in Fig. 12.6. Because it is neither even nor odd, a full Fourier series must be used to represent it.

First, we construct functions that compute the Fourier sine and cosine coefficients:

```
> bb:=  n -> int(hh * sin(n * Pi * x), x = -1 .. 1);

                              1
                             /
                            |
              bb := n ->    |   hh sin(n Pi x) dx
                            |
                             /
                            -1

> aa:=  n -> if (n = 0) then int(hh, x = -1 .. 1) / 2
                else
                    int(hh * cos(n * Pi * x), x = -1 .. 1)
                fi;

aa := proc(n)
        options operator,arrow;
            if n = 0 then 1/2*int(hh,x = -1 .. 1)
            else int(hh*cos(n*Pi*x),x = -1 .. 1)
            fi
        end
```

Now we use the **seq()** function to evaluate these coefficients:

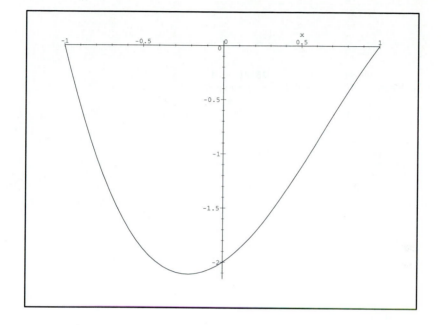

FIGURE 12.6
Plot of $h(x) = (1 - x)(x + 1)(x - 2)$ on the interval $-1 \leq x \leq 1$.

```
> co3 := seq(bb(n), n = 1 .. 10);

              12       3       4        3       12       1        12
      co3 := ---, - -----, -----, - ------, -------, - ------, -------,
               3     2 Pi   9 Pi     16 Pi   125 Pi    18 Pi   343 Pi
              Pi

               3        4        3
          - -------, -------, - -------
               3        3         3
            128 Pi   243 Pi    250 Pi

> co4 := seq(aa(n), n = 0 .. 10);

                      2         2          2            2
                    Pi  + 3   Pi  - 1   4 Pi  + 3    4 Pi  - 1
      co4 := -4/3, - 2 ------- - 6 -------, 1/8 --------- + 3/8 ---------,
                          4          4            4              4
                        Pi         Pi           Pi             Pi
```

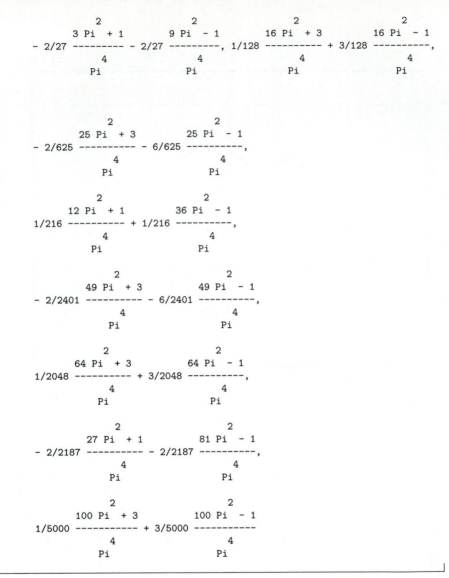

$$- \frac{2}{27} \frac{3 Pi^2 + 1}{Pi^4} - \frac{2}{27} \frac{9 Pi^2 - 1}{Pi^4}, \quad \frac{1}{128} \frac{16 Pi^2 + 3}{Pi^4} + \frac{3}{128} \frac{16 Pi^2 - 1}{Pi^4},$$

$$- \frac{2}{625} \frac{25 Pi^2 + 3}{Pi^4} - \frac{6}{625} \frac{25 Pi^2 - 1}{Pi^4},$$

$$\frac{1}{216} \frac{12 Pi^2 + 1}{Pi^4} + \frac{1}{216} \frac{36 Pi^2 - 1}{Pi^4},$$

$$- \frac{2}{2401} \frac{49 Pi^2 + 3}{Pi^4} - \frac{6}{2401} \frac{49 Pi^2 - 1}{Pi^4},$$

$$\frac{1}{2048} \frac{64 Pi^2 + 3}{Pi^4} + \frac{3}{2048} \frac{64 Pi^2 - 1}{Pi^4},$$

$$- \frac{2}{2187} \frac{27 Pi^2 + 1}{Pi^4} - \frac{2}{2187} \frac{81 Pi^2 - 1}{Pi^4},$$

$$\frac{1}{5000} \frac{100 Pi^2 + 3}{Pi^4} + \frac{3}{5000} \frac{100 Pi^2 - 1}{Pi^4}$$

Now we can assemble the Fourier series with two calls to the **sum**() function:

```
> p := (x, n) -> sum(co3[j] * sin(j * Pi * x), j = 1 .. n) +
                 sum(co4[j + 1] * cos(j * Pi * x), j = 0 .. n);
```

```
                / n                    \  / n                          \
                |-----                 |  |-----                       |
                | \                    |  | \                          |
   p := (x,n) -> |  )   co3[j] sin(j Pi x)| + |  )   co4[j + 1] cos(j Pi x)|
                | /                    |  | /                          |
                |-----                 |  |-----                       |
                \j = 1                 /  \j = 0                       /
```

This result can be plotted with the following call to `plot()`:

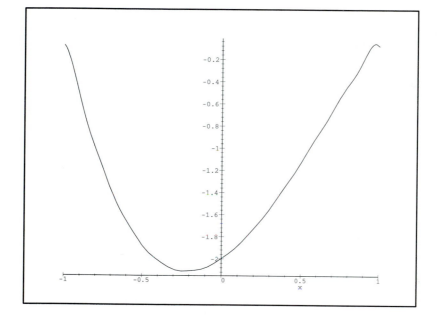

FIGURE 12.7
Tenth partial sum of the Fourier series for $h(x)$.

```
> plot5 := plot(p(x, 10), x = -1 .. 1):

> plot[display](plot5);
```

and the result shown in Fig. 12.7. Finally, $h(x)$ and its ten-term Fourier partial sum can be displayed together using the `plot[display]()` function. The fit between the two curves is excellent, and the regions in which the fit between the two is worst can be seen at the extreme ends of the interval in Fig. 12.8.

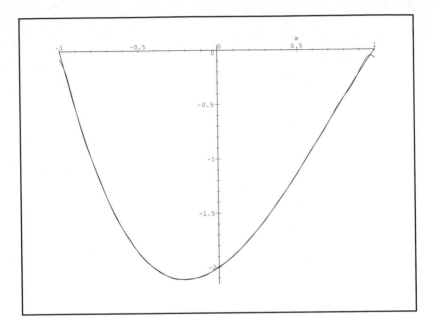

FIGURE 12.8
The tenth Fourier partial sum of $h(x)$ and $h(x)$ are plotted together in this graph. Approximation error caused by truncation of the trigonometric series is most noticeable at the endpoints of the interval.

```
> plot[display]({plot4, plot5});
```

EXERCISES

12.1. Compute the Fourier sine series coefficients for $f(x) = 4x(1 - x)$, $x \in [0, 1]$. How fast do these coefficients decrease?

12.2. Compute the Fourier cosine series coefficients for the previous problem. Compare the magnitudes. Discuss your results.

12.3. Compute the Fourier series coefficients for $g(x) = e^x$, $x \in [-\pi, \pi]$. How many terms in the series are needed to "reasonably" reproduce the behavior of $g(x)$. Support your answer with sketches of $g(x)$ and the partial sums of the Fourier series.

12.4. Compute the Fourier cosine series coefficients for $h(x) = H$, $-1/H < x < 1/H$, and $h(x) = 0$ everywhere else in $[0, 1]$. Discuss what happens to the coefficients as $H \to 0$. Provide sketches to illustrate the behavior of the partial sums.

12.5. Compute the Fourier sine and cosine series coefficients for the periodic Dirac delta function. Let the period be π.

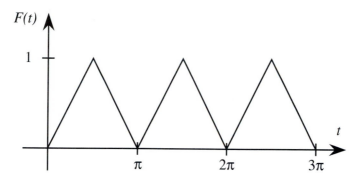

FIGURE 12.9
Sawtooth driving force.

12.6. A periodic sawtooth driving force $F(t)$, as shown in Fig. 12.9, is applied to a damped spring-mass system with mass $m = 1/2$ kg, and damping coefficient $\beta = 1$ N-sec/m. Assuming the mass starts form its equilibrium position at rest, determine the motion of the mass when the spring constant is
(a) 7 N/m.
(b) 8 N/m.
(c) 9 N/m.
Describe any qualitative differences you observe in the solutions. [Hint: Expand $F(t)$ in a Fourier series, and retain at least 8 terms.]

CHAPTER
13

THE HEAT
EQUATION

13.1 LABORATORY GOALS

a. To compute approximate solutions to the one-dimensional heat equation.

b. To visualize solutions in space and time with the `plot3d()` function.

13.2 ONE-DIMENSIONAL SOLUTION

As a consequence of the balance of energy and Fourier's Law of heat conduction,[1] the flow of heat in a thin, laterally-insulated homogeneous rod is modeled by the one-dimensional heat equation:

$$u_t = k u_{xx}, \tag{13.1}$$

together with an initial condition $u(x,0) = f(x)$ and homogeneous boundary conditions. In Eq. (13.1), the subscripts denote partial differentiation with respect to the indicated variable. Thus $u_t = \partial u / \partial t$.

---

[1]For a derivation, see e.g. Ray C. Wiley, and Louis C. Barrett, *Advanced Engineering Mathematics*, McGraw-Hill, New York, 1982, pp. 500–502.

Supposing the temperatures at either end are to be held at zero degrees so that $u(0,t) = u(L,t) = 0$, the separation-of-variables solution for this problem is

$$u(x,t) = \sum_{n=1}^{\infty} b_n \sin(n\pi x/L) \exp(-kn^2\pi^2 t/L^2), \qquad (13.2)$$

with

$$b_n = (2/L) \int_0^L f(x) \sin(n\pi x/L)\, dx. \qquad (13.3)$$

We will use *Maple* to determine the Fourier coefficients b_n and to examine the

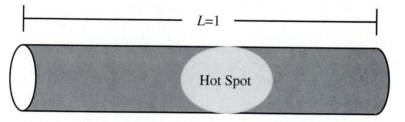

FIGURE 13.1
Uniform rod with asymmetric initial temperature.

partial sums of Eq. (13.2).

13.3   ASYMMETRIC INITIAL TEMPERATURE

Let us examine the behavior of the heat equation solution given by Eq. (13.2) when the rod is heated so that a small region of high temperature occurs near the middle of the bar as suggested in Fig. 13.1. One way to model this "hot spot" is with the function

$$f(x) = 4x^3(1-x)^2, \qquad (13.4)$$

which gives the bar an asymmetric temperature distribution. This can be set up in *Maple* as

```
> f := 4 * x^3 * (1 - x)^2;

                    3        2
            f := 4 x  (1 - x)
```

A sketch of $f(x)$ can be generated by `plot()`

```
plot(f, x = 0 .. 1);
```

with the result shown in Fig. 13.2.   The Fourier sine coefficients can be computed

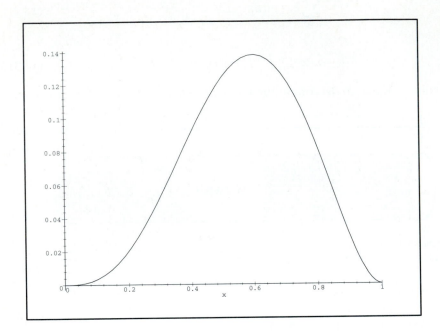

FIGURE 13.2
Initial condition $f(x)$ for example heat equation.

with the *Maple* expression

```
> b:=  n -> 2 * int(sin(f * n * Pi * x), x = 0 .. 1);

                            1
                            /
                            |
              b := n -> 2   |   sin(f n Pi x) dx
                            |
                            /
                            0
```

Since we will be using ten-term partial sums later in this chapter, we can use the **seq()** function to generate those values of **b(n)** now:

```
> co1 := seq(b(n), n = 1 .. 10);
```

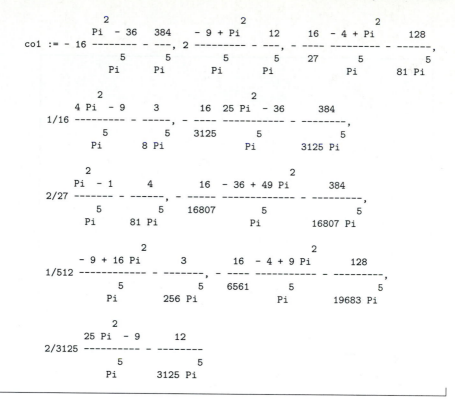

Assuming that $k = 1$, the partial sums can be expressed in *Maple* as

```
> F := (x, t, n) -> sum(co1[j] * sin(j * Pi * x) * exp(-j^2 * Pi^2 * t),
                    j = 1 .. n);
```

$$F := (x,t,n) \to \sum_{j=1}^{n} co1[j]\ \sin(j\ Pi\ x)\ \exp(-\ j^2\ Pi^2\ t)$$

To see, for example, the temperature distribution at $t = 0.1$, a plot of the partial sums can be generated with

```
plot(F(x, 0.1, 10), x = 0 .. 1);
```

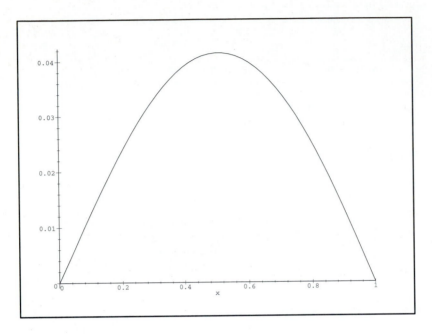

FIGURE 13.3
Solution to example heat equation for $t = 0.1$.

with the result shown in Fig. 13.3. The peak temperature has fallen considerably from its initial value and the shape of the temperature distribution appears very nearly sinusoidal. To see better the evolution of heat distribution in the bar, a time-lapse surface can be generated with the plot3d() function.

13.4   DISPLAYING HEAT FLOW DYNAMICS

The time-lapse surface can be constructed with the following *Maple* command:

```
> plot3 := plot3d(F(x, t, 10), x = 0 .. 1, t = 0 .. 0.1):

> plots[display3d](plot3, style = PATCH, axes = frame);
```

plot3d() takes a function of two variables as its first argument, followed by a pair of equations. Each list gives the range for that respective variable. In this example, we display the surface with the call to plots[display3d](), to which we have also passed the options `style = PATCH` and `axes = frame`.[2] This generates a surface over the x-t plane, with $0 \le x \le 1$ and $0 \le t \le 0.1$ which is shown in Fig. 13.4. *Maple* attempts to draw the "best possible" surface

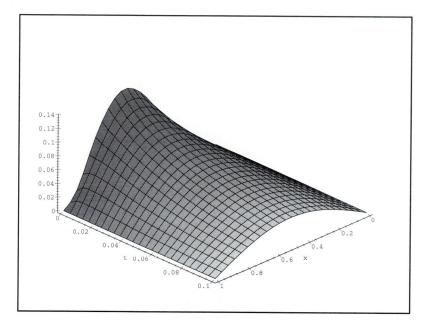

FIGURE 13.4
Solution to example heat equation.

according to a reasonable set of aesthetic and technical criteria. However, the default decisions *Maple* makes occasionally are not adequate.

To improve the appearance of this surface, we can change the orientation of the surface with respect to the viewer. With many windows-based interfaces to *Maple*, the surface can be "grabbed" with the cursor and rotated to any desired orientation. In the event that such a feature is not available, the points calculated with the `plot3d()` command can be re-used by combining those points with the `orientation` option within the `plots[display3d]()` command. The orientation is specified as list of two angles, each representing the relative position of the viewer in spherical coordinates.

For example, this call to `plots[display3d]()` with the indicated setting of `orientation` gives a better look at the surface for small values of time:

---

[2]See Chapter 1.

```
> plots[display3d](plot3, style = PATCH, axes= frame,
                   orientation = [-117, 63]);
```

The orientation angles here are given (in degrees) as $\theta = -17$ and $\phi = 63$. The result is shown in Fig. 13.5.[3]   This perspective gives a better feel for the

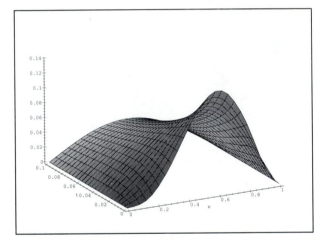

FIGURE 13.5
Solution to example heat equation; plot produced with `orientation = -117, 64]`.

asymmetry of the initial temperature and how that temperature evolves in time.

13.5   DISCUSSION

The time-lapse surface shown in Fig. 13.5 reveals some interesting details about the behavior of solutions to the heat equation. Notice how the shape of the

---

[3]The *Maple* front-end for the Macintosh, MicroSoft Windows, and some Unix workstations provide a mechanism for changing the orientation of surfaces. If the cursor is placed on the surface, the cursor icon can then be used to rotate a wire frame surrounding the surface. The corresponding coordinates of the orientation are shown in the graphics window. *Maple* automatically redraws the figure with the new orientation. Without such an interactive tool, *Maple* users usually have to experiment with a few orientations in order to find just the right one.

initial temperature distribution initially changes. As t increases, the temperature decreases rapidly, and a definite sinusoidal shape emerges almost immediately. The time-dependent terms in Eq. 13.2 decay exponentially. However, the higher order terms ($n = 2, 3, \ldots$) decay much faster than the first term ($n = 1$). That term has a pure sinusoidal shape in this example and it comes to dominate the dynamic behavior of the heat flow.

This suggests that when trying to model heat flow in other problems, if t is sufficiently big, then only the first term in the Fourier series need be kept. Many terms need be kept only when t is very small.

EXERCISES

13.1. Suppose the initial temperature were described by $f(x) = 4x^3(1 - x)^3$. Use *Maple* to show that every other coefficient vanishes. Why? How might the partial sums be set up in *Maple* in order to exploit this fact?

13.2. Solve the sample problem if both ends of the bar are insulated (so that $u_x = 0$ at each end).

13.3. Solve the sample problem if the initial condition is

$$f(x) = \exp[-128(x - 1/4)^2] + \exp[-128(x - 3/4)^2]$$

subject to both ends being held at zero degrees.

13.4. Consider two identical rods but with different initial temperature distributions. For the first bar, the initial temperature is precisely equal to the first mode of its Fourier Sine series with unit amplitude. For the second bar, the initial temperature is equal to the second mode with unit amplitude. Suppose both bars start with an equal amount of heat. Which bar cools faster? Think of a good *physical* reason to explain your result.

13.5. What determines when t is big or small? In the example $t = 0.1$ was big. [Hint: Examine an assumption that was made.]

13.6. Consider a bar of length $L = 2$ whose left end is held at constant temperature zero degrees and whose right end is free to radiate heat into the ambient medium. The appropriate boundary condition is $-u_x(2, t) = \kappa(u(2, t) - u_0)$, where κ is a constant and u_0 is the temperature of the ambient medium. Supposing that $\kappa = 1$ and $u_0 = 0$, determine the solution to the heat equation if the initial temperature is given by Eq. (13.4).

CHAPTER
14

THE VIBRATING BAR

14.1 LABORATORY GOALS

a. Compute solutions to a fourth-order ordinary differential equation.

b. Determine eigenvalues and eigenfunctions for different boundary conditions.

14.2 VIBRATING BAR

In this chapter, we consider the shapes undertaken by a thin uniform bar which is set in motion through some sort of initial impulse. If we let $u(x,t)$ represent the vertical displacement of the bar from its horizontal, equilibrium position, and neglect all forces but the restoring elastic force, the partial differential equation for the displacement is given by

$$\frac{\partial^4 u}{\partial x^4} = \frac{-1}{c^2}\frac{\partial^2 u}{\partial t^2}, \tag{14.1}$$

where c^2 is a constant which depends upon the material properties of the bar.

Since Eq. (14.1) is fourth-order, *four* boundary conditions are required.[1] The boundary conditions typically take one of the forms shown in Table 14.1.

[1] Note that two initial conditions are also required if the full dynamic behavior of the bar is to be examined. Since we are concerned only with determining the mode shapes and frequencies, we can limit ourselves to considering just the interaction among the solution and the boundary conditions.

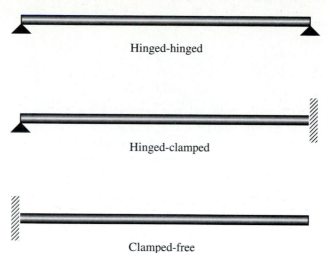

Hinged-hinged

Hinged-clamped

Clamped-free

FIGURE 14.1
Three examples illustrating different kinds of boundary conditions for a vibrating bar.

TABLE 14.1
Boundary conditions used with the vibrating bar.

Boundary	Formulation
clamped	$u = u_x = 0$
hinged	$u = u_{xx} = 0$
free	$u_{xx} = u_{xxx} = 0$

Consider the three particular sets of boundary conditions listed below:

$$u(0,t) = u_{xx}(0,t) = 0, u(L,t) = u_{xx}(L,t) = 0, \qquad (14.2)$$

$$u(0,t) = u_{xx}(0,t) = 0, u(L,t) = u_x(L,t) = 0, \qquad (14.3)$$

$$u(0,t) = u_x(0,t) = 0, u_{xx}(L,t) = u_{xxx}(L,t) = 0, \qquad (14.4)$$

The first set corresponds to a bar which is hinged at both ends as suggested in Fig. 14.1. The second set describes a bar which is hinged at one end and clamped at the other, as indicated in the middle illustration. Finally, the third set of boundary conditions describes a cantilevered bar, i.e. one that is clamped at one end and free at the other, as shown in the bottom bar in Fig. 14.1.

14.3 SEPARATION OF VARIABLES

In order to determine the properties of solutions to Eq. 14.1, we assume that $u(x,t) = y(x)g(t)$. Applying the standard separation of variables method, we obtain two ordinary differential equations:

$$y'''' - \lambda^4 y = 0, \tag{14.5}$$

and

$$g'' + \lambda^4 c^2 = 0, \tag{14.6}$$

where λ^4 is the separation constant whose values must be determined. We note here that solutions to Eq. 14.6 have the form $g(t) = d_1 \cos(\lambda^2 ct) + d_2 \sin(\lambda^2 ct)$. Thus, the vibration frequencies of the various modes are proportional to λ^2.

First, we use *Maple* to determine the general solution to Eq. 14.5. This is done with the `dsolve()` function:

```
> sol := dsolve(diff(y(x), x$4) - lam^4 * y(x) = 0, y(x));

sol :=

    y(x) = _C1 exp(lam x) + _C2 cos(lam x) + _C3 sin(lam x) + _C4 exp(- lam x)
```

Note that the fourth derivative is indicated by the symbol `diff(y(x), x$4)`. The four arbitrary constants are denoted by the symbols _C1, _C2, _C3, and _C4.

We assign the value of the general solution to the symbol g and its first and second derivatives to the symbols g1 and g2:

```
> g:= rhs(sol);

  g := _C1 exp(lam x) + _C2 cos(lam x) + _C3 sin(lam x) + _C4 exp(- lam x)

> g1 := diff(g, x);
       g1 := _C1 lam exp(lam x) - _C2 sin(lam x) lam + _C3 cos(lam x) lam

           - _C4 lam exp(- lam x)

> g2 := diff(g, x$2);
                2                          2                          2
    g2 := _C1 lam  exp(lam x) - _C2 cos(lam x) lam  - _C3 sin(lam x) lam

              2
      + _C4 lam  exp(- lam x)
```

We shall use these expressions in subsequent steps in order to determine non-trivial solutions for different combinations of boundary conditions.

14.4 THE HINGED-HINGED BAR

We consider the hinged-hinged bar with boundary conditions given by Eq. 14.2. First, we establish a set of the four arbitrary constants:

```
> coefs := {_C1, _C2, _C3, _C4};

                      coefs := {_C1, _C2, _C3, _C4}
```

Now, we construct a set of equations corresponding to the four boundary conditions. This set is assigned to the symbol `bc1`:

```
> bc1 := {subs(x = 0, g) = 0, subs(x = L, g) = 0,
          subs(x = 0, g2) = 0,
          subs(x = L, g2) = 0};

bc1 := {
```

$$\_C1\ lam^2\ \exp(0) - \_C2\ \cos(0)\ lam^2 - \_C3\ \sin(0)\ lam^2 + \_C4\ lam^2\ \exp(0) = 0,$$

$$\_C1\ \exp(0) + \_C2\ \cos(0) + \_C3\ \sin(0) + \_C4\ \exp(0) = 0,$$

$$\_C1\ \exp(lam\ L) + \_C2\ \cos(lam\ L) + \_C3\ \sin(lam\ L) + \_C4\ \exp(-\ lam\ L) = 0,$$

$$\_C1\ lam^2\ \exp(lam\ L) - \_C2\ \cos(lam\ L)\ lam^2 - \_C3\ \sin(lam\ L)\ lam^2$$

$$+ \_C4\ lam^2\ \exp(-\ lam\ L) = 0\}$$

Keeping in mind that we are seeking *non-trivial* solutions to this system of equations, we determine those values of λ that make this system of equations singular. To do this, we first build the coefficient matrix. This is done with the **seq()** and **coeff()** functions:

```
> A :=
  array([seq([seq(coeff(lhs(bc1[k]), coefs[j]), j = 1 .. 4)], k = 1 .. 4)]);

A :=
```

$$[lam^2, -\ lam^2, 0, lam^2]$$

$$[1, 1, 0, 1]$$

$$[\exp(lam\ L), \cos(lam\ L), \sin(lam\ L), \exp(-\ lam\ L)]$$

$$[lam^2\ \exp(lam\ L), -\ \cos(lam\ L)\ lam^2, -\ \sin(lam\ L)\ lam^2, lam^2\ \exp(-\ lam\ L)]$$

What we have done is manipulate *Maple*'s representation of a system of equations and systematically isolated and extracted the desired terms. At any rate, we now have the coefficient matrix **A**. Now we take its determinant with the `det()` function:

```
> detA := linalg[det](A);
                4                                    4
    detA := 4 lam  sin(lam L) exp(- lam L) - 4 exp(lam L) lam  sin(lam L)
```

We seek those values of λ that make the determinant vanish. First, we use the `solve()` function to see what *Maple* can find:

```
> solve(detA = 0, lam);
                                    I Pi
                0, 0, 0, 0, 0, 0,  ----, 0
                                     L
```

Maple has found seven solutions (six of which are repeated), none of which is useful in this problem. The first, $\lambda = 0$ will yield only trivial solutions, while the second is complex-valued—but we need *real* eigenvalues.[2]

It is worth noting here that we have run into a real limitation of *Maple*, and indeed, any computer algebra system. The determinant equation possesses infinitely many solutions, some real and some complex. We need to examine the equation by hand, at least for a while, in order to ascertain the nature of the roots we seek. In this case, it is clear from inspecting `detA` that this expression will be zero when $\sin(\lambda L)$ is zero. This implies that $\lambda = n\pi/L$ with $n = 1, 2, \ldots$. Since we are interested in obtaining the fundamental mode, we select $\lambda = \pi/L$ and substitute this back into the system of equations and then use the `solve()` function to determine solutions:

```
> solve(subs(lam = Pi / L, bc1), coefs);
            {_C1 = 0, _C2 = 0, _C3 = 0, _C4 = 0}
```

This is still not good enough, as these values for the constants will yield the trivial solution. However, if we simplify our expression for `bc1` before passing the equations to `solve()`, *Maple* will find non-trivial solutions:

[2]Why?

```
> mode1con := solve(simplify(subs(lam = Pi / L, bc1)), coefs);

        mode1con := {_C3 = _C3, _C1 = 0, _C2 = 0, _C4 = 0}
```

We substitute this result back into the expression for our eigenfunction as follows:

```
> mode1 := subs(mode1con, g);

                    mode1 := _C3 sin(lam x)
```

Finally, we substitute the lowest eigenvalue in as well:

```
> mode1 := subs(lam = Pi / L, mode1);

                              Pi x
              mode1 := _C3 sin(----)
                               L
```

We remove the coefficient (which is arbitrary at this point):

```
> mode1 := coeff(mode1, _C3);

                          Pi x
             mode1 := sin(----)
                           L
```

and obtain the fundamental mode of the hinged-hinged bar: $y = \sin(\pi x / L)$. This result is plotted with the following call to `plot()`, setting $L = 1$, and the result is shown in Fig. 14.2.

```
plot(subs(L = 1, mode1), x = 0 .. 1)
```

Note that the eigenvalues and eigenfunctions for the hinged-hinged bar are identical to those of the uniform vibrating string. However, while the characteristic frequencies of the string are proportional to the eigenvalues, those of the bar are proportional to the square of the eigenvalues. Thus, the spectrum of bar harmonics, i.e. higher-order modes, is much different than that for string harmonics.

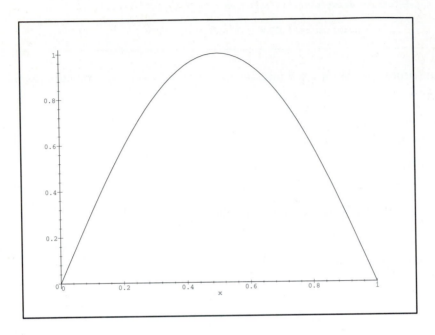

FIGURE 14.2
Fundamental mode of the hinged-hinged bar.

14.5   THE HINGED-CLAMPED BAR

We turn now to the solution of the boundary value problem of the hinged-clamped bar. The boundary conditions to be satisfied are given in Eq. 14.3 and are set up in *Maple* as:

```
> bc2 := {subs(x = 0, g) = 0, subs(x = L, g) = 0,
          subs(x = 0, g1) = 0,
          subs(x = L, g2) = 0};

bc2 := {_C1 exp(0) + _C2 cos(0) + _C3 sin(0) + _C4 exp(0) = 0,

   _C1 exp(lam L) + _C2 cos(lam L) + _C3 sin(lam L) + _C4 exp(- lam L) = 0,

   _C1 lam exp(0) - _C2 sin(0) lam + _C3 cos(0) lam - _C4 lam exp(0) = 0,

                2                          2                        2
   _C1 lam  exp(lam L) - _C2 cos(lam L) lam  - _C3 sin(lam L) lam

              2
     + _C4 lam  exp(- lam L) = 0}
```

As we did in the previous section, we use the list manipulating ability of *Maple* to extract the coefficients of the four equations to obtain the coefficient matrix:

```
> B :=
  array([seq([seq(coeff(lhs(bc2[k]), coefs[j]), j = 1 .. 4)], k = 1 .. 4)]);

  B :=

                            [1, 1, 0, 1]

              [exp(lam L), cos(lam L), sin(lam L), exp(- lam L)]

                        [lam, 0, lam, - lam]

       2                  2                          2            2
   [lam  exp(lam L), - lam  cos(lam L), - sin(lam L) lam , lam  exp(- lam L)]
```

Next, we examine the simplified determinant:

```
> > detB := simplify(linalg[det](B));

                        3                            3
  detB := 2 cos(lam L) lam  exp(- lam L) + 2 exp(lam L) lam  sin(lam L)

                     3                        3
      - 2 exp(lam L) lam  cos(lam L) + 2 lam  sin(lam L) exp(- lam L)
```

Those real roots of this expression will determine the eigenvalues for the hinged-clamped bar. In order to see more clearly where these roots lie, we collect like powers of λ:

```
> detB := collect(detB, lam);

  detB := (2 cos(lam L) exp(- lam L) + 2 exp(lam L) sin(lam L)

                                                              3
          - 2 exp(lam L) cos(lam L) + 2 sin(lam L) exp(- lam L)) lam
```

Since we are not interested in trivial solutions, we are really concerned with the coefficient of λ^3 in this last result. We extract it be dividing this result by λ^3 and assign it to the variable `eigeneq`:

```
> eigeneq := detB / lam^3;

    eigeneq := 2 cos(lam L) exp(- lam L) + 2 exp(lam L) sin(lam L)

        - 2 exp(lam L) cos(lam L) + 2 sin(lam L) exp(- lam L)
```

Not surprisingly, the `solve()` function will not find symbolic roots to this expression. In fact, roots must be found numerically. To do so, we first set $L = 1$:

```
> eigeneq := subs(L = 1, eigeneq);

eigeneq := 2 cos(lam) exp(- lam) + 2 exp(lam) sin(lam) - 2 exp(lam) cos(lam)

        + 2 sin(lam) exp(- lam)
```

Since the equation must have real roots, we try a graphical solution to see

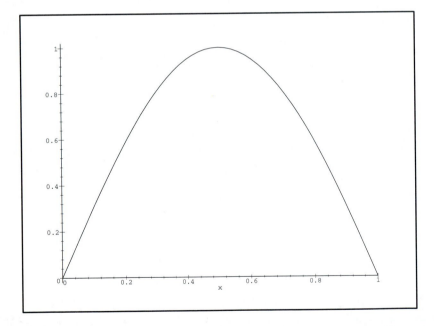

FIGURE 14.3
The first zero of this curve corresponds to the fundamental eigenvalue of the the hinged-clamped bar.

where they might be:

```
> plot2 := plot(eigeneq, lam = 0 .. 4):

> plot[display](plot2);
```

As shown in Fig. 14.3, the first root appears for $3 < \lambda < 4$. This give us enough information to use the `fsolve()` function to estimate the eigenvalue:

```
> lam1 := fsolve(eigeneq, lam = 3 .. 4);

                    lam1 := 3.926602312
```

and we see that $\lambda \approx 3.9266$. We substitute this value of λ back into the boundary conditions and attempt to solve for non-trivial values of the coefficients:

```
> solve(simplify(subs(lam = lam1, bc2)), coefs);

               {_C1 = 0, _C2 = 0, _C4 = 0, _C3 = 0}
```

Unfortunately, *Maple* reports only the trivial solution. What happened? Since we used the `fsolve()` function to determine the eigenvalue, the result was only *approximate*—not exact. Therefore, when we substituted this value back into the boundary conditions, the resulting system was still non-singular, and so *Maple* returned the trivial solution.

In order to work around this difficulty, we will have to manipulate the boundary conditions by hand. First, we substitute $L = 1$ and $\lambda = 3.9266$ into BC2:

```
> bc2a := subs({lam = lam1, L = 1}, bc2);

bc2a := {3.926602312 _C1 + 3.926602312 _C3 - 3.926602312 _C4 = 0,

 _C1 + _C2 + _C4 = 0,

 15.41820572 _C1 exp(3.926602312) - 15.41820572 _C2 cos(3.926602312)

     - 15.41820572 _C3 sin(3.926602312) + 15.41820572 _C4 exp(-3.926602312)

     = 0,

_C1 exp(3.926602312) + _C2 cos(3.926602312) + _C3 sin(3.926602312)

     + _C4 exp(-3.926602312) = 0}
```

Next, we solve the second and third equation of this system for _C1 and _C2:

```
> res1 := solve({bc2a[2], bc2a[3]}, {_C1, _C2});

           res1 := {_C1 = .01374601639 _C4 - .01412903215 _C3,

               _C2 = - 1.013746016 _C4 + .01412903215 _C3}
```

Now, we substitute this result into the second and fourth equations of BC2:

```
> reduceset := subs(res1, {bc2a[1], bc2a[4]});

           reduceset := { - 3.872627172 _C4 + 3.871123222 _C3 = 0,

               1.434210238 _C4 - 1.433653257 _C3 = 0}
```

Now we solve this last set for the remaining variables:

```
> solve(reduceset, {_C3, _C4});

                    {_C3 = _C3, _C4 = .9996116461 _C3}
```

We note that _C3 is arbitrary—a good sign that this approach will yield non-trivial solutions. We can now substitute this result back into **res1**:

```
> res3 := subs(res2, res1);

       res3 := {_C2 = - .9992232919 _C3, _C1 = - .00038835408 _C3}
```

Our constants can now be represented by the following set, which is built with the **union** operator:

```
> mode2con := res2 union res3;

   mode2con := {_C3 = _C3, _C2 = - .9992232919 _C3, _C4 = .9996116461 _C3,

       _C1 = - .00038835408 _C3}
```

Finally, having expressed all our constants in terms of _C3, we can eliminate all but one constant from the eigenfunction:

```
> mode2 := subs(mode2con union {L = 1, lam = lam1}, g);

     mode2 :=   - .00038835408 _C3 exp(3.926602312 x)

         - .9992232919 _C3 cos(3.926602312 x) + _C3 sin(3.926602312 x)

         + .9996116461 _C3 exp( - 3.926602312 x)
```

Since _C3 is arbitrary, we collect and keep just the coefficients of _C3:

```
> mode2 := coeff(collect(mode2, _C3), _C3);

mode2 :=   - .00038835408 exp(3.926602312 x) - .9992232919 cos(3.926602312 x)

         + sin(3.926602312 x) + .9996116461 exp( - 3.926602312 x)
```

In order to see the shape of this mode, we use the **plot()** function to sketch it over the interval $0 \le x \le 1$:

```
> plot(mode2, x = 0 .. 1);
```

The result of this command is shown in Fig. 14.4. The behavior of the clamped boundary is easily seen at the left end of the interval.

14.6 EXAMINING MANY EIGENVALUES

We turn now to the problem of obtaining many eigenvalues. In some cases, careful manipulation of the expression for the eigenvalues is required. For example, suppose we wish to determine the first five eigenvalues for the hinged-clamped bar. Recall from Fig. 14.3 that the magnitude of the expression plotted grew exponentially with λ. This can make a graphical analysis very difficult, since scaling requirements may render some zeroes impossible to see. To work around this difficulty, we scale the expression for the eigenvalues, **eigeneq**, by a factor of $\exp(L\lambda)$, which ensures that its magnitude remains bounded. We then plot the result:

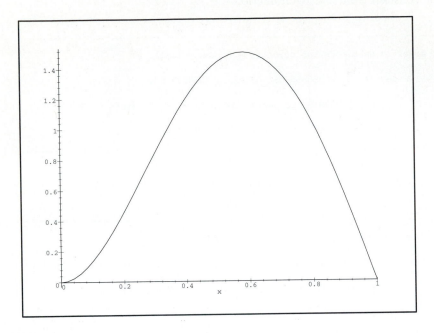

FIGURE 14.4
Fundamental mode of the hinged-clamped bar.

```
> eigeneq1 := eigeneq / exp(lam);
        eigeneq1 := (2 cos(lam) exp(- lam) + 2 exp(lam) sin(lam)

              - 2 exp(lam) cos(lam) + 2 sin(lam) exp(- lam))/exp(lam)

> plot(eigeneq1, lam = 0 .. 20);
```

We can now easily see the approximate location of all the eigenvalues for $\lambda < 20$, as shown in Fig. 14.5. First we build a list whose elements are the intervals in which `fsolve()` should look for roots:

```
> rootrange := [lam = 3.5 .. 4.5, lam = 6.5 .. 7.5, lam = 9.5 .. 10.5,
            lam = 13 .. 14, lam = 16 .. 17, lam = 19 .. 20];

     rootrange := [lam = 3.5 .. 4.5, lam = 6.5 .. 7.5, lam = 9.5 .. 10.5,

        lam = 13 .. 14, lam = 16 .. 17, lam = 19 .. 20]
```

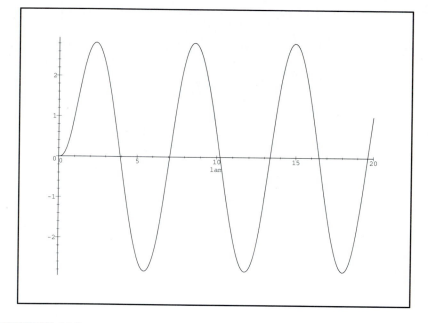

FIGURE 14.5
Zeroes of this curve correspond to the eigenvalues of the hinged-clamped bar.

Now, we use `seq()` together with `fsolve()` to find the root in each of these ranges and collect the results into a list:

```
> eiglist2 := [seq([j, fsolve(eigeneq1, rootrange[j])], j = 1 .. 6)];

    eiglist2 := [[1, 3.926602312], [2, 7.068582746], [3, 10.21017612],

        [4, 13.35176878], [5, 16.49336143], [6, 19.63495408]]
```

Note that list contains six smaller lists. Each of these will be interpreted as a coordinate when we plot this result below.

We also build a list of the eigenvalues for the hinged-hinged bar. Recall that $\lambda = n\pi$. This list is easily built with the `seq()` function:

```
> eiglist1 := [seq([j, j * Pi], j = 1 .. 6)];

    eiglist1 := [[1, Pi], [2, 2 Pi], [3, 3 Pi], [4, 4 Pi], [5, 5 Pi], [6, 6 Pi]]
```

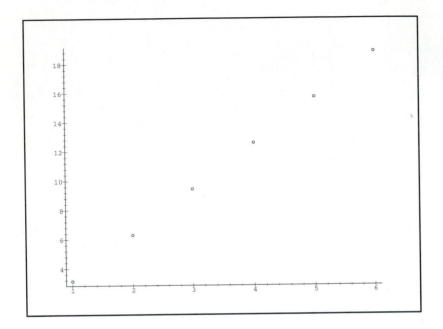

FIGURE 14.6
First six eigenvalues of the hinged-hinged bar.

These eigenvalues can be plotted with the `plot()` function. The `symbol` option causes *Maple* to use circles for the individual points it draws as can be seen in Fig. 14.6.

```
> plot5 := plot(eiglist1, style = POINT, symbol = CIRCLE):

> plot[display](plot5);
```

A similar command is used to plot the eigenvalues of the hinged-clamped bar and this plot is shown in Fig. 14.7:

```
> plot6 := plot(eiglist2, style=POINT, symbol = DIAMOND);

> plot[display](plot6);
```

Finally, we can use the `display()` function to overlay the two plots with the result shown in Fig. 14.8:

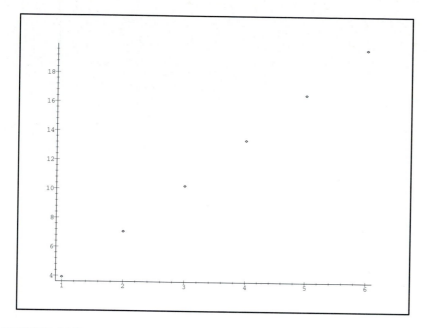

FIGURE 14.7
First six eigenvalues of the clamped-clamped bar.

```
    > plot[display]({plot5, plot6});
```

Note that the eigenvalues of the hinged-clamped bar appear to be shifted up by a uniform amount over the equivalent eigenvalues of the hinged-hinged bar. As we observed earlier, since the vibration frequencies are proportional to the square of the eigenvalues, we can see that the harmonic structure—the distribution of vibration frequencies—is substantially different in these two cases. This is one way in which to see that changing just one boundary condition in this type of problem can substantially alter the quantitative and qualitative nature of solutions.

EXERCISES

14.1. Determine the fundamental mode for the cantilevered bar (assume that $L = 1$). Compare the fundamental frequency to that of the other two bars. Which is highest? Which is lowest?

14.2. Determine the fundamental mode for a clamped-clamped bar (assume that $L = 1$.)

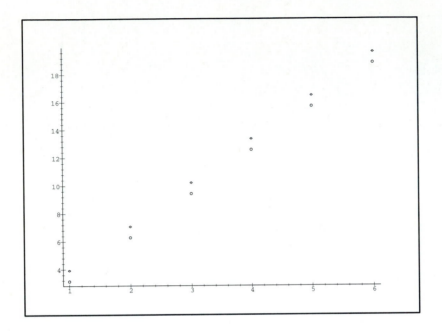

FIGURE 14.8
First six eigenvalues of both the hinged-hinged and clamped-clamped bars.

14.3. What would the length of a cantilevered bar have to be in order to have the same fundamental frequency of the hinged-hinged bar discussed in the text?

14.4. Determine the shape of the second mode of the cantilevered bar.

CHAPTER
15

THE VIBRATING
ANNULUS

15.1 LABORATORY GOALS

a. To determine the characteristic frequencies of a vibrating annular membrane.

b. To employ the `BesselJ()` and `BesselY()` functions for the computation of Bessel functions of different orders.

c. To use the `cylinderplot()` function to plot modal surfaces of a vibrating annulus.

15.2 DESCRIPTION OF THE ANNULUS

Consider the annular membrane whose cross section is shown in Fig. 15.1.

Assuming that the membrane is of uniform composition and under uniform tension, the partial differential equation which governs the small-amplitude vibrations of this membrane is, in cylindrical coordinates,

$$(1/c^2)u_{tt} = u_{rr} + (1/r)u_r + (1/r^2)u_{\theta\theta}, \tag{15.1}$$

where $u(r, \theta, t)$ represents the height of the membrane above or below its equilibrium position and c represents the speed of vibrations in the membrane. The boundary conditions are given by

$$u(a, \theta, t) = u(b, \theta, t) = 0, \tag{15.2}$$

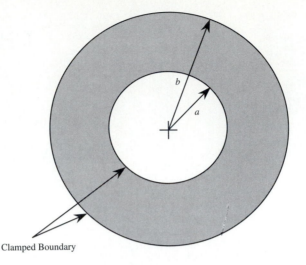

Clamped Boundary

FIGURE 15.1
Annulus with clamped edges.

which indicate that the membrane is clamped along its inner and outer edge. The initial condition is given as $u(r, \theta, 0) = f(r, \theta)$. Suppose the inner radius $a = 2$ and the outer radius $b = 4$. In addition, if we take the wave speed $c = 1$,[1] what statements can we make about the eigenfrequencies and eigenmodes of this membrane as it vibrates?

15.3   SEPARATION OF VARIABLES SOLUTION

By assuming solutions of the form $u(r, \theta, t) = \phi(r, \theta)G(t)$, Eq. 15.1 is reduced to the following pair of equations:

$$\phi_{rr} + (1/r)\phi_r + (1/r^2)\phi_{\theta\theta} + \lambda\phi = 0, \tag{15.3}$$

and

$$G''(t) + \lambda G(t) = 0. \tag{15.4}$$

The boundary conditions also become $\phi(a, \theta) = \phi(b, \theta) = 0$.

A further assumption is made concerning the form of ϕ: that $\phi(r, \theta) = R(r)\Theta(\theta)$. When this result is substituted into Eq. 15.3, we obtain two more ordinary differential equations:

$$r^2 R''(r) + rR'(r) + (\lambda r^2 + \mu)R(r) = 0, \tag{15.5}$$

which is a parametric Bessel's equation, and

$$\Theta''(\theta) + \mu\Theta(\theta) = 0. \tag{15.6}$$

---

[1] The problem can always be rescaled to make this so.

This assumption results in the explicit boundary conditions $R(a) = R(b) = 0$ and the implicit condition that Θ possess 2π-periodicity. The latter condition on Θ demands that

$$\mu = m^2, \quad m = 0, 1, 2, \ldots. \tag{15.7}$$

The solution to the radial portion of the problem is

$$R(r) = c_1 J_m(\sqrt{\lambda_{mn}}r) + c_2 Y_m(\sqrt{\lambda_{mn}}r), \tag{15.8}$$

where J_m and Y_m are the Bessel functions of the first and second kind respectively of order m. (Note that we now double-index λ.) Imposition of the boundary conditions at $a = 2$ and $b = 4$ results in the following pair of equations:

$$c_1 J_m(2\sqrt{\lambda_{mn}}) + c_2 Y_m(2\sqrt{\lambda_{mn}}) = 0, \tag{15.9}$$

and

$$c_1 J_m(4\sqrt{\lambda_{mn}}) + c_2 Y_m(4\sqrt{\lambda_{mn}}) = 0. \tag{15.10}$$

In order to have non-trivial solutions for c_1 and c_2, it is necessary and sufficient that

$$J_m(2\sqrt{\lambda_{mn}})Y_m(4\sqrt{\lambda_{mn}}) - J_m(4\sqrt{\lambda_{mn}})Y_m(2\sqrt{\lambda_{mn}}) = 0. \tag{15.11}$$

The roots of Eq. 15.11 will correspond to the eigenvalues.

15.4   DETERMINATION OF THE EIGENVALUES

In order to find values for the four lowest eigenvalues, we first use *Maple* to provide a graphical solution to Eq. 15.11. The function to be plotted is first determined by passing the coefficient matrix to `det()`:

```
> a := linalg[det]([[BesselJ(n, 2 * lam), BesselY(n, 2 * lam)],
        [BesselJ(n, 4 * lam), BesselY(n, 4 * lam)]]);

a :=

    BesselJ(n, 2 lam) BesselY(n, 4 lam) - BesselY(n, 2 lam) BesselJ(n, 4 lam)
```

The arguments of `BesselJ()` and `BesselY()` are identical. The first is the order, and the second is the argument.

In order to be sure that the *first* four eigenvalues are found, it is not enough to look for the first four zeroes of Eq. 15.11 when $m = 0$. We also need to check the zeroes when $m = 1, 2, 3$ as well. This is done with the following call to `plot()`:

```
> plot({seq(a, n = 0 .. 3)}, lam = 0.1 .. 4);
```

`plot()` is passed a list built up by successively substituting incremented values of the index.[2]

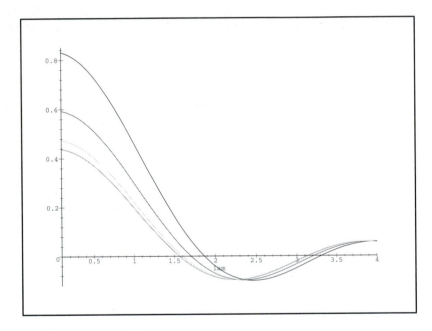

FIGURE 15.2
Graphical solution of Eq. 15.11 for values of $m = 0, 1, 2, 3$ and $0 < \sqrt{\lambda_{mn}} < 4$.

In Fig. 15.2, the first four roots correspond to the order of the increasing index m. Since all roots are less than 2, we can use the `fsolve()` function to generate numerical approximations to these roots. In this example, we use the `seq()` function to generate the four roots in a list:

```
> eigs := [seq(fsolve(a, lam = 1.5 .. 2), n = 0 .. 3)];
    eigs := [1.561515460, 1.598289190, 1.703460713, 1.864435034]
```

These results correspond to the four smallest values of $\sqrt{\lambda_{mn}}$. The eigenfrequencies can then be determined from the relation $f_{mn} = \sqrt{\lambda_{mn}}/(2\pi c)$.

[2]Note that since Y_m is undefined at the origin, the plotting domain begins at 0.1.

15.5 SKETCHING THE EIGENMODES

In order to determine the appearance of the fourth eigenmode, we must first return to Eq. 15.8 and eliminate one of the arbitrary constants. This can be done, of course, since the values of $\sqrt{\lambda_{mn}}$ found above are precisely those that make the system represented by Eqs. 15.9 and 15.10 have nontrivial solutions. In particular, for the fourth eigenvalue ($m = 3$ and $n = 1$),

$$c_1/c_2 = -Y_3(\sqrt{4\lambda_{31}})/J_3(\sqrt{4\lambda_{31}}), \tag{15.12}$$

which is represented in *Maple* with

```
> b := - BesselY(3, 4 * eigs[4]) / BesselJ(3, 4 * eigs[4]);

                    b := .6740716628
```

The mode function ϕ is then given by

$$\phi = \cos(3\theta)[(c_1/c_2)J_3(\sqrt{\lambda_{31}}r) + Y_3(\sqrt{\lambda_{31}}r)]. \tag{15.13}$$

This is set up in *Maple* with the following:

```
> phi := cos(3 * th) * (b * BesselJ(3, r * eigs[4]) +
              BesselY(3, r * eigs[4]));

   phi := cos(3 th)

      (.6740716628 BesselJ(3, 1.864435034 r) + BesselY(3, 1.864435034 r))
```

The `cylinderplot()` function presents a very nice rendition of ϕ. It is called here with several arguments. The first is a list of the three coordinates used in the plot (note that `phi` is the same as the z-coordinate), while the second and third arguments provide the plotting range for the radius r and azimuthal angle θ. The last two arguments are plotting options:

```
> plot3 := plots[cylinderplot]([r, th, phi], r = 2 .. 4, th = 0 .. 2 * Pi,
              axes = BOXED, style = PATCH);

> plots[display3d](plot3);
```

Note that the surface features can clearly be seen in Fig. 15.3. By changing the orientation so that our viewpoint is in the plane of the annulus at rest, we can also see how the boundaries behave:

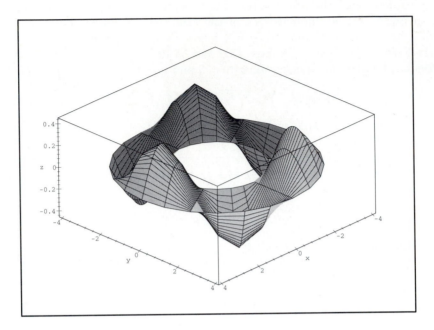

FIGURE 15.3
Perspective view of the fourth eigenmode of the annulus.

```
> plots[display3d](plot3, orientation = [90, 90]);
```

This result is displayed in Fig. 15.4, in which it is readily seen that clamped boundary conditions along the inner and outer radii have been satisfied.

EXERCISES

15.1. Determine the first four vibration frequencies if the inner boundary condition is changed to $u_r(a, \theta) = 0$. (This is called a free boundary.) Sketch each mode. Discuss differences between this result and the one presented in the text.

15.2. Determine the first four vibration frequencies for the half-annulus shown in Fig. 15.5. Sketch the fourth mode.

15.3. Consider a second annulus with inner radius $a = 4$. What would the outer radius have to be in order to ensure that the fundamental frequency of this annulus matches the one discussed in the text?

15.4. Compare the eigenfrequencies of the annular membrane to those of a rectangular membrane of similar dimensions. In what ways are the structure of the two spectra similar?

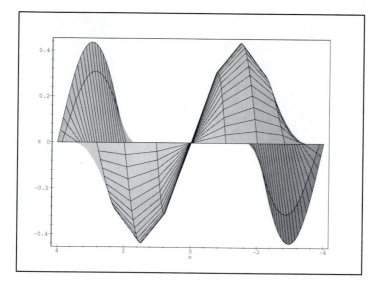

FIGURE 15.4
Side view of the fourth eigenmode of the annulus.

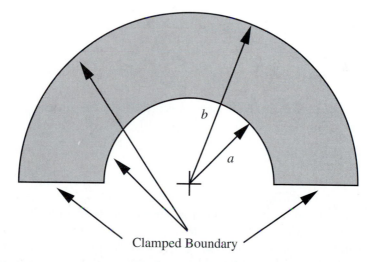

FIGURE 15.5
Half-annulus for Exercise 2; $a = 2$ and $b = 4$.

CHAPTER
16

APPROXIMATING EIGENVALUES

16.1 LABORATORY GOALS

a. To use difference equations to estimate eigenvalues of a boundary value problem.

b. To use the `seq()` function to construct a tridiagonal matrix of arbitrary size.

16.2 MOTIVATION

As seen in Chapters 14 and 15, the eigenvalues of a boundary value problem are extremely useful to the engineer seeking to understand the behavior of complicated systems. The examples presented so far assume that an analytical representation of the eigenfunctions can be found. The search for eigenvalues is then reduced to finding the roots of certain complicated transcendental equations. In many cases, the boundary-value problem may not yield a solution in terms of known functions. In such an instance, an approximation method for estimating eigenvalues, especially the lowest few, is needed. One such method involves the use of difference equations.

16.3 USING DIFFERENCE EQUATIONS

Consider the Sturm-Liouville boundary value problem

$$y'' + \lambda y = 0, \tag{16.1}$$

with $y(0) = y(1) = 0$. The eigenvalues for this problem are well known: $\lambda_n = n^2\pi^2, n = 1, 2, \ldots$, and the eigenfunctions are $y_n(x) = c_n \sin\sqrt{\lambda_n}x$. To illustrate the method of difference equations, we first note that the second derivative term is equal to the following limit:

$$y'' = \lim_{h \to 0} \frac{y(x-h) - 2y(x) + y(x+h)}{h^2}. \tag{16.2}$$

If h is small enough, then the second derivative can be approximated by the difference quotient on the right-hand side of Eq. (16.2).

Suppose now we let $h = 1/2$. Divide the interval $0 \le x \le 1$ into two halves, and let $x_0 = 0$, $x_1 = 1/2$, and $x_2 = 1$, and if we let $y(x_j) = y_j$, we can write Eq. (16.1) as:

$$\frac{y_0 - 2y_1 + y_2}{1/4} + \lambda y_1 = 0. \tag{16.3}$$

Using the fact that $y_0 = y(0) = 0$ and $y_2 = y(x_2) = 0$, the equation reduces to

$$(8 - \lambda)y_1 = 0. \tag{16.4}$$

This method predicts that the lowest eigenvalue is $\lambda = 8$, while the true value is π^2. To increase the accuracy of the method, we choose a smaller step size. This time, choose $h = 1/3$, so that we are using the difference approximation on a mesh of 4 points. This time, we are led to a pair of equations:

$$\frac{y_0 - 2y_1 + y_2}{1/9} + \lambda y_1 = 0, \tag{16.5}$$

$$\frac{y_1 - 2y_2 + y_3}{1/9} + \lambda y_2 = 0. \tag{16.6}$$

Using our boundary conditions, this reduces to

$$\frac{-2y_1 + y_2}{1/9} + \lambda y_1 = 0, \tag{16.7}$$

$$\frac{y_1 - 2y_2}{1/9} + \lambda y_2 = 0. \tag{16.8}$$

This can be written in matrix form as

$$\begin{bmatrix} -2 + \lambda/9 & 1 \\ 1 & -2 + \lambda/9 \end{bmatrix} \begin{bmatrix} y_1 \\ y_2 \end{bmatrix} = \begin{bmatrix} 0 \\ 0 \end{bmatrix} \tag{16.9}$$

In order for this system to have non-trivial solutions, the coefficient matrix must be singular. This provides a way of determining the eigenvalues. We enter the coefficients as a 2×2 matrix in *Maple*:

```
> a := [[-2 + lam / 9, 1], [1, -2 + lam / 9]];

              a := [[- 2 + 1/9 lam, 1], [1, - 2 + 1/9 lam]]
```

We set the determinant, taken with the `det()` function, equal to zero and use `solve()` to find the admissible values of λ:

```
> sol1 := solve(linalg[det](a) = 0, lam);

                       sol1 := 27, 9
```

The smaller root is an improved approximation to the first eigenvalue, while the larger root is a first approximation to the second eigenvalue.

If we extend this process to a mesh of five points, so that $h = 1/4$, we obtain the following coefficient matrix:

$$a = \begin{bmatrix} -2 + \lambda/16 & 1 & 0 \\ 1 & -2 + \lambda/16 & 1 \\ 0 & 1 & -2 + \lambda/16 \end{bmatrix}. \tag{16.10}$$

We enter the following *Maple* expression:

```
> a := [[-2 + lam / 16, 1, 0], [1, -2 + lam / 16, 1],
        [0, 1, -2 + lam / 16]];

a :=

     [[- 2 + 1/16 lam, 1, 0], [1, - 2 + 1/16 lam, 1], [0, 1, - 2 + 1/16 lam]]
```

and then use `det()` and `solve()` to determine the approximate eigenvalues:

```
> sol2 := solve(linalg[det](a) = 0, lam);

                              1/2              1/2
              sol2 := 32, 32 + 16 2   , 32 - 16 2
```

We can get a clearer picture of the results by converting them to decimal form using `evalf()` and using `sort()` to put this list in ascending order:

```
> sort([evalf(sol2)]);
```

$$[9.37258301, 32., 54.62741699]$$

We can see three eigenvalue approximations in this result. Our estimate for the lowest has improved even more, our estimate for the second has improved, although it is still not very good, while the third result gives a first estimate for the third eigenvalue.

16.4 GENERATING THE COEFFICIENT MATRIX

We can continue this procedure indefinitely, obtaining better and better estimates for the eigenvalues, but the entry of the elements of the coefficient matrix can become unwieldy. We note the special structure of the coefficient matrix for $h = 1/n$, so that there are $n + 1$ mesh points:

$$a = \begin{bmatrix} -2 + \lambda/n^2 & 1 & 0 & 0 & \cdots \\ 1 & -2 + \lambda/n^2 & 1 & 0 & \cdots \\ \vdots & \vdots & \ddots & \vdots & \vdots \\ \cdots & 1 & -2 + \lambda/n^2 & 1 & 0 \\ \cdots & 0 & 0 & 1 & -2 + \lambda/n^2 \end{bmatrix}. \qquad (16.11)$$

The coefficient matrix has a *tridiagonal* structure. The diagonals immediately above and below the main diagonal have non-zero entries, while the rest of the matrix has zero entries. We define a function that will build tridiagonal matrices of any size. This function uses the *Maple* function band(). The band() function takes two arguments: the first is a vector whose elements will be used to initialize the diagonals of the matrix, and the second is the size of the matrix. The main diagonal is initialized with the middle element of the vector, while the superdiagonals and subdiagonals are initialized with the first and last elements respectively. Thus,

```
> tridiag := (n) -> linalg[band]([1, -2 + lam / (n + 1)^2, 1], n):
```

The following command generates a 5×5 tridiagonal coefficient matrix:

```
> b:= tridiag(5);
```

$$b := [- \, 2 + 1/36 \; lam, \; 1, \; 0, \; 0, \; 0]$$

$$[1, -2 + 1/36 \text{ lam}, 1, 0, 0]$$

$$[0, 1, -2 + 1/36 \text{ lam}, 1, 0]$$

$$[0, 0, 1, -2 + 1/36 \text{ lam}, 1]$$

$$[0, 0, 0, 1, -2 + 1/36 \text{ lam}]$$

We are now in a position to apply this method to coefficient matrices of arbitrary size. For example, the following command builds a 6×6 coefficient matrix, sets the determinant to zero, uses `fsolve()` to find the roots.[1] When calling `fsolve()` with a polynomial argument, it is not necessary to specify an interval for the roots. `fsolve()` will find all the roots and return them in increasing order:

```
> eig6 := fsolve(linalg[det](tridiag(6)));

eig6 :=

  9.705050946, 36.89799942, 76.19294847, 119.8070515, 159.1020006, 186.2949491
```

This procedure can be used to determine eigenvalues to arbitrary degrees of precision. For example, we can examine just the first eigenvalue of the 15×15 coefficient matrix by appending [1] to our expression:

```
> eig15a := fsolve(linalg[det](tridiag(15)))[1];

                    eig15a := 9.837936434
```

The relative error of this estimate is less than 0.4%.

16.5   APPLICATION TO VIBRATING STRING

We now apply the method described here for computing the fundamental frequency of a vibrating string with variable mass. In particular, suppose the thickness of a string increases linearly with its length, as suggested in Fig. 16.1. In this case the linear density of the string is assumed to have the form $\rho(x) = \rho_0(1+\alpha x)$, where ρ_0 and α are constants. If the string is under a uniform tension T, the

---

[1]Once the matrix is 5×5 or larger, the polynomial obtained by taking the determinant is at least fifth degree. The `solve()` function will usually return results using the `RootOf()` function.

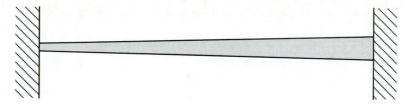

FIGURE 16.1
Vibrating string of variable thickness. Both ends are fixed to solid supports.

governing wave equation for small amplitude transverse oscillations of the string is

$$u_{tt} = \frac{T}{\rho(x)} u_{xx}. \tag{16.12}$$

We will consider the case in which both ends of the string are fixed to non-moving supports, so that $u(0,t) = u(L,t) = 0$. We assume that $u(x,t) = \phi(x)G(t)$, and apply the method of separation of variables to obtain the following pair of ordinary differential equations:

$$\phi'' + \frac{\rho(x)\lambda}{T}\phi = 0, \tag{16.13}$$

and

$$G'' + \lambda G = 0. \tag{16.14}$$

From the second equation, we see that $G(t) = c_1 \sin(\sqrt{\lambda}t) + c_2 \cos(\sqrt{\lambda}t)$ and so the vibration frequencies are given by $f = \sqrt{\lambda}/(2\pi)$.

Let us suppose that $L = 1$, $T = 1$, $\rho_0 = 1$, and $\alpha = 0.2$. The boundary value problem is then written as

$$\phi'' + (1 + 0.2x)\lambda\phi = 0, \tag{16.15}$$

together with the boundary conditions $\phi(0) = \phi(1) = 0$. If we divide the interval into $n+2$ steps, then $h = 1/(n+1)$, and the difference equations can be written as

$$\phi_{k-1} - 2\phi_k + \phi_{k+1} + \left(1 + 0.2\frac{k}{n+1}\right)\lambda\phi_k = 0, \tag{16.16}$$

for $k = 1, 2, \ldots, n$. These difference equations lead to a tridiagonal coefficient matrix whose determinant must vanish. As before, the values for λ which make this matrix singular will be the approximate eigenvalues.

We use the same approach as in the previous section to define a coefficient matrix by modifying the function we had defined for `tridiag()` to define a new function `tridiag2()`:

```
> tridiag2 := (n) -> linalg[band]([1, -2 + (1 + 0.2 * i / (n + 1)) *
                       lam / (n + 1)^2, 1], n):
```

Since we are interested only in the first eigenvalue, we first try n = 5:

```
> fsolve(linalg[det](tridiag2(5)))[1];
                         8.765823425
```

Is this value of λ reasonable? If the string had a constant linear density $\rho = 1$, then $\lambda = \pi^2 \approx 9.8696$. If the string had a constant linear density $\rho = 1.2$, then $\lambda = \pi^2/1.2 \approx 8.2247$. Since our string has a density that varies between these values, it is reasonable to expect that the eigenvalue should have a value between these two extremes, which is precisely what we find. A more accurate estimate is obtained from a 15×15 coefficient matrix:

```
> fsolve(linalg[det](tridiag2(15)))[1];
                         8.940337962
```

We conclude that the fundamental frequency is approximately

```
> evalf(sqrt(") / (2 * Pi));
                        .4758796131
```

EXERCISES

16.1. Determine estimates for the two lowest eigenvalues for the boundary value problem

$$y'' + \lambda y = 0, y(0) = 0, y(1) = 0 \qquad (16.17)$$

for all coefficient matrix sizes from 2×2 through 25×25. Determine the relative error in the approximations and plot this as a function of n. Can you conjecture a rate at which the approximations converge to the true answer? What implications does this have for the practicality of this method? Can you formulate a rule-of-thumb regarding the size of the coefficient matrix required for a given relative error?

16.2. Use the method of difference equations to estimate the first two eigenvalues of the following boundary-value problem:

$$y'' + \lambda y = 0, y(0) = 0, y'(\pi) = 0. \qquad (16.18)$$

Compare your results to the exact eigenvalues. How big must the coefficient matrix be in order to obtain an estimate of the lowest eigenvalue that is accurate to 1%? 0.1%?

16.3. Use the method of difference equations to estimate the first three eigenvalues of the following boundary value problem:

$$y'' + \lambda y = 0, y(0) = 0, y'(1) - y(1) = 0. \qquad (16.19)$$

Compare these results with numerical estimates obtained from the transcendental equation for the eigenvalues. How big must the coefficient matrix be in order to obtain an estimate of the lowest eigenvalue that is accurate to 1%? 0.1%?

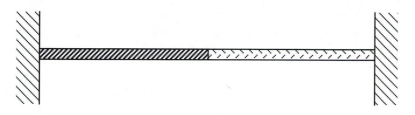

FIGURE 16.2
Vibrating rope system. The left half is made of wire and the right half is made of hemp.

16.4. Suppose a wire rope of density 1 kg/m is tied to a hemp rope of density 0.2 kg/m and configured as suggested in Fig. 16.2. If the combination rope is subject to a uniform tension of 100 N, determine the fundamental frequency of the combination rope for small amplitude transverse oscillations.

16.5. The method of difference equations can also be used for higher order equations. See if you can implement this method to determine the eigenvalues for the vibrating bar. In particular, estimate the smallest eigenvalue for

$$y'''' - \lambda^4 y = 0, \qquad (16.20)$$

subject to $y(0) = y''(0) = 0$ and $y(1) = y''(1) = 0$. Compare to the exact result. [Hint: The coefficient matrix will be *pentadiagonal* in this case.]

CHAPTER
17

VECTOR DIFFERENTIATION

17.1 LABORATORY GOALS

a. To determine the gradient of a scalar function.

b. To determine the divergence and curl of a vector function.

c. To establish vector identities using *Maple*.

17.2 THE GRADIENT, DIVERGENCE, AND CURL

Before proceeding further, the `linalg` package should be loaded:

```
> with(linalg):

Warning: new definition for    norm
Warning: new definition for    trace
```

The package just loaded contains three functions which can be used to perform many common vector differentiation operations. The `grad()` function can be used to evaluate the gradient of a scalar function of three variables. For example, let $f(x, y, z) = 2xz + z^2 e^y$. Then ∇f is determined as follows:

```
> f := 2 * x * z + z^2 * exp(y);

                              2
              f := 2 x z + z  exp(y)

> gradf := grad(f, [x, y, z]);

                        2
        gradf := [ 2 z, z  exp(y), 2 x + 2 z exp(y) ]
```

The components can be picked out as needed. Directional derivatives can now be obtained. For example, suppose we require the rate of change of f in the direction of $2\mathbf{i}+3\mathbf{j}-\mathbf{k}$ at the point $(2,1,1)$. First, define the vector in *Maple* and then normalize it with the `norm()` function.[1] Recall that the second argument of `norm()` is used to specify the type of norm. Here we want the euclidean norm (or the 2-norm):

```
> v := [2, 3, 1];

              v := [2, 3, 1]

> v := v / norm(v, 2);

                                    1/2
        v := 1/14 [2, 3, 1] 14
```

Now take the dot product of the gradient with this unit vector using the `dot-prod()` function, and use `subs()` to evaluate the result at the point $(2,1,1)$:

```
> subs({x = 2, y = 1, z = 1}, dotprod(gradf, v));

        1/2                1/2                          1/2
    2/7 14    + 3/14 exp(1) 14    + 1/14 (4 + 2 exp(1)) 14

> simplify(");

                    1/2                1/2
            4/7 14    + 5/14 exp(1) 14
```

This result is equivalent to $(8+5e)/\sqrt{14}$.

The `diverge()` function can be used to find the divergence of a vector function of three variables. For example, let $\mathbf{g} = y\mathbf{i}+2xz\mathbf{j}+ze^x\mathbf{k}$. The divergence of $\mathbf{g}$ is found as:

---

[1] That is, we scale it so that it is a unit vector.

```
> g := [y, 2 * x * z, z * exp(x)];
                        g := [y, 2 x z, z exp(x)]

> diverge(g, [x, y, z]);

                              exp(x)
```

The `curl()` function can be used to determine the curl of any three-component vector. For example, applied to **g**, we obtain:

```
> curl(g, [x, y, z]);

                    [ - 2 x, - z exp(x), 2 z - 1 ]
```

Even with functions not explicitly defined, these functions can be used. For example, the familiar identity $\nabla \times \nabla \phi(x, y, z) = 0$ can be verified as follows:

```
> grad(phi(x, y, z), [x, y, z]);

          d                 d                 d
     [ ---- phi(x, y, z), ---- phi(x, y, z), ---- phi(x, y, z) ]
        dx                dy                dz

> curl(", [x, y, z]);

                            [ 0, 0, 0 ]
```

Note that *Maple* does not use any special symbols to denote partial differentiation. In standard mathematical notation, the result of the `grad()` function would be written as

$$\frac{\partial \phi}{\partial x}\mathbf{i} + \frac{\partial \phi}{\partial y}\mathbf{j} + \frac{\partial \phi}{\partial z}\mathbf{k}.$$

17.3 OTHER VECTOR DIFFERENTIATION OPERATORS

In addition to those operators discussed in the previous section, *Maple* also can apply the Laplacian operator and biharmonic operator. For example, to compute $\nabla^2 f$, the Laplacian of f, we use the `laplacian()` function:

```
> laplacian(f, [x, y, z]);

                        2
                       z  exp(y) + 2 exp(y)
```

Let $h = e^x \cos y$. Then $\nabla^2 h$ is found to be

```
> h := exp(x) * cos(y);
                          h := exp(x) cos(y)

> laplacian(h, [x, y]);
                                  0
```

(Note that since h depends only on x and y, the second argument of `laplacian` is just a two-component list.) Recall that $h(x, y)$ is the real part of the analytic function e^z, and so is harmonic, i.e. the Laplacian vanishes.

The biharmonic operator is defined to be the Laplacian of the Laplacian. *Maple* does not have this available as a built-in function, but it can be defined using the `laplacian()` function:

```
> biharmonic := (f, [x, y, z]) ->
             laplacian(laplacian(f, [x, y, z]), [x, y, z]);

  biharmonic := (f,[x,y,z]) -> laplacian(laplacian(f, [x, y, z]), [x, y, z])

> biharmonic(f, [x, y, z]);

                        2
                       z  exp(y) + 4 exp(y)
```

17.4 ESTABLISHING VECTOR IDENTITIES

These operators can be used to establish many useful vector identities that would be extremely tedious to verify by hand. For example, the claim is made that if **F** and **G** are any two differentiable vector fields,

$$\nabla(\mathbf{F} \cdot \mathbf{G}) = (\mathbf{F} \cdot \nabla)\mathbf{G} + (\mathbf{G} \cdot \nabla)\mathbf{F} + \mathbf{F} \times (\nabla \times \mathbf{G}) + \mathbf{G} \times (\nabla \times \mathbf{F}). \qquad (17.1)$$

First, we define **F** and **G**:

```
> F := [F1(x, y, z), F2(x, y, z), F3(x, y, z)];
            F := [F1(x, y, z), F2(x, y, z), F3(x, y, z)]

> G := [G1(x, y, z), G2(x, y, z), G3(x, y, z)];
            G := [G1(x, y, z), G2(x, y, z), G3(x, y, z)]
```

Before proceeding, we note that $\nabla \mathbf{G}$ is represented as a 3×3 matrix.[2] Since the grad() function cannot be used on a vector, we define a function called vectorgrad() as follows:

```
> vectorgrad := (F, [x, y, z]) -> [seq(grad(F[j], [x, y, z]), j = 1 .. 3)];
Warning, 'j' is implicitly declared local
    vectorgrad :=

        (F,[x,y,z]) -> local j; [seq(grad(F[j], [x, y, z]), j = 1 .. 3)]
```

First, we compute the left-hand side of the identity:

```
> leftside := grad(dotprod(F, G), [x, y, z]);

leftside := [

   /  d          \                          /  d          \
   |---- F1(x, y, z)| G1(x, y, z) + F1(x, y, z) |---- G1(x, y, z)|
   \ dx          /                          \ dx          /

           /  d          \                          /  d          \
        + |---- F2(x, y, z)| G2(x, y, z) + F2(x, y, z) |---- G2(x, y, z)|
           \ dx          /                          \ dx          /

           /  d          \                          /  d          \
        + |---- F3(x, y, z)| G3(x, y, z) + F3(x, y, z) |---- G3(x, y, z)|,
           \ dx          /                          \ dx          /

   /  d          \                          /  d          \
   |---- F1(x, y, z)| G1(x, y, z) + F1(x, y, z) |---- G1(x, y, z)|
   \ dy          /                          \ dy          /

           /  d          \                          /  d          \
        + |---- F2(x, y, z)| G2(x, y, z) + F2(x, y, z) |---- G2(x, y, z)|
           \ dy          /                          \ dy          /

           /  d          \                          /  d          \
        + |---- F3(x, y, z)| G3(x, y, z) + F3(x, y, z) |---- G3(x, y, z)|,
           \ dy          /                          \ dy          /
```

[2]Or a tensor of rank two.

```
   /  d          \                            /  d              \
   |---- F1(x, y, z)|  G1(x, y, z) + F1(x, y, z) |---- G1(x, y, z)|
   \  dz         /                            \  dz             /


     /  d          \                            /  d              \
   + |---- F2(x, y, z)|  G2(x, y, z) + F2(x, y, z) |---- G2(x, y, z)|
     \  dz         /                            \  dz             /


     /  d          \                            /  d               \
   + |---- F3(x, y, z)|  G3(x, y, z) + F3(x, y, z) |---- G3(x, y, z)| ]
     \  dz         /                            \  dz              /
```

Now we determine the right-hand side. The `crossprod()` function is called to evaluate cross products. We must also call the `matrix()` and `vector()` functions so that the `&*` operation will be well-defined.[3] Note that we terminate the expression with the colon operator : in order to suppress the very lengthy output:

```
> rightside := matrix(vectorgrad(G, [x, y, z])) &* vector(F) +
        matrix(vectorgrad(F, [x, y, z])) &* vector(G) +
     crossprod(F, curl(G, [x, y, z])) + crossprod(G, curl(F, [x, y, z])):
```

Now, we pass the difference between both sides to `evalm()` and use `map()` and `simplify()` to simplify each of the components:

```
> map(simplify, evalm(rightside - leftside));

                    [ 0, 0, 0 ]
```

This establishes the result.

EXERCISES

17.1. Compute ∇f and verify that $\nabla \times \nabla f = 0$:
   (a) $f = \cos(x + y + z)$
   (b) $f = 2e^x \log(yz)$
   (c) $f = \sqrt{\sin(x + \cos y)}$

17.2. Compute $\nabla \cdot \mathbf{F}$ and $\nabla \times \mathbf{F}$, and verify that $\nabla \cdot (\nabla \times \mathbf{F}) = \mathbf{0}$.
   (a) $\mathbf{F} = x\mathbf{i} + y\mathbf{j} + 3z\mathbf{k}$
   (b) $\mathbf{F} = \sinh x\mathbf{i} + \cosh z\mathbf{j} + y^2\mathbf{j}$ [Hint: Use the *Maple* functions `cosh()` and `sinh()`.]

---

[3] See Chapter 2.

(c) $\mathbf{F} = J_0(x)\mathbf{i} + J_1(y)\mathbf{j} + J_2(z)\mathbf{k}$ where J_n is the Bessel function of the first kind of order n.

17.3. Let f and g be scalar fields. Prove that

$$\nabla \cdot (\nabla f \times \nabla g) = 0$$

17.4. Let $\mathbf{F}$ and $\mathbf{G}$ be vector fields. Prove that

$$\nabla \times (\mathbf{F} \times \mathbf{G}) = (\mathbf{G} \cdot \nabla \mathbf{F}) - (\mathbf{F} \cdot \nabla \mathbf{G}) + (\nabla \cdot \mathbf{G})\mathbf{F} - (\nabla \cdot \mathbf{F})\mathbf{G}.$$

17.5. Verify that

$$f = \tan^{-1}\left(\frac{2y}{x^2 + y^2 - 1}\right)$$

is a solution to Laplace's equation $\nabla^2 f = 0$.

17.6. Suppose the temperature along the surface of a metal plate is given by $T(x, y) = 90 - x^2 - 3y^2$. An insect, located at $(x, y) = (0, 1)$, travels along a path which lowers its temperature as quickly as possible. Along what direction will the insect set out?

VECTOR FUNCTIONS OF A SINGLE VARIABLE

18.1 LABORATORY GOALS

a. Determine the derivatives of vector-valued functions of a single variable.
b. Manipulate these derivatives to obtain the curvature and torsion of space curves.
c. Develop proficiency with the `spacecurve()` function.
d. Compute the length of a curve from its parametric representation.

18.2 THREE-DIMENSIONAL PARTICLE MOTION

First, we load the `linalg` package:

```
> with(linalg):

Warning: new definition for    norm
Warning: new definition for    trace
```

Consider the vector $\mathbf{r} = x(t)\mathbf{i} + y(t)\mathbf{j} + z(t)\mathbf{k}$. We will assume that the position functions x, y, and z are all sufficiently differentiable. This vector corresponds to the motion of a particle in three-dimensional space, with the position vector of the particle represented by $\mathbf{r}$. The velocity and acceleration of this particle are computed by taking the derivative of $\mathbf{r}$ with respect to t: $\mathbf{v} = d\mathbf{r}/dt$ and $\mathbf{a} = d\mathbf{v}/dt$. To illustrate the use of *Maple* to do these kinds of manipulations, suppose that $\mathbf{r} = \cos(t)\mathbf{i} + \sin(t)\mathbf{j} + (t/4)\mathbf{k}$. In *Maple*, this would be represented as:

```
> r1 := [cos(t), sin(t), t / 4];

              r1 := [cos(t), sin(t), 1/4 t]
```

First, we sketch the curve traced out by $\mathbf{r}$ over the interval $0 \le t \le 2\pi$ with the `spacecurve()` function, which is part of the `plots` package:

```
plots[spacecurve](r1, t =  0 .. 2 * Pi, axes=NORMAL);
```

The option `axes` is set to the value `NORMAL`, which causes *Maple* to display a set of Cartesian axes in the appropriate place in the figure. We recognize in Fig. 18.1 that $\mathbf{r}$ traces out a helix. The velocity of this particle can be obtained simply by taking the derivative of $\mathbf{r}$ with respect to time with the `diff()` function:

```
> v1 := diff(r1, t);

              v1 := [- sin(t), cos(t), 1/4]
```

and the acceleration is given by

```
> a1 := diff(v1, t);

              a1 := [- cos(t), - sin(t), 0]
```

The speed of our particle can be computed by noting that $|\mathbf{v}| = \sqrt{\mathbf{v} \cdot \mathbf{v}}$. In *Maple*, this is done with the `dotprod()` function,[1] and so

---

[1] The `norm()` function produces a correct result, but one that won't simplify in this case.

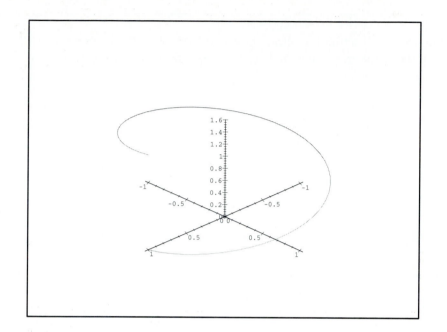

FIGURE 18.1
Helix traced out by $\mathbf{r} = \cos(t)\mathbf{i} + \sin(t)\mathbf{j} + (t/4)\mathbf{k}$ for $t \in [0, 2\pi]$.

```
> speed := sqrt((dotprod(v1, v1)));

                        2            2      1/2
            1/4 (16 sin(t)  + 16 cos(t)  + 1)
```

and this result can be simplified with the **simplify()** function:

```
> speed1 := simplify(");

                              1/2
                speed1 := 1/4 17
```

To determine when the velocity and acceleration vectors are orthogonal, we can examine the dot product between them:

```
> dotprod(v1, a1);
```

$$0$$

and thus the two vectors are always perpendicular. Finally, to determine the length of the helix traced out in Fig. 18.1, we apply the arc length formula $s = \int_a^b |\mathbf{v}| dt$ and we obtain

```
> s1 := int(speed, t = 0 .. 2 * Pi);

                                   1/2
                     s1 := 1/2 17    Pi
```

18.3   THE TNB COORDINATE SYSTEM

We now examine ways in which *Maple* can be used to examine the geometric properties of curves in 3-dimensional space.

In many applications it is useful to employ the **TNB** coordinate system, which is built upon three mutually orthogonal unit vectors which follow the path of a particle in space. The unit tangent vector, **T**, is defined as

$$\mathbf{T} = \mathbf{v}/|\mathbf{v}|. \tag{18.1}$$

This vector always points in the direction of particle travel. The unit normal vector **N** is defined as

$$\mathbf{N} = d\mathbf{T}/dt/|d\mathbf{T}/dt|, \tag{18.2}$$

and this vector always points inward and perpendicular to the path of travel. The third vector, **B**, called the binormal vector is defined as

$$\mathbf{B} = \mathbf{T} \times \mathbf{N}. \tag{18.3}$$

These three unit vectors can be constructed in *Maple* for any space curve which is sufficiently differentiable. Referring to the helix described in the previous section, we first construct **T**:

```
> t1 := v1 / speed1;

                                            1/2
              t1 := 4/17 [- sin(t), cos(t), 1/4] 17
```

In order to keep the *Maple* expressions manageable, we construct $d\mathbf{T}/dt$:

```
> dt1 := diff(t1, t);
```

$$dt1 := 4/17 \ [- \cos(t), \ - \sin(t), \ 0] \ 17^{1/2}$$

and then build the unit normal **N**:

```
> n1 := dt1 / simplify(sqrt(dotprod(dt1, dt1)));
```

$$n1 := [- \cos(t), \ - \sin(t), \ 0]$$

We can quickly verify that these two vectors are orthogonal by taking the dot product between them:

```
> dotprod(t1, n1);
```

$$0$$

Next, we construct the binormal **B**. To do this, we will use the `crossprod()` function:

```
> b1 := crossprod(t1, n1);
```

$$b1 := [\ 1/17 \ 17^{1/2} \ \sin(t), \ - \ 1/17 \ 17^{1/2} \ \cos(t),$$
$$4/17 \ 17^{1/2} \ \sin(t)^2 \ + \ 4/17 \ 17^{1/2} \ \cos(t)^2 \ ]$$

These three vectors are now available for additional computations.

18.4   CURVATURE AND TORSION

A basic result from advanced calculus is that the curvature κ of a space curve is given by

$$\kappa = \frac{|\mathbf{v} \times \mathbf{a}|}{|\mathbf{v}|^3} \tag{18.4}$$

Using the results already obtained for the helix described in the previous section, we can compute its curvature as follows:

```
> kappa1 := simplify(sqrt(dotprod(crossprod(v1, a1), crossprod(v1, a1))) /
                     (speed1^3));
```

$$kappa1 := \frac{16}{17}$$

which shows the curvature of this helix is constant. Since the radius of curvature is simply the reciprocal of the curvature, i.e. $\rho = 1/\kappa$,

```
> roc1 := 1 / kappa1;
```

$$roc1 := \frac{17}{16}$$

Next, we consider computing the torsion τ of space curves. If the component functions are sufficiently differentiable, the torsion can be computed with the following formula:

$$\tau = \frac{\begin{vmatrix} \dot{x} & \dot{y} & \dot{z} \\ \ddot{x} & \ddot{y} & \ddot{z} \\ \dddot{x} & \dddot{y} & \dddot{z} \end{vmatrix}}{|\mathbf{v} \times \mathbf{a}|^2}, \tag{18.5}$$

where x, y, and z are the three coordinate components of $\mathbf{r}$ and the dots denote time derivatives.

Equation (18.5) is surprisingly straightforward to implement in *Maple*. The first and second rows of the determinant are just the components of $\mathbf{v}$ and $\mathbf{a}$, while the third row is $d\mathbf{a}/dt$. We build this row first:

```
> i1 := diff(a1, t);
```

$$i1 := [\sin(t), -\cos(t), 0]$$

and then construct the expression for the torsion using det():

```
> torsion := simplify(det([v1, a1, i1]) /
                       dotprod(crossprod(v1, a1), crossprod(v1, a1)));
```

$$torsion := 4/17$$

and we see that the torsion for our helix is a constant.

EXERCISES

18.1. Suppose a particle moves with the position components described below. Determine the tangential and normal acceleration components and the radius of curvature for each case:

(a) $x = t^2$, $y = t$, $z = t + 1$

(b) $x = \cos t$, $y = \sin t$, $z = \sqrt{t}$

(c) $x = e^t$, $y = \cos t$, $z = t$.

18.2. Determine the arc length for each of the curves in Exercise 1 over the interval $0 < t < 2\pi$.

18.3. Compute the torsion for each of the curves in Exercise 1. In each instance, determine those values of t for which the torsion is maximized and minimized.

CHAPTER
19

VECTOR
INTEGRATION

19.1 LABORATORY GOALS

a. To evaluate surface and volume integrals.
b. To apply the divergence theorem and Stoke's theorem to evaluation of surface and volume integrals.

19.2 THE DIVERGENCE THEOREM

Before proceeding further, we require the `linalg` package:

```
> with(linalg):

Warning: new definition for    norm
Warning: new definition for    trace
```

Let $\mathcal{V}$ be a closed region in three-dimensional space with piece-wise smooth boundary $\mathcal{S}$. Let $\mathbf{v} = x(y+1)z^3\mathbf{j}$ be a continuously differentiable vector field defined in a region $\mathcal{R}$ of three-dimensional space. If **n** denotes the unit normal on $\mathcal{S}$, then the divergence theorem says that

$$\int_{\mathcal{V}} \nabla \cdot \mathbf{v}\, dV = \int_{\mathcal{S}} \mathbf{n} \cdot v\, dA. \tag{19.1}$$

We illustrate the divergence theorem with the following example. Let $\mathcal{V}$ be the triangular prism shown in Fig. 19.1. Its faces are given by the planes $x = 0$, $x = 2$, $y = 0$, $z = 0$, and $y + z = 1$.   First we determine $\nabla \cdot \mathbf{v}$:

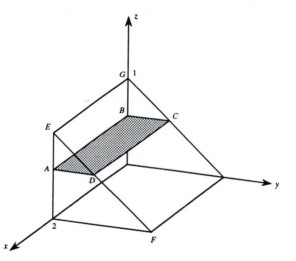

FIGURE 19.1
Triangular prism in the first octant.

```
> v := [0, x * (y+1) * z^3, 0];

                                    3
                    v := [0, x (y + 1) z , 0]

> divv := diverge(v, [x, y, z]);

                              3
                    divv := x z
```

To compute the volume integral on the left-hand side of Eq. (19.1), we let $dV = dx\, dy\, dz$ in such a way that the shaded plane $ABCD$ sweeps out the prism by beginning at the segment EG and ending at the xy-plane. In this case, $0 \le x \le 2$, $0 \le y \le 1 - z$, and $0 \le z \le 1$. We can now evaluate this as an iterated integral:

```
> int(int(int(divv, x = 0 .. 2), y = 0 .. 1 - z), z = 0 .. 1);
```

$$1/10$$

The right-hand side of Eq. (19.1) is evaluated in five pieces. Note that on the face where $x = 0$, $\mathbf{n} = -\mathbf{i}$, and by inspection $\mathbf{n} \cdot \mathbf{v} = 0$. The same result holds for the face at $x = 2$ since $\mathbf{n} = \mathbf{i}$ there. In addition, on the face $z = 0$, $\mathbf{n} = -\mathbf{k}$, and $\mathbf{n} \cdot \mathbf{v} = 0$ there as well. On the face $y = 0$, the unit normal is $-\mathbf{j}$. In this instance, the surface integral is straightforward to evaluate:

```
> res1 := int(int(dotprod([0, -1, 0], subs(y = 0 , v)),
                    x = 0 .. 2), z = 0 .. 1);

                    res1 := -1/2
```

Since the slanted face is part of the plane $y + z = 1$, the unit normal is $\mathbf{n} = (\mathbf{j} + \mathbf{k})/\sqrt{2}$. Noting that $dA = \sqrt{2}\,dx\,dy$ on the slanted face, we can evaluate the surface integral on that face with the following *Maple* expression:

```
> res2 := int(int(sqrt(2) * dotprod([0, 1, 1] / sqrt(2),
            subs(z = 1 - y, v)), x = 0 .. 2), y = 0 .. 1);



                    res2 := 3/5

> res1 + res2;

                    1/10
```

and the result is seen to be $1/10$, the same as obtained above.

19.3   STOKE'S THEOREM

Let $\mathbf{v}$ be a continuously differentiable vector field defined in a region $\mathcal{R}$ of three-dimensional space. Let $\mathcal{S}$ be a piecewise-smooth surface in $\mathcal{R}$ and suppose that the edge of $\mathcal{S}$ is a piece-wise smooth simple closed curve $\mathcal{C}$. Then Stoke's theorem says that

$$\int_S \mathbf{n} \cdot \nabla \times \mathbf{v}\, dA = \oint_C \mathbf{v} \cdot d\mathbf{r}, \tag{19.2}$$

where **n** is the unit normal to the surface S. For example, suppose that S is the portion of the paraboloid $z = 1 - x^2 - y^2$ which lies in the octant bounded by $0 \le x$, $0 \le y$, and $0 \le z$. As suggested in Fig. 19.2, the curve S will be the edge of the paraboloid $ABCA$. Let $v = yz\mathbf{k}$.   We will use *Maple* to evaluate both

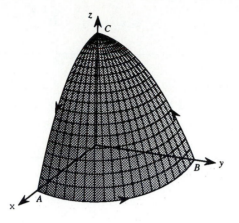

FIGURE 19.2
The paraboloid $z = 1 - x^2 - y^2$ in the first octant. Note the orientation of the boundary $C = ABCA$.

sides of Eq. (19.2). First, we determine $\nabla \times \mathbf{v}$:

```
> v := [0, 0, y * z];

                        v := [0, 0, y z]

> curlv := curl(v, [x, y, z]);

                        curlv := [ z, 0, 0 ]
```

Now we compute the unit normal vector **n**. If the surface is written as $f(x, y, z) = z + x^2 + y^2 - 1$, then $\mathbf{n} = \nabla f / |\nabla f|$. Thus

```
> f := z + x^2 + y^2 - 1;

                                2    2
                        f := z + x  + y  - 1

> gradf := grad(f, [x, y, z]);
```

```
                    gradf := [ 2 x, 2 y, 1 ]
```

```
> nn := gradf / sqrt(dotprod(gradf, gradf));
```

$$nn := \frac{gradf}{(4 \ x^2 + 4 \ y^2 + 1)^{1/2}}$$

If we write the equation for the paraboloid as $z = g(x, y) = 1 - x^2 - y^2$, then the area element is expressed as $dA = \sqrt{1 + g_x^2 + g_y^2} \, dx \, dy$. The coefficient here is found as follows:

```
> g := 1 - x^2 - y^2;
```

$$g := 1 - x^2 - y^2$$

```
> acoeff := sqrt(1 + diff(g, x)^2 + diff(g, y)^2);
```

$$acoeff := (4 \ x^2 + 4 \ y^2 + 1)^{1/2}$$

Finally noting that in xy-plane, the limits of integration are $0 \le x \le \sqrt{1 - y^2}$ and $0 \le y \le 1$, we can evaluate the left-hand side of Eq. (19.2) as an iterated integral:

```
> int(int(subs(z = g, dotprod(nn, curlv)) * acoeff,
        x = 0 .. sqrt(1 - y^2)), y = 0 .. 1);
```

$$4/15$$

Now to evaluate the right-hand side of Eq. (19.2), note that

$$\oint_C \mathbf{v} \cdot d\mathbf{r} = \oint_C yz \, dz. \tag{19.3}$$

Along CA, $y = 0$, and along AB, $z = 0$. On BC, $z = 1 - y^2$. Thus

$$\oint_C \mathbf{v} \cdot d\mathbf{r} = \int_{BC} yz \, dz. \tag{19.4}$$

We evaluate this last result as follows:

```
> int(y * (1 - y^2) * diff(1 - y^2, y), y = 1 .. 0);
```

$$\frac{4}{15}$$

The two computations agree as they should.

EXERCISES

19.1. Verify the divergence theorem by working out both sides for $\mathbf{v} = x^2 z \mathbf{i} + 3y(z + 1)\mathbf{j} + z^2 \mathbf{k}$ for the triangular prism discussed in Section 19.2.

19.2. The following result can be derived from the divergence theorem:

$$\int_{\mathcal{V}} \nabla^2 u \, dV = \int_S \frac{\partial u}{\partial n} \, dA,$$

where $\partial u / \partial n$ denotes the normal derivative of u along the surface S. Let $u = z \cos(xy + z)$. Verify this result for the unit cube.

19.3. Verify Stoke's theorem by working out both sides for $\mathbf{v} = e^{-x} y \mathbf{i} + e^{-y} \mathbf{j} + z e^z \mathbf{k}$ for the unit cube, but excluding the face $y = 1$.

19.4. Let $\mathbf{v} = [y^2 + x^2 \cos(yz)]\mathbf{i} - y^2 \mathbf{k}$. Evaluate $\int_S \mathbf{n} \cdot \nabla \times v \, dA$ where S is the surface $z = 1 - x^4 - y^4$ with $0 \le z$.

CHAPTER
20

MULTI-VARIABLE OPTIMIZATION

20.1 LABORATORY GOALS

a. To use *Maple* to solve multi-variable optimization problems.

b. Use the `plot3d()` function to visualize solutions to optimization problems.

20.2 DESCRIPTION OF THE TROUGH

It is desired to determine the cross-sectional shape of a long strip of sheet metal which is to be used as a trough. The shape of the trough is shown in Fig. 20.1. The width of the sheet metal piece is L units and two ends of equal length y are bent upward at equal angles θ, measured from the vertical.

We seek to determine the values of y and θ that will maximize the cross sectional area of the trough. The area A is given by the following expression:

$$A = y \cos \theta (L - 2y) + y^2 \cos \theta \sin \theta, \qquad (20.1)$$

subject to the constraints that $0 < \theta < \pi/2$ and that $0 < y < L/2$. In *Maple*, we express the area as

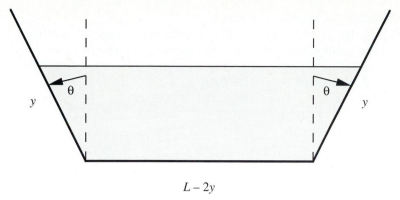

$$L - 2y$$

FIGURE 20.1
Cross-sectional view of a symmetric trapezoidal trough. The end-to-end length is L.

```
> A := y * cos(t) * (L - 2 * y)+ y^2 * cos(t) * sin(t);

                                      2
             A := y cos(t) (L - 2 y) + y  cos(t) sin(t)
```

where **t** is used to represent θ.

20.3   LOCATING CRITICAL POINTS

Recall that a maximum point, if it exists, must occur at critical points inside
the constraint intervals. Since A is continuously differentiable in both y and θ,
we need not be concerned with critical points at which derivatives fail to exist.
The most straightforward way to attack the problem, then, is to set $\partial A/\partial\theta =
\partial A/\partial y = 0$ and solve for θ and y. This can be set up in *Maple* by combining the
diff() function and **solve()** function:

```
> solve({diff(A, t) = 0, diff(A, y) = 0}, {y, t});

     {y = 0, t = 1/2 Pi}, {y = 0, t = - 1/2 Pi}, {y = L, t = 1/2 Pi},

         {y = 1/3 L, t = - 1/2 Pi},

                                       2
         {y = 1/3 L, t = 2 arctan(RootOf(_Z  - 4 _Z + 1))}
```

While this certainly gives a list of critical points, six in fact, it does not tell us at which point the maximum occurs.[1]

When the direct approach fails, results may often be obtained through intermediate manipulation of the computations. For example, we can simplify the two derivatives which we are setting equal to zero and try again. To illustrate this alternative, we first determine $\partial A/\partial y$:

```
> tmp1 := diff(A, y);

    tmp1 := cos(t) (L - 2 y) - 2 y cos(t) + 2 y cos(t) sin(t)
```

We then factor out the $\cos\theta$ term (because we set this derivative equal to zero) and assign the symbolic name `eq1` to the resulting expression:

```
> eq1:= coeff(tmp1, cos(t));

    eq1 := L - 4 y + 2 y sin(t)
```

We now compute the other partial derivative:

```
> tmp2 := diff(A, t);
                                    2       2    2        2
    tmp2 := - y sin(t) (L - 2 y) - y   sin(t)   + y   cos(t)
```

and simplify it by eliminating a y from each term:

```
> tmp3 := simplify(tmp2 / y);
                                                        2
    tmp3 := - sin(t) L + 2 y sin(t) - y + 2 y cos(t)
```

We now solve `eq1` for y:

```
> ysub := solve(eq1, y);
                              L
              ysub := - --------------
                        - 4 + 2 sin(t)
```

---

[1] Recall that the `RootOf()` function is *Maple*'s way of handling certain expressions that arise from the roots of polynomials. See Exercise 1.

and then substitute this result into previous result:

```
> tmp4 := subs(y = ysub, tmp3);
                                                                    2
                    L sin(t)            L              L cos(t)
   tmp4 := - sin(t) L - 2 -------------- + -------------- - 2 --------------
                    - 4 + 2 sin(t)   - 4 + 2 sin(t)     - 4 + 2 sin(t)
```

We simplify the result as follows:[2]

```
> tmp4 := simplify(tmp4);

                        L (2 sin(t) - 1)
            tmp4 := 1/2 ----------------
                          - 2 + sin(t)
```

We now ask *Maple* to solve this expression for θ:

```
> tsub := solve(tmp4, t);
                    tsub := 1/6 Pi
```

Maple determined the root $\theta = \pi/6$. This is now used to obtain the value for y at which the critical point occurs:

```
> ysub := subs(t = tsub, ysub);
                            L
            ysub := - --------------------
                        - 4 + 2 sin(1/6 Pi)

> ysub := simplify(ysub);

                    ysub := 1/3 L
```

---

[2]We are still going to solve two equations in two unknowns. We have explicitly substituted one equation into the other before asking *Maple* to go to work.

20.4   THE SECOND DERIVATIVE TEST

We must now determine the nature of the critical point, noting that if $A_{yy} < 0$ and $A_{yy}A_{\theta\theta} - A_{y\theta}^2 > 0$, then A will have a local maximum at that point.

First, we set up an expression to evaluate A_{yy}:

```
> tmp5 := simplify(subs({t = tsub, y = ysub}, diff(A, y$2)));

                                    1/2
                    tmp5 := - 3/2 3
```

which is evidently negative. Now we compute the second test expression:

```
> tmp6 := simplify(subs({t = tsub, y = ysub},
                tmp5 * diff(A, t$2) - diff(diff(A, y), t)^2));

                                 2
                    tmp6 := 1/2 L
```

which is clearly positive. We conclude that a local maximum occurs at this critical point. By inspection we observe that no global maximum can occur at the limits of the constraints and so we have determined the optimal shape of the trough.

20.5   DISCUSSION

The maximum cross-sectional area of the trough is given by this expression:

```
> maxa := simplify(subs({t = tsub, y = ysub}, A));

                              2  1/2
                    maxa := 1/12 L   3
```

In order to see more clearly that this is the maximum point, we examine a surface plot of the area. In order to set this up, we need to assign a numerical value to L. Thus for this example, we let $L = 1$:

```
> A1 := subs(L = 1, A);
                                        2
            A1 := y cos(t) (1 - 2 y) + y  cos(t) sin(t)
```

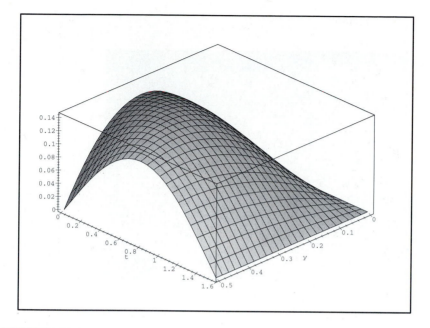

FIGURE 20.2
Surface corresponding to the cross-sectional area of the trough as a function of leg length and leg angle.

and we use the `plot3d()` function to examine A over the admissible ranges of both y and θ:

```
> plot3d(A1, y = 0 .. 1/2, t = 0 .. Pi / 2, style = PATCH, axes = BOXED);
```

with the result shown in Fig. 20.2   In order to see more clearly where the maximum value of A occurs, we employ the `densityplot()` function:

```
> plots[densityplot](A1, y = 0 .. 1/2, t = 0 .. Pi / 2);
```

From Fig. 20.3 it can be seen that the lightest area, which corresponds to the maximum value of the area, occurs when y is a little bigger than 0.3 and θ is about 0.5. These values correspond to the solution obtained in the previous section.

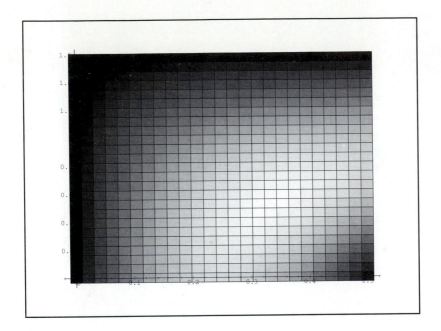

FIGURE 20.3
Density plot corresponding to the cross-sectional area of the trough as a function of leg length and leg angle.

EXERCISES

20.1. Which of the critical points found by *Maple* corresponds to the point found above? Of what significance are the other critical points?

20.2. Determine the dimensions of a right circular cylinder of volume V such that the surface area is minimized.

20.3. Determine the dimensions of a right circular cylinder of surface area A such that the volume is maximized.

20.4. Re-do the previous two problems for a right circular cone.

20.5. Suppose that the trough design specification is changed to require that one of the two angles must be 90 degrees, with the height of each lip remaining equal. Determine the shape of maximum cross-sectional area.

VISUALIZING
FIELDS

21.1 LABORATORY GOALS

a. To plot the gradient field of a scalar function of two variables and to compare it to the density plot of that function.

b. To plot the field of a vector function of two variables and to compare it to the divergence of that function.

21.2 GRADIENT FIELDS

We must first load the two *Maple* packages `linalg` and `plots`:

```
> with(linalg):

Warning: new definition for    norm
Warning: new definition for    trace

> with(plots):
```

Suppose we wish to examine the gradient field for the function $f(x, y) = \sin(x^2 + y^2)$. First we define the function and compute its gradient. Note that the second argument in the call to `grad()` is a list with only two elements. This ensures that a two-dimensional gradient vector is returned.

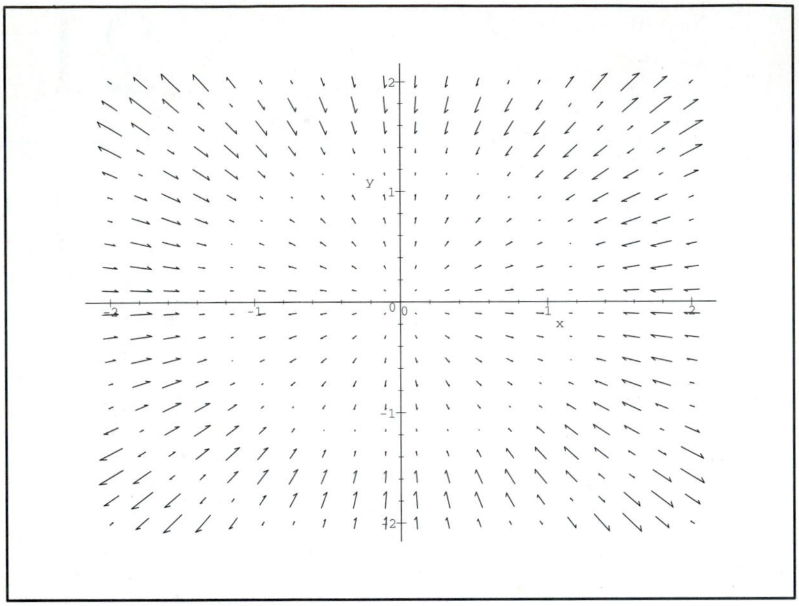

FIGURE 21.1
Gradient field for $f(x, y) = \sin(x^2 + y^2)$ on the domain $-2 \leq x \leq 2$ and $-2 \leq y \leq 2$.

```
> f := sin(x^2 + y^2);

                              2    2
                    f := sin(x  + y )

> gradf := grad(f, [x, y]);

                    2    2              2    2
        gradf := [ 2 cos(x  + y ) x, 2 cos(x  + y ) y ]
```

This vector field can be visualized with the `fieldplot()` function:

```
> fieldplot(gradf, x = -2 .. 2, y = -2 .. 2);

> plot1 := ":
```

Note that `fieldplot()` takes the same arguments as `plot3d()`. Also, we assigned the result of this call to `fieldplot()` to the symbol `plot1`. Storing the plot in this way will make it easier later on to overlay this with other plots.

In Fig. 21.1, the tail of each arrow is located at the point for which the gradient is evaluated. The direction and length of the arrows correspond to those of the respective gradient. In order to see the relationship between the gradient field and the surface shape determined by $f(x, y)$, we first generate a density plot over the same domain with the `densityplot()` function:

```
> densityplot(f, x = -2 .. 2, y = -2 .. 2);

> plot2 := ":
```

In Fig. 21.2 the darker areas correspond to the smaller values of $f(x, y)$ while the lighter areas designate the larger values. We can overlay the two illustrations with the `display()` function, taking care to place the density plot first:

```
> display({plot1, plot2});
```

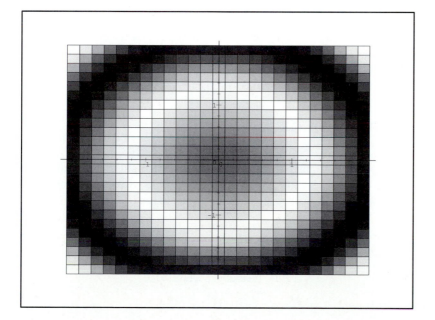

FIGURE 21.2
Density plot for $f(x, y) = \sin(x^2 + y^2)$ on the domain $-2 \leq x \leq 2$ and $-2 \leq y \leq 2$.

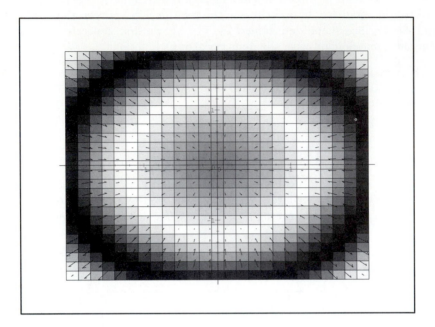

FIGURE 21.3
Superposition of Fig. 21.1 over Fig. 21.2. The domain is as in those figures.

Several important properties of the gradient field can be seen in Fig. 21.3. Note that the arrows always point toward lighter regions, that is, point in the direction of greatest increase in the function value. Also, the arrow lengths are proportional to the rate of change of shading seen in the figure.

21.3   DIVERGENCE OF A VECTOR FIELD

Maple makes it possible to visualize both a given vector field and the divergence of that field. For example, let $\mathbf{g}(x, y) = (\sin xy, \cos xy)$ be a vector function. The vector field formed by $\mathbf{g}$ can be seen with the `fieldplot()` function:

```
> g := [cos(x * y), sin(x * y)];

                       g := [cos(x y), sin(x y)]

> fieldplot(g, x = 0 .. Pi, y = 0 .. Pi);;

> plot4 := ":
```

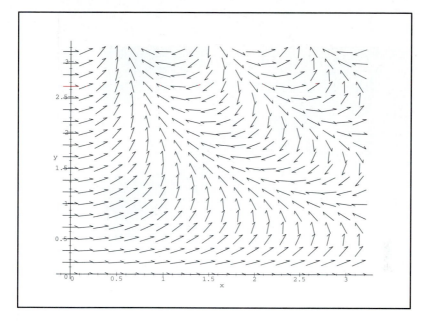

FIGURE 21.4
Vector field plot for $\mathbf{g}(x,y) = (\sin xy, \cos xy)$ on the domain $0 \le x \le \pi$ and $0 \le y \le \pi$.

The result of this call to `plotfield()` is shown in Fig. 21.4. Note that the arrows all have the same length. This follows from the fact that $|\mathbf{g}| = 1$ for x and y.

The divergence of $\mathbf{g}$, $\nabla \cdot \mathbf{g}$ is computed with the `diverge()` function.

```
> divg := diverge(g, [x, y]);

              divg := - sin(x y) y + cos(x y) x
```

Since $\nabla \cdot \mathbf{g}$ is a scalar function of x and y, we can examine its density plot:

```
> densityplot(divg, x = 0 .. Pi, y = 0 .. Pi);

> plot5 := ":
```

Now we overlay both Figs. 21.5 and 21.4 with the `display()` function:

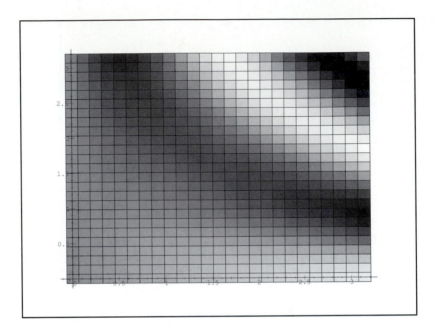

FIGURE 21.5
Density plot of $\nabla \cdot \mathbf{g}$ on the domain $0 \leq x \leq \pi$ and $0 \leq y \leq \pi$.

```
> display({plot4, plot5});
```

Figure 21.6 provides some useful insights into the nature of the divergence. Note that $\nabla \cdot \mathbf{g}$ achieves its largest and smallest values (in the regions of lightest and darkest shading respectively) at regions where the arrows are spreading outward or inward respectively.[1] In the regions of intermediate gray shading, $\nabla \cdot \mathbf{g}$ is nearly zero and it is in precisely these locations that the gradient vectors are more or less parallel.

EXERCISES

21.1. Plot the gradient field for $f(x, y) = xy$. Overlay it with the density plot of $f(x, y)$.
21.2. Plot the gradient field for $f(x, y) = \sin(x \cos y)$. Overlay it with the density plot of $f(x, y)$.
21.3. Plot the vector field for $\mathbf{g}(x, y) = (\exp(-x^2), x+y)$. Overlay it with the density plot of $\nabla \cdot \mathbf{g}$.

---

[1] Figure 21.6 provides good geometric motivation for the term *divergence*.

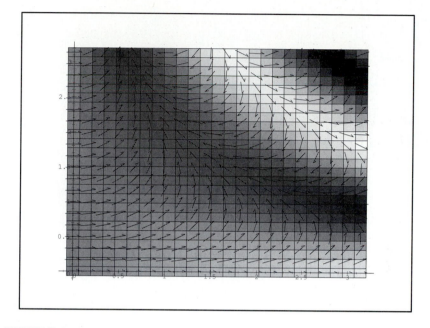

FIGURE 21.6
Superposition of Fig. 21.4 over Fig. 21.5. The domain is as in those figures.

21.4. Plot the vector field for $\mathbf{g}(x, y) = (J_0(x), J_1(y))$. Overlay it with the density plot of $\nabla \cdot \mathbf{g}$.

CHAPTER
22

COMPLEX ARITHMETIC

22.1 LABORATORY GOALS

a. To become familiar with the manipulations of complex numbers.

b. To become familiar with the *Maple* functions Re() and Im().

c. To become familiar with the syntax of the elementary complex functions.

22.2 MANIPULATING COMPLEX NUMBERS

Complex numbers are numbers of the form $z = x + iy$ where x and y are real, and $i = \sqrt{-1}$. x is called the *real* part of z and y the *imaginary* part. Complex numbers can be added, multiplied, and divided by performing operation on the real and imaginary part. *Maple* can often perform much of this tedious process for you.

In *Maple* $i = \sqrt{-1}$ is represented by I. Virtually all functions that can take a complex argument can operate on I or any other complex number:

```
   > tmp1 := sqrt(I);

                              1/2           1/2
                 tmp1 := 1/2 2      + 1/2 I 2
```

Note that *Maple* returns the *principal value* of $\sqrt{i}$. The real and imaginary part of $\sqrt{i}$ can be obtained with the `Re()` and `Im()` functions:

```
> Re(tmp1);

                                    1/2
                              1/2  2

> Im(tmp1);

                                    1/2
                              1/2  2
```

Let $z_1 = 1 + 2i$ and $z_2 = 3 - i$. First we enter

```
> z1 := 1 + 2 * I;;

                        z1 := 1 + 2 I

> z2 := 3 - I;

                        z2 := 3 - I
```

Next, we wish to compute $z_1 z_2$ and z_1/z_2:

```
> z1 * z2;

                          5 + 5 I

> z1 / z2;

                     1/10 + 7/10 I
```

The modulus and phase (or argument) can be found with the the `abs()` and `argument()` functions:

```
> abs(z1);

                            1/2
                           5

> argument(z2);

                       - arctan(1/3)
```

Maple will normally give exact symbolic results. Often, it leaves the result of the argument in the form of the `arctan()` function because no simpler form (say in terms of fractions of π) exists or can be found using its internal rules. A numerical estimate of the argument can always be obtained with the `evalf()` function:

```
> evalf(");
```

$$-.3217505544$$

Note that *Maple* returns the principal value of the argument, i.e. $-\pi < \arg(z) \le \pi$. Finally, we note that complex numbers can be used as exponents:

```
> tmp2 := I^I;
```

$$tmp2 := I^I$$

```
> Re(tmp2);
```

$$\exp(-\,1/2\;Pi)$$

```
> Im(tmp2);
```

$$0$$

Again *Maple* gives the principal value of i^i.

22.3   COMPLEX FUNCTIONS

First, define the complex variable $z = x + iy$:

```
> z := x + I * y;
```

$$z := x + I\;y$$

First we point out what appears to be an anomaly in *Maple*. Evaluating the real and imaginary parts of z, we obtain:

```
> Re(z);
```

$$Re(x) - Im(y)$$

```
> Im(z);
```

$$Im(x) + Re(y)$$

At this point, *Maple* has no way of knowing whether x and y are purely real or possible complex-valued. With no other information at hand, it makes the safest possible assumption, which accounts for the form of the results above. This situation can be improved by using the **assume()** function. This function allows you to give *Maple* specific information about a symbol. Here, we use it to explicitly tell *Maple* that x and y are real, i.e. that their imaginary parts are zero:

```
> assume(x, real);

> assume(y, real);
```

Now, the **Re()** and **Im()** functions work as expected:

```
> Re(z);
```

$$x\~$$

```
> Im(z);
```

$$y\~$$

Note that *Maple* adds a tilde (after x and y in order to indicate that something has been assumed about them.[1]

  Maple correctly handles complex inputs to most functions. For example the complex exponential is evaluated with

```
> tmp3 := exp(z);
```

$$tmp3 := exp(x\~ + I\ y\~)$$

---

[1]When referring to these variables, don't add or use the tilde! Refer to the original symbol names.

```
> Re(tmp3);
```

$$\exp(x^\sim)\ \cos(y^\sim)$$

```
> Im(tmp3);
```

$$\exp(x^\sim)\ \sin(y^\sim)$$

which is easily seen to be a commonly-appearing form for this function. *Maple* becomes even more useful when real and imaginary parts of more complicated functions are required. For example, suppose we need to determine the real and imaginary parts of $f(z) = \sin(z^2 + 1)$.

```
> f := sin(z^2 + 1);
```

$$f := \sin((x^\sim + I\ y^\sim)^2 + 1)$$

```
> evalc(Re(f));
```

$$\sin(x^{\sim 2} - y^{\sim 2} + 1)\ \cosh(2\ x^\sim\ y^\sim)$$

```
> evalc(Im(f));
```

$$\cos(x^{\sim 2} - y^{\sim 2} + 1)\ \sinh(2\ x^\sim\ y^\sim)$$

Note that we had to also use the `evalc()` function when evaluating the real and imaginary parts of a more complicated function.

The inverse trigonometric and hyperbolic functions also handle complex arguments. For example:

```
> g := arccos(z + I);
```

$$g := \arccos(x^\sim + I\ y^\sim + I)$$

```
> evalc(Re(g));
```

$$\arccos($$
$$\tfrac{1}{2}\ (x^{\sim 2} + 2\ x^\sim + 2 + y^{\sim 2} + 2\ y^\sim)^{1/2} - \tfrac{1}{2}\ (x^{\sim 2} - 2\ x^\sim + 2 + y^{\sim 2} + 2\ y^\sim)^{1/2}$$
$$)$$

```
> evalc(Im(g));
```

```
                            2                 2         1/2
  csgn(I x~ - y~ - 1) ln(1/2 (x~  + 2 x~ + 2 + y~  + 2 y~))

            2           2       1/2
  + 1/2 (x~  - 2 x~ + 2 + y~  + 2 y~)     + ((

        2           2      1/2         2           2       1/2
  1/2 (x~  + 2 x~ + 2 + y~  + 2 y~)   + 1/2 (x~  - 2 x~ + 2 + y~  + 2 y~)

  )^2 - 1)^1/2)
```

The `csgn()` function returns -1 if the real part of the argument is negative (or the real part is zero and the imaginary part is negative) and 1 if the real part is positive (or the real part is zero and imaginary part is positive, or the expression is zero).

EXERCISES

22.1. Determine the real and imaginary parts of $d^2[e^{z^2}]/dz^2$.

22.2. Let $f(z) = e^{(z-1)}$. Show that $\text{Re}[f(z)]$ is an harmonic function, i.e. show that if $u(x,y) = \text{Re}[f(z)]$, then $u_{xx} + u_{yy} = 0$.

22.3. Use the `Plot()` function to sketch the graphs of the real and imaginary parts of $f(z) = \cos^{-1} z$ along the three lines $y = 0$, $y = 1/2$, and $y = 1$ for $0 \le x \le 1$.

22.4. Write the given complex number in both polar form and in the form $a + ib$:
(a) $[\cos(\pi/12) + i\sin(\pi/12)]^9\{3[\cos(\pi/9) + i\sin(\pi/9)]\}^6$
(b) $\{2[\cos(2\pi/15) + i\sin(2\pi/15)]\}^7/\{6[\cos(4\pi/9) + i\sin(4\pi/9)]\}^{12}$.

22.5. Let $f(z) = z^2 - 1$. Find $f(f(f(1-i)))$. Determine the real and imaginary parts of $f(f(z))$.

22.6. Determine all zeroes of the polynomial $f(z) = z^7 + 3z + 1$. Which zero has the largest magnitude? Which has the largest argument? Use *Maple* to plot the zeroes.

22.7. Let $g(z) = \bar{z}$. Let the real and imaginary parts of $g(z)$ correspond to the x and y components of a vector at the point z. Plot the resulting vector field on the domain $-3 \le x \le 3$ and $-3 \le y \le 3$.

22.8. Use the `solve()` function to determine the three *third* roots of 1. Show that this set of roots is closed under multiplication. [This set, the three cube roots of one, forms a cyclic group of order 3.]

CHAPTER
23

TAYLOR AND
LAURENT
SERIES

23.1 LABORATORY GOALS

a. To expand analytic functions in Taylor series about arbitrary points in the complex plane.

b. To use the `TaylorRatioTest()` function to estimate the radius of convergence of a Taylor Series.

c. To expand analytic functions in Laurent series about arbitrary points in the complex plane.

23.2 TAYLOR SERIES

The first few terms of a Taylor Series are easy to find with *Maple*. The basic form of the `series()` function takes two arguments. The first is the function for which the expansion is sought, and the second is an equation that specifies the independent variable and the point about the expansion is to be taken. (The the number of terms in the expansion can be given as an optional third argument).[1] For example to find the first five terms of the Taylor series of $f(z) = \sin z$ about the point $z = 0$, we issue the following:

---

[1] This is not the number of *non-zero* terms.

```
> series(sin(z), z = 0, 6);
```

$$z - 1/6 \; z^3 + 1/120 \; z^5 + O(z^6)$$

This expression displays only three terms. Five terms were actually computed, but the even powers of z all have zero coefficients for this example. The term $O(z^6)$ is *Maple*'s way of indicating that the remainder of this expansion begins with that power of the expansion variable.[2]

As another example, the expansion about the point $z = i$ is given by

```
> series(sin(z), z = I, 6);
```

$$I \; \sinh(1) + \cosh(1) \; (z - I) - 1/2 \; I \; \sinh(1) \; (z - I)^2 - 1/6 \; \cosh(1) \; (z - I)^3$$

$$+ \; 1/24 \; I \; \sinh(1) \; (z - I)^4 + 1/120 \; \cosh(1) \; (z - I)^5 + O((z - I)^6)$$

Note that *Maple* preserves exact results for all coefficients.

The **series()** function is very powerful, permitting the determination of Taylor coefficients for many complicated expressions. For example, the ten-term Taylor series of $g(x) = \tan^{-1}(\sin z)$ about $z = 0$ is generated by this call to **series()**:

```
> series(arctan(sin(z)), z = 0, 10);
```

$$z - 1/2 \; z^3 + 3/8 \; z^5 - \frac{83}{240} \; z^7 + \frac{8375}{24192} \; z^9 + O(z^{10})$$

Maple does not permit operations on series. They must first be converted to polynomial form before they can be manipulated. For example, consider the seven-term Taylor series for $f(z) = e^z$ and $g(z) = \sin z$:

```
> f := series(exp(z), z = 0, 7);
```

$$f := 1 + z + 1/2 \; z^2 + 1/6 \; z^3 + 1/24 \; z^4 + 1/120 \; z^5 + 1/720 \; z^6 + O(z^7)$$

[2]This is not unlike the Landau notation $O(z^6)$.

```
> g := series(sin(z), z = 0, 7);
```

$$g := z - 1/6\ z^3 + 1/120\ z^5 + O(z^7)$$

We convert them to polynomials with the **convert()** function:

```
> F := convert(f, polynom);
```

$$F := 1 + z + 1/2\ z^2 + 1/6\ z^3 + 1/24\ z^4 + 1/120\ z^5 + 1/720\ z^6$$

```
> G := convert(g, polynom);
```

$$G := z - 1/6\ z^3 + 1/120\ z^5$$

Now we can compute the product of the two truncated series using the **expand()** function:

```
> expand(F * G);
```

$$z + 1/3\ z^3 - 1/30\ z^5 + z^2 - 1/90\ z^6 - 1/720\ z^7 + 1/8640\ z^9 + 1/14400\ z^{10}$$
$$+ 1/86400\ z^{11}$$

We can keep just terms up to z^6 with the **rem()** function:

```
> rem(", z^7, z);
```

$$z + 1/3\ z^3 - 1/30\ z^5 + z^2 - 1/90\ z^6$$

Compare this with the result obtained by computing the seven-term Taylor series directly:

```
> series(exp(z) * sin(z), z = 0, 7);
```

$$z + z^2 + 1/3\ z^3 - 1/30\ z^5 - 1/90\ z^6 + O(z^7)$$

Except for the order of terms, the results are identical.

Maple can also generate the Taylor series for a large family of special functions. For example, the ten-term Taylor expansion of $f(z) = J_0(z)$ about $z = 0$ is given by:

```
> series(BesselJ(0, z), z = 0, 10);
```

$$1 - 1/4\ z^2 + 1/64\ z^4 - 1/2304\ z^6 + 1/147456\ z^8 + O(z^{10})$$

The radius of convergence of a Taylor series for the function $f(z)$ is the radius of the largest circle about the point $z = z_0$ in which the function is analytic. The radius of convergence can be estimated from the Taylor series in several ways. For example, if the symbolic form of the Taylor coefficients is known, then the ratio test can usually be applied to yield the radius of convergence. Maple has a function called `taylcoef()` that will compute the coefficients. This allows us to build a small procedure for applying the ratio test. The Maple source code for this procedure is given below:

```
> TaylorRatioTest := proc(expr, x, a, terms)
       local result, u, i;
       result := [];
       i := 1;
       for i from 1 to terms do
         u := coeftayl(expr, x = a, i);
         if (simplify(u) <> 0) then
           result := [op(result), u];
        fi;
       od;
       RETURN(seq(abs(result[i] / result[i + 1]),
                    i = 1 .. nops(result) - 1));
       end:
```

Before using this procedure, the `taylcoef()` function must be loaded with `readlib()`:

```
> readlib(coeftayl);

proc(e,eqn,k) ... end
```

Recall that the radius of convergence $\rho = \lim_{n \to \infty} |a_n/a_{n+1}|$ where a_n is the Taylor coefficient of the nth *non-zero* term of the Taylor expansion. The function `TaylorRatioTest()` takes four arguments: an expression, the independent variable, the expansion point, and the number of terms to examine. It returns a sequence containing no more than the number of terms of this sequence given by the fourth argument. Examination of these terms will almost always suggest the correct value of the radius of convergence. For example, Let $F(z) = \sin z/(2-z)$. The Taylor expansion of $F(z)$ about $z = 0$ is given by

```
> f1 := sin(z) / (2 - z);

                              sin(z)
                    f1  :=  ------
                             2 - z

> series(f1, z = 0, 10);

              2         3          4          5           6     143   7
  1/2 z + 1/4 z  + 1/24 z  + 1/48 z  + 7/480 z  + 7/960 z  + ----- z
                                                             40320

        143   8     1289    9         10
   + ----- z  + ------- z  + O(z  )
      80640     1451520
```

The `TaylorRatioTest()` returns the following list:

```
> evalf(TaylorRatioTest(f1, z, 0, 10));

   2.000000000, 6.000000000, 2.000000000, 1.428571429, 1.999999999,

      2.055944056, 2.000000000, 1.996896819, 2.000000000
```

This result confirms the known result that $\rho = 2$.

23.3   LAURENT SERIES

Consider the function:
$$f(z) = \frac{7z - 2}{(z+1)z(z-2)}, \tag{23.1}$$
and the annulus shown in Fig. 23.1.   First we enter $f(z)$ into *Maple*:

```
> f2 := (7 * z - 2) / ((z + 1) * z * (z - 2));

                       7 z - 2
             f2  :=  ------------------
                     (z + 1) z (z - 2)
```

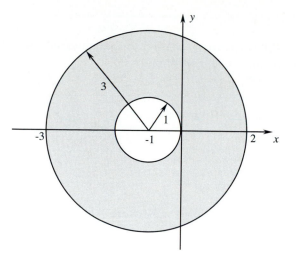

FIGURE 23.1
Regions of convergence for the three Laurent series represented by Eq. 23.1.

We seek Laurent series which converge in the three regions shown in Fig. 23.1, i.e. series converging in the disk $0 < |z + 1| < 1$, in the annulus $1 < |z + 1| < 3$ and in the region $3 < |z + 1|$.

To find the series within the region $0 < |z + 1| < 1$, we simply expand $f(z)$ about the point $z = -1$ with the `series()` function (we will take the first 5 terms):

```
> series(f2, z = -1, 6);

                -1                              29        2    83        3
      - 3 (z + 1)   - 5/3 - 11/9 (z + 1) - ---- (z + 1)  - ---- (z + 1)
                                            27             81

          245        4    731        5             6
        - --- (z + 1)  - --- (z + 1)  + O((z + 1) )
          243            729
```

Note that this series contains only one negative power of $(z + 1)$. Next, we seek the series which converges for $3 < |z + 1|$. First, we use the `convert()` function which separates $f(z)$ into partial fractions:

```
> ff := convert(f2, parfrac, z);

                        3                2
        ff  :=  - ----- + 1/z + -----
                  z + 1         z - 2
```

Before we can do the expansion, we need to change variables, letting $z = 1/y - 1$. This substitution is made and we obtain

```
> fff := subs(z = 1/y - 1, ff);
```

$$fff := -3 \ y + \frac{1}{1/y - 1} + \frac{2}{1/y - 3}$$

Now we expand this result using the **series()** about the point $y = 0$:

```
> L2 := series(fff, y = 0, 6);
```

$$L2 := 7 \ y^2 + 19 \ y^3 + 55 \ y^4 + 163 \ y^5 + O(y^6)$$

Now we change the variable back to z:

```
> L2 := subs(y = 1/(z + 1), L2);
```

$$L2 := \frac{7}{(z+1)^2} + \frac{19}{(z+1)^3} + \frac{55}{(z+1)^4} + \frac{163}{(z+1)^5} + O(\frac{1}{(z+1)^6})$$

This Laurent series converges for $3 < |z + 1|$. By changing variables, we force *Maple* to perform the correct manipulations.

This approach is evident when we generate the expansion in the annular domain $1 < |z + 1| < 3$.

First, we decompose $f(z)$ into three fractions as before:

```
> fff := convert(f2, parfrac, z);
```

$$fff := -\frac{3}{z+1} + 1/z + \frac{2}{z-2}$$

Now, we change variables, letting $z = y - 1$:

```
> fff := subs(z = y - 1, fff);
```
$$fff := -\ 3/y + \frac{1}{y - 1} + \frac{2}{y - 3}$$

Now we need to separately treat the third term $2/(y-3)$ in order to ensure that it is expanded properly. We perform another change of variables for just this term, letting $y = 3w$:

```
> tmp := subs(y = 3 * w, op(3, fff));
```
$$tmp := \frac{2}{3\ w\ -\ 3}$$

We now expand this term in a series about the point $w = 0$. We will convert this and subsequent series into polynomials as well:[3]

```
> L3a := convert(series(tmp, w = 0, 6), polynom);
```
$$L3a := -\ 2/3 - 2/3\ w - 2/3\ w^2 - 2/3\ w^3 - 2/3\ w^4 - 2/3\ w^5$$

We then change variables back to y:

```
> L3a := subs(w = y / 3, L3a);
```
$$L3a := -\ 2/3 - 2/9\ y - 2/27\ y^2 - 2/81\ y^3 - 2/243\ y^4 - 2/729\ y^5$$

and then restore this result to our original variable, z:

```
> L3a := subs(y = z + 1, L3a);
```
$$L3a := -\ 8/9 - 2/9\ z - 2/27\ (z + 1)^2 - 2/81\ (z + 1)^3 - 2/243\ (z + 1)^4$$

---

[3]If we don't do it now, we will wind up with an expression which has several O() terms in it. *Maple* cannot properly convert such an expression to polynomial form.

$$- 2/729 \; (z + 1)^5$$

We now restore z to the second term of the partial fraction decomposition and then let $z = 1/w - 1$:

```
> tmp := subs(z = 1/w - 1, subs(y = z + 1, op(2, fff)));

                              1
                tmp := -------
                       1/w - 1
```

Now we expand this result about the point $w = 0$:

```
> L3b := convert(series(tmp, w = 0, 6), polynom);

                       2    3    4    5
           L3b := w + w  + w  + w  + w
```

We revert to the variable z, and obtain the correct expansion for the second term of the partial fraction expansion:

```
> L3b := subs(w = 1 / (z + 1), L3b);

               1        1          1          1          1
     L3b := ----- + -------- + -------- + -------- + --------
            z + 1         2          3          4          5
                    (z + 1)    (z + 1)    (z + 1)    (z + 1)
```

The first term is straightforward to expand, since, when it is re-expressed in terms of z, it has the correct form:

```
> L3c := convert(series(subs(y = z + 1, op(1, fff)), z = -1, 6), polynom);

                          3
              L3c := - -----
                       z + 1
```

The full Laurent expansion is then obtained by adding the three individual results just obtained:

```
> L3 := L3a + L3b + L3c;

                      2              3              4
   L3 := - 8/9 - 2/9 z - 2/27 (z + 1)  - 2/81 (z + 1)  - 2/243 (z + 1)

              5      2      1           1           1           1
     - 2/729 (z + 1)  - ----- + -------- + -------- + -------- + --------
                        z + 1          2          3          4          5
                              (z + 1)    (z + 1)    (z + 1)    (z + 1)
```

This result is the Laurent expansion which converges in $1 < |z + 1| < 3$, and we have discarded terms like $O((z + 1)^6)$ and $O((z + 1)^{-6})$. When possible, *Maple* has combined like terms in this expression.

EXERCISES

23.1. Use the twelve-term Taylor expansions of $f(z) = e^z$ and $g(z) = \cos z$ to form the twelve-term composition $f[g(z)] = e^{\cos z}$. Also determine the composite series directly and verify that the results match.

23.2. The *error function* erf z is defined by

$$\text{erf } z = \frac{2}{\sqrt{\pi}} \int_0^z e^{-s^2} \, ds.$$

Determine the first ten terms of the Taylor expansion for erf z using the definition given above. Repeat the calculation using the *Maple* function `erf()`. Compare your results.

23.3. Determine the ten-term Taylor expansion of $f(z) = z^2/(z^2 + 4i)$ about the point $z = 2i$. What is the radius of convergence?

23.4. Determine two distinct Laurent expansions (five terms) for $f(z) = (3z+1)/(z^2 - 1)$ around $z = -1$ and determine where each converges.

23.5. Determine two distinct Laurent expansions (five terms) for $f(z) = 1/[z(z + 1)(z - 2)]$ around $z = 0$ and determine where each converges.

23.6. The Taylor expansion of $f(z) = z/(e^z - 1)$ is used to define the *Bernoulli numbers* B_n as follows:

$$\frac{z}{e^z - 1} = 1 + B_1 z + \frac{B_2}{2!} z^2 + \frac{B_3}{3!} z^3 + \dots$$

Use this definition to determine the first ten Bernoulli numbers.

CHAPTER
24

RESIDUES

24.1 LABORATORY GOALS

a. To evaluate residues at isolated singularities in the complex plane.

b. To evaluate certain real integrals with residues.

24.2 DETERMINING RESIDUES

The residue of a function of a complex variable $f(z)$ is defined to be the coefficient of $(z - a)^{-1}$ in the expansion of $f(z)$ around an isolated singular point. Consequently, if all such singularities can be identified and the Laurent expansions determined, the residues can be found. Determining residues by hand can be a laborious process. Fortunately, *Maple* has a function called `residue()` which substantially simplifies this process. We must first load this function with `readlib()`:

```
> readlib(residue);

proc(f,a) ... end
```

For example, let $f(z) = (-3z + 4)/[z(z-1)(z-2)]$. By inspection, we see that $f(z)$ has singular points at $z = 0$, $z = 1$, and $z = 2$. We first determine the residue at $z = 0$. The **residue()** function is called with two arguments. The first is the function, and the second is a list which specifies the independent variable and the point at which the residue is desired. Thus:

```
> f := (-3 * z + 4) / (z * (z-1) * (z-2));

                          - 3 z + 4
                  f := ------------------
                       z (z - 1) (z - 2)

> residue(f, z = 0);

                              2
```

and so the residue is 2. The other two residues are found as follows:

```
> residue(f, z = 1);

                             -1

> residue(f, z = 2);

                             -1
```

Unfortunately, residues of more complicated functions (those that involve more than just algebraic functions) cannot always be found using the **residue()** function. For example, let $g(z) = (1 + z)/(1 - \cos z)$. Here is what *Maple* reports for the residue at $z = 0$:

```
> g := (1 + z) / (1 - cos(z));

                            z + 1
                    g := ----------
                         1 - cos(z)

> residue(g, z = 0);

                        z + 1
            residue(----------, z = 0)
                     1 - cos(z)
```

In this instance, we must use the **series()** function to find the coefficient for the z^{-1} term:

```
> series(g, z = 0, 0);

                       -2       -1
                    2 z    + 2 z    + O(1)
```

The residue is therefore 2.

As a final example, let $h(z) = z/[(z - \sin z)(\cosh z - \cos z)]$. We seek the residue of $h(z)$ at the origin.[1] We use *Maple* to expand $h(z)$ in a series and then look for the appropriate coefficient:

```
> h := z / ((z - sin(z)) * (cosh(z) - cos(z)));

                              z
              h := ----------------------------
                   (z - sin(z)) (cosh(z) - cos(z))

> series(h, z = 0, 1);

                     -4          -2    37       2
                  6 z    + 3/10 z    - ---- + O(z )
                                       4200
```

Since there is no term containing z^{-1}, the residue must be zero. This suggests the definition of a new procedure for calculating residues:

```
> impresidue := proc(expr, z, a)
              local tmp;
              tmp := series(expr, z = a, 10);
              RETURN(coeff(tmp, z, -1));
              end:
```

`impresidue()` is called with three arguments: an expression whose residue we seek, the independent variable, and the point at which the residue is required. For our two previous examples, we obtain the following:

```
> impresidue(f, z, 0);

                              2

> impresidue(h, z, 0);
```

[1]Computing this residue by hand would be a formidable task.

0

24.3   INTEGRATING WITH RESIDUES

The residue theorem tells us that, if $f(z)$ is an analytic within and on a closed curve C except at a finite number of singular points within C, then

$$\int_C f(z)\,dz = 2\pi i[\text{Res}(z_1) + \text{Res}(z_2) + \ldots + \text{Res}(z_n)], \qquad (24.1)$$

where $\text{Res}(z_k)$ denotes the residue of $f(z)$ at its k-th singular point. To use this theorem, we first determine the singular points within the contour, determine the residues and then compute the integral. For example, let C be the contour $|z| = 4$ and $f(z) = 1/[z(z-2)^3]$. We seek $\int_C f(z)\,dz$. Note that $f(z)$ has two singular points: at $z = 0$ and $z = 2$. We proceed as follows:

```
> f1 := 1 / (z * (z - 2)^3);

                            1
              f1 :=  ----------
                            3
                     z (z - 2)

> result := 2 * Pi * I * (residue(f1, z = 0) + residue(f1, z = 2));

                    result := 0
```

Thus this particular integral is zero. As another example, let C be the contour $|z| = 2$ and $g(z) = \tan z$. This function has two singularities within C: one at $z = \pi/2$ and the other at $-\pi/2$. The computation is set up in the following manner:

```
> result := 2 * Pi * I *
        (residue(tan(z), z = Pi / 2) + residue(tan(z), z = -Pi / 2));

              result := - 4 I Pi
```

Thus $\int_C g(z)\,dz = -4\pi i$. Note that, in this instance, the `residue()` function properly handled the function `tan()`.

24.4   EVALUATING REAL INTEGRALS

Residues can be used to determine a wide class of integrals that *Maple* cannot directly handle. For example, suppose we wish to evaluate

$$\int_{-\infty}^{\infty} \frac{\cos mx}{1 + x^2}\, dx.$$

Setting this up directly in *Maple* with the `int()` function gives the following result:

```
> int(cos(m * x) / (1 + x^2), x = -infinity .. infinity);

    I Pi (I signum(m) sinh(m) - cosh(m) signum(m) - I cosh(m) csgn(m))
```

A simpler result can be obtained with residue theory. One result says that if $Q(z)$ is analytic in the upper half of the z-plane except at a finite number of poles none of which falls on the real axis, and if $zQ(z)$ converges to zero uniformly as $z \to \infty$, then

$$\int_{-\infty}^{\infty} \cos mx\, Q(x)\, dx = -2\pi \sum \text{Im}[\text{Res}(e^{imz}Q(z))], \tag{24.2}$$

and

$$\int_{-\infty}^{\infty} \sin mx\, Q(x)\, dx = 2\pi \sum \text{Re}[\text{Res}(e^{imz}Q(z))], \tag{24.3}$$

where the sum in both instances is taken over all the residues of $e^{imz}Q(z)$ in the upper half-plane, and Re and Im denote the real and imaginary part, respectively.

In our example, there is one pole of $Q(z)$ at $z = i$. Thus the integral is found by:

```
> -2 * Pi * Im(residue(exp(I * m * z) / (1 + z^2), z = I));

                        Pi Re(exp(- m))
```

Assuming that m is real, the result is therefore πe^{-m}.

As a rule, these types of integrals should be tried first with the `int()` function. The many methods provided by residue theory may then be used if *Maple* finds the integral intractable.

EXERCISES

Note: In these exercises, try and compute the integral directly with *Maple* and with residues. Other residue integration theorems may be helpful!

24.1. Determine the residue of $f(z) = 1/J_0(z)$ at the smallest real zero of $J_0(z)$.

24.2. Evaluate

$$\int_0^{2\pi} \frac{d\theta}{1 - 2p\sin\theta + p^2}, \quad -1 < p < 1.$$

24.3. Evaluate

$$\int_{-\infty}^{\infty} \frac{\cos mx}{(x-a)^2 + b^2}\,dx.$$

24.4. Evaluate

$$\int_{-\infty}^{\infty} \frac{\cos mx}{(a^2 + x^2)^2}\,dx.$$

24.5. Evaluate

$$\int_{-\infty}^{\infty} \frac{x\sin mx}{1 + x^4}\,dx.$$

24.6. Evaluate

$$\int_0^{\infty} \frac{x^{a-1}}{1 + x^3}\,dx, \quad 0 < a < 3.$$

CHAPTER
25

VISUALIZING COMPLEX MAPPINGS

25.1 LABORATORY GOALS

a. To use the `conformal()` function to map certain plane regions under complex mappings.

b. To obtain the parametric equations for images of curves under complex mappings.

25.2 MAPPING RECTANGULAR REGIONS

Many applications of complex analysis are built around the shapes that regions in the z-plane assume in the w-plane under mappings by analytic functions. The `conformal()` function will generate the shape of any *rectangular* region in the z-plane under a given mapping. The first argument is the mapping function, and the second argument is a *complex* range giving the lower left- and upper right-hand coordinate of the rectangular region to be mapped.

25.3   THE EXPONENTIAL MAP

For example, consider, the image of the rectangle $0 \leq x \leq 1$ and $0 \leq y \leq \pi$ under the mapping $w = e^z$. Note that by setting `scaling` to the value `constrained`, the circular arcs in the half-annulus are undistorted:[1]

```
> conformal(exp(z), z = 0 .. 1 + I * Pi, scaling = constrained);
```

The image under this mapping is shown in Fig. 25.1. The mapping e^z takes the

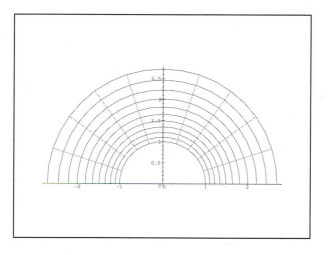

FIGURE 25.1
Image of the rectangle $0 \leq x \leq 1$ and $0 \leq y \leq \pi$ under the mapping e^z.

rectangle into a half-annulus. In order to understand better the detailed behavior of e^z, separate the real and imaginary parts of e^z:

```
> assume(x, real);

> assume(y, real);

> z := x + I * y;
```

$$z := x\text{\textasciitilde} + I\ y\text{\textasciitilde}$$

```
> u := Re(exp(z));
```

[1] This feature can be changed interactively as well.

```
                              u := exp(x~) cos(y~)

  > v := Im(exp(z));

                              v := exp(x~) sin(y~)
```

Note that these expressions for u and v form a pair of parametric equations in the w-plane. When y is held fixed, they represent rays in the w-plane, while when x is held fixed, they correspond to circular arcs centered at the origin. Thus the rays seen in Fig. 25.1 are the images of the horizontal line segments in the rectangle and the semi-circles are images of the vertical line segments.

25.4   THE SINE MAP

As another example, consider the region $0 \le x \le \pi$ and $0 \le y \le 1$ under the mapping $w = \sin z$:

```
  > conformal(sin(z1), z1 = 0 .. Pi + I);

  > plot2 := ":
```

As shown in Fig. 25.2, the images of the horizontal and vertical line segments in the z-plane appear to be a family of confocal ellipses and hyperbolas in the w-plane. To verify this, we proceed as before:

```
  > u := Re(sin(z));

                              u := sin(x~) cosh(y~)

  > v := Im(sin(z));

                              v := cos(x~) sinh(y~)
```

Note that for fixed y,

$$\frac{u^2}{\cosh^2 y} + \frac{v^2}{\sinh^2 y} = 1, \tag{25.1}$$

which is the equation for an ellipse, while for fixed x,

$$\frac{u^2}{\sin^2 x} - \frac{v^2}{\cos^2 x} = 1, \tag{25.2}$$

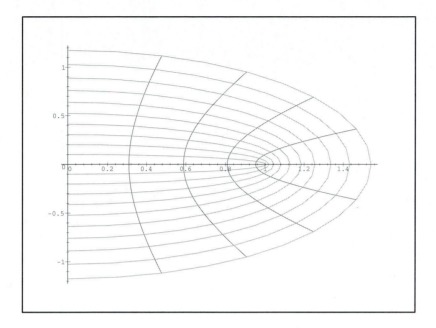

FIGURE 25.2
Image of the rectangle $0 \le x \le \pi$ and $0 \le y \le 1$ under the mapping $\sin z$.

which is the equation of a pair of hyperbolas. Therefore, vertical line segments map to branches of an hyperbola, while horizontal line segments map to portions of an ellipse. Suppose now we divide the rectangle in the z-plane in two by the line $y = x/\pi$. What would be the image of the diagonal line under our mapping and the images of each of the triangles thus formed? To answer this question, we use the **plot()** function, considering u and v as parametric equations. We also substitute x/π for y in u and v:

```
> tmp := subs(y = x / Pi, [u, v, x = 0 .. Pi]);

                              x~                      x~
             tmp := [sin(x~) cosh(----), cos(x~) sinh(----), x~ = 0 .. Pi]
                              Pi                      Pi

> plot(tmp);

> plot3 := ":
```

The result of this call to **plot()** is shown in Fig. 25.3. Having obtained this result, we can overlay the two graphs and determine the images of each triangle:

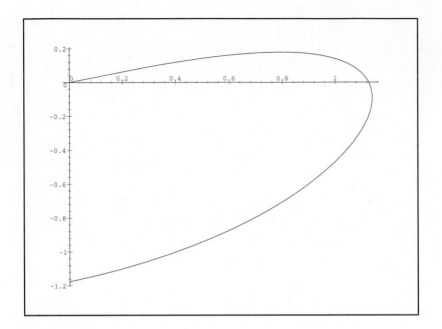

FIGURE 25.3
Image of the linear segment $y = x/\pi$ with $0 \le x \le \pi$ under the mapping $\sin z$.

```
> display({plot2, plot3});
```

As shown in Fig. 25.4, the image of the diagonal segment divides the image in the w-plane into two regions. One (the larger of the two) conforms to the upper triangle, while the other conforms to the lower as suggested in the figure.

25.5 OTHER MAPPINGS

Consider the function $w = z^2$. The image of the unit square can now be found with the following call to `conformal()`

```
> conformal(z1^2, z1 = 0 .. 1 + I * 1);
```

The image of the unit square is shown in Fig. 25.5. The images of both vertical and horizontal line segments are parabolas.

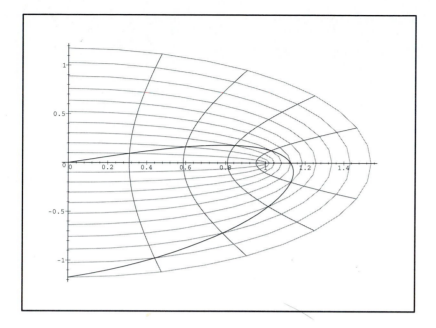

FIGURE 25.4
Overlay of Fig. 25.2 and Fig. 25.3.

For some mappings, like the logarithm function, the natural coordinates with which to work are polar coordinates. Unfortunately, the `conformal()` function is limited to cartesian coordinates in this release of *Maple*.

EXERCISES

25.1. Determine the parametric equations for the parabolas shown in Fig. 25.5.

25.2. What is the image of the unit circle under the mapping $w = \cosh^{-1} z$? [Hint: Use `arccosh()`.]

25.3. What is the image of the unit square under the mapping $w = \tan z$?

25.4. Determine the parametric equations for the images of the lines $y = x$ and $y = -x$ under the mapping $w = z + 1/z$.

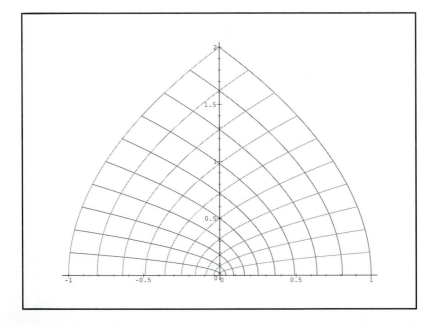

FIGURE 25.5

Image of the square $0 \leq x \leq 1$ and $0 \leq y \leq 1$ under the mapping z^2.

CHAPTER
26

CONFORMAL
MAPPINGS

26.1 LABORATORY GOALS

a. To determine the form of linear fractional transformations satisfying given conditions.

b. To evaluate and plot two-dimensional equilibrium temperatures.

b. To evaluate and plot stream functions for two-dimensional incompressible fluid flow.

26.2 LINEAR FRACTIONAL
TRANSFORMATIONS

We begin this chapter by assuming x and y to be *real* variables:

```
> assume(x, real);

> assume(y, real);
```

Linear fractional transformations , or LFTs, are used extensively in mapping applications.[1] LFTs have the following form:

$$w = \frac{az + b}{cz + d} \tag{26.1}$$

One way to define an LFT in *Maple* is with the following statement:

```
> LFT := (z, a, b, c, d) -> (a * z + b) / (a * z + d);

                                        a z + b
                  LFT := (z,a,b,c,d) -> -------
                                        a z + d
```

It is well-known that LFTs map circles and straight lines into either circles or straight lines. The particular image of either a circle or line can be obtained with this definition of the LFT. For example, suppose we seek parametric equations for the image of the line $y = x + 1$ under the mapping $w = 1/z$. We express the mapping in terms of its real and imaginary parts:

```
> w := LFT(z, 0, 1, 1, 0);

                        w := 1/z

> w := subs(z = x + I * y, w);

                              1
                    w := ----------
                          x~ + I y~

> u := evalc(Re(w));

                            x~
                    u := ---------
                          2     2
                         x~  + y~

> v := evalc(Im(w));

                            y~
                    v := - ---------
                            2     2
                           x~  + y~
```

Now suppose we parameterize $y = x + 1$ as $x = t$ and $y = t + 1$, with $-\infty < t < \infty$. This leads immediately to parametric equations for u and v:

---

[1]They are also called bilinear transformations or Möbius transformations.

```
> u := subs({x = t, y = t + 1}, u);

                    t
        u  :=  --------------
                2         2
               t  + (t + 1)

> v := subs({x = t, y = t + 1}, v);

                     t + 1
        v  :=  -  --------------
                  2         2
                 t  + (t + 1)
```

Note that this form is not unique since the parameterization of x and y by t is not unique.

This form of the LFT can also be used to establish the fixed point result for LFTs which states that every LFT has at most two fixed points (unless it is the identity transform $w = z$). Since a fixed point is a value of z for which $f(z) = z$, we can use the solve() function and our LFT definition as follows:

```
> solve(LFT(z, a, b, c, d) = z, z);

                      2            2       1/2
             - a + d + (a  - 2 a d + d  + 4 c b)
      - 1/2 ---------------------------------------,
                            c

                      2            2       1/2
             - a + d - (a  - 2 a d + d  + 4 c b)
      - 1/2 ---------------------------------------
                            c
```

From this result, we see that the condition for a single fixed point is that $a^2 + 4bc - 2ad + d^2 = 0$.

We often seek an LFT which maps three distinct points in the z-plane into three distinct points in the w-plane. The form to be satisfied is

$$\frac{(w - w_1)(w_2 - w_3)}{(w - w_3)(w_2 - w_1)} = \frac{(z - z_1)(z_2 - z_3)}{(z - z_3)(z_2 - z_1)} \tag{26.2}$$

First we define a *Maple* function which has this form:

```
> LFT3 := (z, z1, z2, z3) -> (z - z1) * (z2 - z3) / ((z - z3) * (z2 - z1));
```

```
                                     (z - z1) (z2 - z3)
             LFT3 := (z,z1,z2,z3) -> ------------------
                                     (z - z3) (z2 - z1)
```

Now suppose we seek an LFT that maps 0 into -1, 1 into $-i$ and 2 into 1. We use the form just described to form the left and right sides of an equation for w in terms of z and then use the `solve()` function:

```
> solve(LFT3(w, -1, -I, 1) = LFT3(z, 0, 1, 2), w);

        - I z + 2 I - z
      - ---------------
        - I z + 2 I + z
```

The desired transformation is evidently

$$w = \frac{(1+i)z - 2i}{(1-i)z + 1 + 2i}. \tag{26.3}$$

Suppose instead that we require the point 2 to map into the point at infinity in the w-plane. Determining the transformation now involves two steps. First, require the point 2 to map into an arbitrary point, say a:

```
> sol :=  solve(LFT3(w, -1, -I, a) = LFT3(z, 0, 1, 2), w);

           I z - 2 I + 3 a z - 2 a - z + 2 + I a z - 2 I a
   sol := - -----------------------------------------------
           I z - 2 I + a z - 2 a - 3 z + 2 + I a z - 2 I a
```

Now use the `limit()` function, and let $a \to \infty$:

```
> limit(sol, a = -infinity);

        3 z - 2 + I z - 2 I
      - -------------------
          z - 2 + I z - 2 I

> collect(", z);

        (3 + I) z - 2 - 2 I
      - -------------------
        (1 + I) z - 2 - 2 I
```

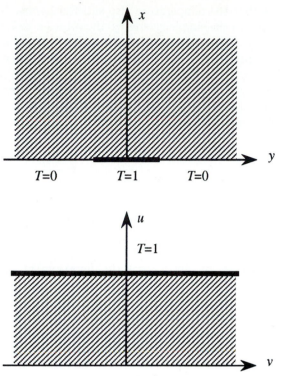

FIGURE 26.1
The mapping $w = \log[(z-1)/(z+1)]$ takes upper half of the z- plane into the infinite strip $0 \le v \le \pi$. The temperature is $T = 1$ along the segment $-1 \le x \le 1$. This boundary maps to the top edge of the strip.

26.3 EQUILIBRIUM TEMPERATURES

An important application of complex mappings is to the solution of Laplace's equation. For example, consider the semi-infinite plate shown in the top half of Fig. 26.1. The temperature T is held at zero everywhere along the lower portion of the plate, except along the segment $-1 \le x \le 1$, where the temperature is 1. The temperature satisfies Laplace's equation

$$T_{xx} + T_{yy} = 0,$$

subject to the indicated boundary conditions. It can be shown that the mapping

$$w = \log\left(\frac{z-1}{z+1}\right), \tag{26.4}$$

maps the half-plane to the semi-infinite strip shown in the lower half of Fig. 26.1. The segment maps to the upper boundary of the strip which is π units wide in the

w-plane. We know that the temperature also satisfies Laplace's equation in the strip. Further, owing to the simple geometry, the solution to Laplace's equation in the strip is $T = v/\pi$. By substituting the imaginary part of w into this result, we can obtain an expression for the temperature in the z-plane. Thus

```
> v := evalc(Im(subs(z = x + I * y, ln((z - 1)/(z + 1)))));
  v := arctan(

              y~ (x~ + 1)      (x~ - 1) y~     (x~ - 1) (x~ + 1)         y~ 2
            ---------------- - --------------, ------------------ + ----------------)
                2      2         2      2          2      2            2      2
            (x~ + 1)  + y~    (x~ + 1)  + y~   (x~ + 1)  + y~       (x~ + 1)  + y~

> T := v / Pi:
```

The temperature can now be plotted with the **densityplot()** function:

```
> plots[densityplot](T, x = -2 .. 2, y = 0 .. 2, grid = [30, 30]);
```

A density plot of the temperature is shown in Fig. 26.2. Note that the correct temperatures are attained along the bottom boundary.

26.4 FLOW IN A CORNER

Complex mapping methods can also be used to solve steady, inviscid, incompressible flow problems. For example, suppose we desire to describe the flow of such a fluid in the vicinity of a corner, suggested in the top-half of Fig. 26.3. The boundaries of the corner are impenetrable, and so satisfy the Neumann boundary condition. This region can be mapped into the upper half-plane by the mapping $w = z^2$ as suggested in the lower half of Fig. 26.3. In this domain, the solution is trivial to obtain. Recall that the velocity field is described in the w-plane by the expression

$$\frac{d\Phi}{dw} = \phi_u + i\psi_u, \tag{26.5}$$

where $\Phi = \phi + i\psi$ is the complex velocity potential. Since the flow in the w plane is uniform and steady, $\phi_u + i\psi_u = U$. Thus $\Phi = Uw$. In the z-plane, the velocity potential is therefore $\Phi = Uz^2$. Thus velocity potential in the corner is described by the following:

```
> velx := evalc(subs(z = x + I * y, Re(U * z^2)));
```

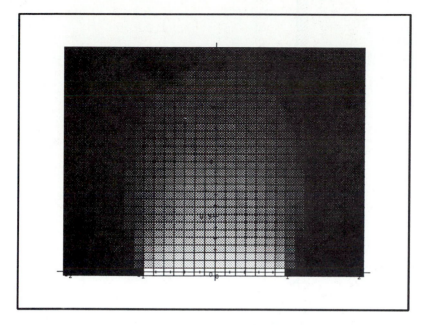

FIGURE 26.2
Density plot of the temperature distribution in the domain $-2 \leq x \leq 2$ and $0 \leq y \leq 2$.

$$velx := U\ (x\tilde{}^{2} - y\tilde{}^{2})$$

```
> vely := evalc(subs(z = x + I * y, Im(U * z^2)));
```

$$vely := 2\ U\ x\tilde{}\ y\tilde{}$$

The imaginary part of the velocity potential is the stream function. The flow in the corner will follow level curves of this function. These curves can be plotted with the `densityplot()` function, but an alternative view can be had by examining the *Hamiltonian* field of the stream function. This vector field is everywhere orthogonal to the gradient of the stream function, and so in a visualization of this field, the vectors will be parallel to the streamlines. (If f is the stream function, then the two components of the Hamiltonian vector are $\partial f / \partial y$ and $-\partial f / \partial x$. First, we compute the Hamiltonian vector:

```
> H := [diff(vely, y), -diff(vely, x)];
```

$$H := [2\ U\ x\tilde{},\ -\ 2\ U\ y\tilde{}]$$

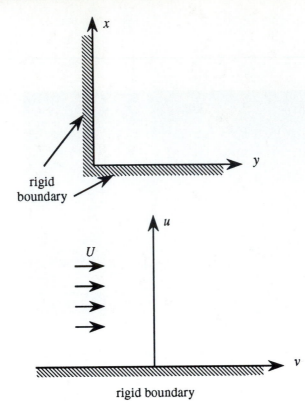

FIGURE 26.3
The mapping $w = z^2$ takes the first quadrant of the z-plane into the upper half-plane. The hatched edges denote a Neumann (or rigid) boundary condition. The flow in the half-plane is uniform.

Now we invoke the **fieldplot()** function, discussed in Chapter 21:

```
> plots[fieldplot](subs(U = 1, H), x = 0 .. 2, y = 0 .. 2);
```

The result is depicted in Fig. 26.4. In addition to indicating the direction of the flow, the magnitude of each arrow also suggests the flow speed. Note the flow is stationary at the point in the lower-left corner of the figure. This is called a stagnation point.

EXERCISES

26.1. Find two distinct LFTs that map $x \leq 0$ onto $|w| \geq 2$.

26.2. Determine the image of the annulus $1 \leq |z| \leq 2$ under the mapping $w = (z + 1)/z - i)$.

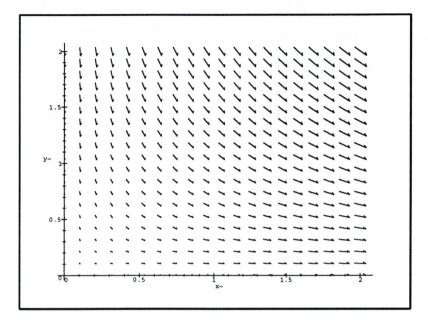

FIGURE 26.4
Hamiltonian field of the stream function for ideal flow in a corner. The arrows are parallel to the stream line. Note that the origin (lower-left) is a stagnation point.

26.3. Determine the equilibrium temperature in the plates discussed in the laboratory. In this case, let the segment $-1 \leq x \leq 1$ be insulated. Sketch the resulting temperature field.

26.4. The corner flow found in Section 26.4 is not the only one. Determine two other possible flows which satisfy Laplace's equation and the rigid boundary conditions.

26.5. The complex potential $F(z) = \log(z-1) - \log(z+1)$ generates a flow in the upper-half plane with a *source* at $z = 1$ and a *sink* at $z = -1$.
(a) Plot this flow on the domain $-2 \leq x \leq 2$ and $0 \leq y \leq 4$.
(b) Show that the streamlines are the family of circles $x^2 + (y-c)^2 = 1 + c^2$.

26.6. Consider the solid cylinder whose cross section is shown in Fig. 26.5. The horizontal boundary is held at a temperature of 20 degrees, while the vertical boundary is held at 60 degrees. The outer edge is insulated. Determine the temperature inside the cylinder. Plot the isothermal lines.

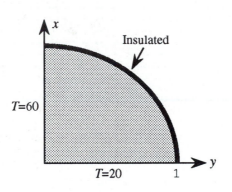

FIGURE 26.5
Cross section of a solid cylinder. The circular edge is insulated.

CHAPTER
27

MATHEMATICAL STATISTICS

27.1 LABORATORY GOALS

a. To become familiar with the `stats` package.

b. To generate lists of random numbers.

c. To compute basic statistical descriptions of data sets.

d. To generate box plots, histograms, and scatter plots.

e. To determine the linear regression equation for two data sets.

27.2 THE `STATS` PACKAGE

Before proceeding further, we load the `stats` package:

```
> with(stats);

    [describe, fit, importdata, random, statevalf, statplots, transform]
```

With Release V, Version 3 of *Maple*, the structure of the `stats` package changed substantially. Since the printed documentation available with this release does not yet discuss the new `stats` package, we will cover it in some detail in this section.

The `stats` package is unique among *Maple* packages insofar as it is composed of seven *subpackages*. These subpackages are listed in the output display above.

We first load the `random` subpackage, which contains a wide variety of random number generators:

```
> with(random);

  [beta, binomiald, cauchy, chisquare, discreteuniform, empirical,

     exponential, fratio, gamma, laplaced, logistic, lognormal,

     negativebinomial, normald, poisson, studentst, uniform, weibull]
```

We use the `uniform()` function to generate a list of 30 uniformly-distributed random numbers:[1]

```
> q1 := [uniform[1, 10](30)];

  q1 := [5.794453386, 3.998152891, 7.994992938, 3.675030000, 1.316215595,

     1.291485071, 1.371354692, 5.183541127, 6.964679669, 1.474469743,

     4.278280404, 8.441237667, 5.302973027, 2.999494986, 2.518339725,

     6.586410719, 8.675465556, 6.680476365, 6.425160092, 6.078470713,

     3.241965596, 1.492823679, 3.963587048, 8.057057096, 4.803105486,

     7.708845802, 7.241660894, 6.692965218, 1.783690820, 9.966570598]
```

(Note that the random numbers you generate with *Maple* will likely be different than the ones in this example.) The beginning and end values of the range for the uniform distribution are passed as parameters within the square brackets, while the number of random numbers desired is passed as an argument to the function.

The following generates a second list of normally distributed random numbers with the `normald()` function:

---

[1] As with other packages, the syntax `random[uniform[1, 10]](30)` also works with function inside subpackages.

```
> q2 := [normald(20)];

  q2 := [-.3379474498, .5192182258, .2557316326, -.5037576607, .2638163703,

       -.1948634063, .08264318837, .5175915149, -.5431259936, -1.725751036,

       .9408754607, -.5272378108, -1.482016075, -.7226830020, -1.491647547,

       -.1205834520, -.9793892252, .5858612336, 1.253735483, -.6332354069]
```

We can analyze the statistical properties of each of this lists (and indeed, any collection of data in a list) with a number of functions from the `describe` subpackage:

```
> with(describe);

  [coefficientofvariation, count, countmissing, covariance, decile,

      geometricmean, harmonicmean, kurtosis, linearcorrelation, mean,

      meandeviation, median, mode, moment, percentile, quadraticmean,

      quantile, quartile, range, skewness, standarddeviation, variance]
```

For example, to determine the mean values of the data in q1 and q2, we will use the **mean()** function:

```
> mean(q1);

                          5.066765219

> mean(q2);
                          -.2421382478
```

The standard deviation is computed with the **standarddeviation()** function:

```
> standarddeviation(q1);

                          2.515216618

> standarddeviation(q2);
                          .7931755770
```

The variance is computed similarly with the `variance()` function.

The median of a data set can be found with the `median()` function. The data must first be sorted with the `sort()` function:

```
> median(sort(q1));

                        5.243257077

> median(sort(q2));

                        -.2664054281
```

For information on other functions in the `describe` subpackage, refer to the on-line help files that come with *Maple*.

27.3 GRAPHICAL REPRESENTATION OF DATA

The `statplots` subpackage provides several functions which greatly aid the study of data samples. The subpackage is loaded as follows:

```
> with(statplots);

Warning: new definition for    quantile
[boxplot, histogram, notchedbox, quantile, quantile2, scatter1d, scatter2d,

    symmetry, xscale, xshift, xyexchange]
```

For example, the `boxplot()` provides a very useful way to visualize the statistical properties of a data set or sample. Consider the box plot of the data in `q1`:

```
boxplot(q1);
```

The result is shown in Fig. 27.1.   A box plot consists of three components. First, a box with a central line showing the median, a lower line showing the first quartile, and an upper line showing the third quartile are all displayed. Second, two lines are drawn which extend from the central box of maximal length 3/2 the interquartile range but not extending past the range of the data. Finally, outliers, i.e. points that lie outside the extent of the previous elements, are displayed.

Histograms provide a convenient way to exhibit frequency of occurrence in data sets. For example, suppose a machine in a certain manufacturing plant

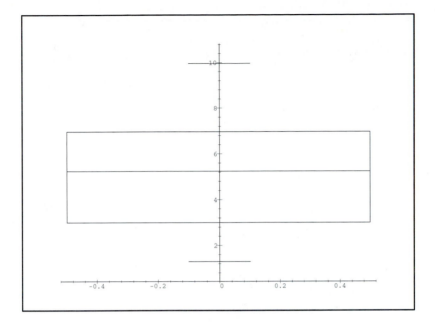

FIGURE 27.1
Boxplot of data set consisting of 30 random numbers uniformly distributed in the interval
$[1, 10]$.

produces 100 ohm resistors. Twenty resistors are sampled and their measured
resistances are obtained and entered in the following list:

```
> resist := [98, 102, 100, 100, 101, 103, 104, 99, 101, 100,
             100, 98, 102, 100, 103, 101, 99, 100, 99, 101];
```

In order to prepare these data for display, they must be processed by the **tally-into()** function, which is contained in the **transform** subpackage:

```
> resist1 := stats[transform, tallyinto](resist,[97.5 .. 98.5, 98.5 .. 99.5,
             99.5 .. 100.5, 100.5 .. 101.5, 101.5 .. 102.5, 102.5 .. 103.5,
             103.5 .. 104.5]):
```

Since we had not previously loaded the **transform** package, we must use the
form indicated above. **tallyinto()** takes two arguments: the first is the list of
data to be processed, while the second is a list of data ranges into which data is
to be counted. The resulting list is passed to the **histogram** function:

```
> histogram(resist1);
```

with the result shown in Fig. 27.2.

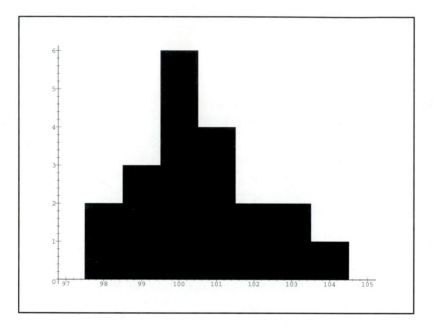

FIGURE 27.2
Frequency histogram of the data sample `resist`.

One-dimensional scatter plots can be drawn with the `scatter1d()` function. When called with no optional parameters, `scatter1d()` generates a simple scatter plot. Repeated items in the data sample are not seen, though. In order to see repeated data items, the `stacked` parameter can be specified. For example, consider the scatter plot of the resistor data generated by the following command:

```
> scatter1d['stacked'](resist);
```

The result is shown in Fig. 27.3. Two-dimensional scatter plots can be viewed with the `scatter2d` function. This function takes two arguments, each of which

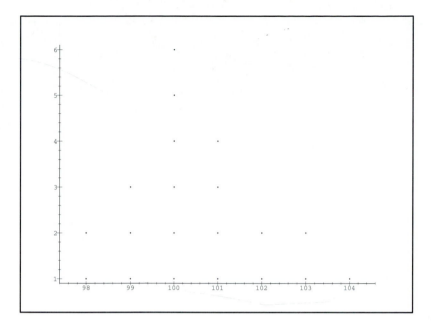

FIGURE 27.3
Stacked scatter plot of the data sample `resist`.

is a list containing data. For example, to see a scatter plot of the uniformly-distributed random numbers used in the previous section, we first generate a list containing the integers from 1 to 30:

```
> p1 := [seq(i, i = 1 .. 30)];

p1 := [1, 2, 3, 4, 5, 6, 7, 8, 9, 10, 11, 12, 13, 14, 15, 16, 17, 18, 19,

    20, 21, 22, 23, 24, 25, 26, 27, 28, 29, 30]
```

We then pass this list and `q1` to `scatter2d()`. The resulting scatter plot is shown in Fig. 27.4.

27.4 CURVE FITTING, REGRESSION, AND CORRELATION

Maple has extensive capabilities for fitting curves to data, for determining regression lines, and for evaluating the correlation of data sets. Consider the following

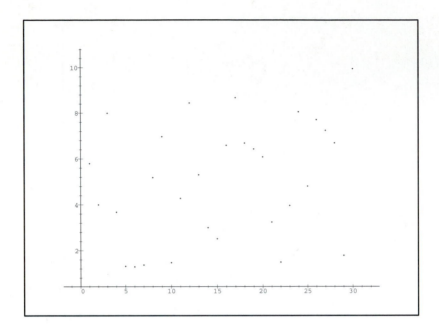

FIGURE 27.4

Two-dimensional scatter plot of the data samples `p1` and `q1`.

example. An experiment was performed which was designed to explore the relationship between applied stress on a certain type of stainless steel and the time until the steel fractured.[2]

First we enter the data into two *Maple* lists:

```
> stress := [2.5, 5, 10, 15, 17.5, 20, 25, 30, 35, 40];
            stress := [2.5, 5, 10, 15, 17.5, 20, 25, 30, 35, 40]

> fract := [63, 58, 55, 61, 62, 37, 38, 45, 46, 19];
            fract := [63, 58, 55, 61, 62, 37, 38, 45, 46, 19]
```

The stress data in `stress` are measured in kg/mm^2 and the fracture times in `fract` are measured in hours.

The result is shown in Fig. 27.5.

The `leastsquare()` function, which is in the `fit` subpackage, will compute the least squares fit of given data sets to any polynomial. In this case, we want to

---

[2]For more details on this experiment, see J.L. Devore, *Probability and Statistics for Engineering and the Sciences*, (Brooks-Cole, Pacific Grove, CA, 1991), pp. 454–455.

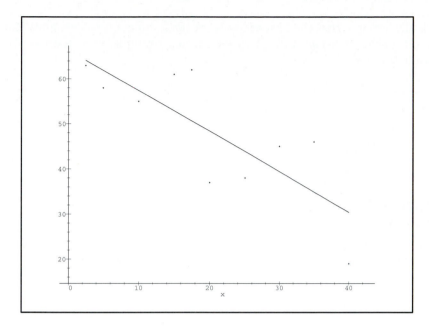

FIGURE 27.5
Overlay of linear regression line and two-dimensional scatter plot of the data samples **stress** and **fract**.

compute the regression line for the sets **stress** and **fract**. The **leastsquare()** function can take several parameters and an argument. In our example, we will pass the list [x, y] as the parameter which tells the function that what the two variables will be called, and a list containing both data sets:

```
> eq1 := fit[leastsquare[[x, y]]]([stress, fract]);

              eq1 := y = 66.41769912 - .900884956 x
```

This result gives a linear regression line for the relationship between the stress and fracture time. To compare it to the data sets themselves, we can overlay a sketch of the regression line with a scatter plot of the data sets:

```
> plot1 := plot(rhs(eq1), x = 2.5 .. 40):

> plot2 := scatter2d(stress, fract):
```

```
> plot[display]({plot1, plot2}):
```

Finally, we note that the `linearcorrelation()` function will compute the correlation coefficient between two data sets. In our example, we determine the correlation as follows:

```
> linearcorrelation(stress, fract);
```

$$-.7953101697$$

EXERCISES

27.1. Generate five lists of 30 uniformly-distributed random numbers in the interval $[-5, 5]$. Determine the mean and standard deviation of each list. How do your results compare with the theoretical values? (You may need to look those up in a probability and statistics text.)

27.2. Repeat Exercise 1, but use normally-distributed random numbers instead.

27.3. Generate a list of 500 uniformly-distributed random numbers in the interval $[0, 50]$. Determine the median. Then, round off each entry to the nearest integer and determine the mode.

27.4. Generate a list of 40 exponentially-distributed random numbers with arrival time 2. (The syntax is `exponential[2](20)`). Construct a box plot of this data set and interpret the plot. Then, construct a histogram with 8 equi-spaced bins in the interval $[0, 4]$.

27.5. Generate a list of 50 uniformly-distributed random numbers in the interval $[0, 10]$. Generate a second list containing the integers $1, 2, \ldots, 50$. Determine the least-squares linear regression line your set of random numbers. Plot the line along with a two-dimensional scatter plot of the data. Determine the correlation coefficient.

APPENDIX
A

SUMMARY OF FUNCTIONS AND OPERATORS

This appendix contains a brief tabular summary of the *Maple* functions, operators, and keywords used in this book. In addition to the discussions in the text, the *Maple* book, the on-line documentation should be consulted for detailed usage and syntax information. A quick-reference guide to functions, operators, and symbols is in Table A.1. Each subsequent table contains the name of the func-

TABLE A.1
Quick Reference Guide

Category	Table	Category	Table
Algebraic Functions	A.2	Manipulations	A.8
Elementary Function	A.3	Graphics	A.9
Special Functions	A.4	Miscellaneous	A.10
Vectors and Matrices	A.5	Operators	A.11
Calculus	A.6	Keywords	A.12
Solvers	A.7	Statistics	A.13

tion, operator, or keyword and a very brief remark about it. Every table entry is also listed in the Index, and page number references can be obtained from there.

TABLE A.2

Algebraic Functions

Maple **Name**	**Function Effect**
coeff()	Determine Coefficients
collect()	Collect Like Terms
evalc()	Evaluates Complex Expression
evalf()	Convert to Numerical Value
expand()	Expand Expression
factor()	Factor Expression
floor()	Floor Function
rem()	Computes Polynomial Remainder
RootOf()	Represents Roots
simplify()	Simplifies Expression
subs()	Perform Substitutions

TABLE A.3

Elementary Functions

Maple **Name**	**Function Effect**
abs()	Absolute Value
arccos()	Inverse Cosine
arccosh()	Inverse Hyperbolic Cosine
arctan()	Inverse Tangent
argument()	Argument
cos()	Cosine
cosh()	Hyperbolic Cosine
csgn()	Complex Sign
exp()	Exponential
Im()	Imaginary Part
ln()	Natural Logarithm
Re()	Real Part
sec()	Secant
sech()	Hyperbolic Secant
sin()	Sine
sinh()	Hyperbolic Sine
sqrt()	Square Root
tan()	Tangent

TABLE A.4
Special Functions

Maple **Name**	**Function Effect**
BesselJ()	Bessel function of the First Kind
BesselY()	Bessel function of the Second Kind
Delta()	Dirac Delta
erf()	Error Function
Heaviside()	Heaviside function
H()	Hermite Polynomials
P()	Legendre Polynomials
Si()	Sine Integral

TABLE A.5
Vector and Matrix Functions

Maple **Name**	**Function Effect**
angle()	Angle Between Vectors
crossprod()	Cross Product
curl()	Curl Operator
det()	Determinant
diverge()	Divergence Operator
dotprod()	Dot Product
eigenvals()	Matrix Eigenvalues
eigenvects()	Matrix Eigenvectors
evalm()	Evaluates Matrix Expression
exponential()	Matrix Exponential
inverse()	Matrix Inverse
laplacian()	Laplacian Operator
norm()	Vector Norm
transpose()	Matrix Transpose
vectdim()	Determine Dimensions

TABLE A.6
Calculus Functions

Maple **Name**	**Function Effect**
asympt()	Generates Asymptotic Expansion
diff()	Take Derivative
int()	Evaluate Integral (symbolic)
invlaplace()	Inverse Laplace Transform
laplace()	Laplace Transform
residue()	Determines Residue
series()	Generates Power Series
spline()	Determine Spline Function
taylcoef()	Determine Taylor Coefficients

TABLE A.7
Symbolic and Numerical Solvers

Maple **Name**	**Function Effect**
dsolve()	Differential Equation Solver (Symbolic and Numeric)
fsolve()	Numerical Equation solver
solve()	Algebraic Equation Solver (Symbolic)

TABLE A.8
Manipulation Functions

Maple **Name**	**Function Effect**
array()	Make Array
band()	Make Band Matrix
col()	Extract Column from Matrix
map()	Apply Function to List
matrix()	Make Matrix
op()	Display Components of an Expression
seq()	Generate a Sequence
sort()	Sort List
swaprow()	Swap Rows in Matrix
zip()	Apply Function to Two Lists

TABLE A.9
Graphical Functions

Maple **Name**	**Function Effect**
contourplot()	Contour Plot
conformal()	Complex Plot
cylinderplot()	Three-dimensional plot in Cylindrical Coordinates
densityplot()	Density Plot
fieldplot()	Plot Vector Field
odeplot()	Plots ODE Solution
plot()	2D Plot
plot3d()	3D Plot
display()	Redisplay 2D Graphics
display3d()	Redisplay 3D Graphics
spacecurve()	Plot a 3D Curve
surfdata()	Plot Surface with Data

TABLE A.10

Miscellaneous Functions

Maple **Name**	**Function Effect**
assume()	Make Assumptions about Symbol
C()	Output C Code
convert()	Performs Conversions
fortran()	Output FORTRAN Code
makeproc()	Makes a Procedure
readdata()	Reads Data from File
readlib()	Loads Procedure
sum()	Iterate a Sum
with()	Loads Package

TABLE A.11

Maple operators used in the text.

Maple **Symbol**	**Effect**
'	String delineation
"	Previous output
" "	Next-to-previous output
^	Exponentiation
*	Multiplication
&*	Matrix Multiplication
-	Subtraction
+	Addition
:=	Assignment
=	Logical comparison
{}	Makes sets
[]	Makes lists
:	Suppress output
?	Get brief help message
/	Division
union	Union of Sets

TABLE A.12

Maple keywords used in text.

Maple **Symbol**	**Use**
Digits	Effective Precision of Computation
E	e
I	$i = \sqrt{-1}$
Pi	π

TABLE A.13

Statistics Functions

Maple **Name**	**Function Effect**
boxplot()	Generates Box Plot
histogram()	Generates Histogram
linearcorrelation()	Compute Correlation Coefficient
mean()	Compute Mean
mode()	Compute Mode
normald()	Generate Normal Random Number
scatter1d()	Generate 1D Scatter Plot
scatter2d()	Generate 2D Scatter Plot
standarddeviation()	Compute Standard Deviation
tallyinto()	Process List
uniform()	Generate Uniform Random Number
variance()	Compute Variance

B

ENHANCING GRAPHICS

In order to simplify things, most graphics functions in this book were called with their many different options set to default values. From time to time, more elegant plots are required, say, for projects, special assignments, or classroom presentations. This appendix includes a short discussion of many plotting options that users might find useful in these situations.

B.1 TWO-DIMENSIONAL PLOTS

Consider the following graph comparing $\sin x$ and $J_0(x)$ on the same axes:

```
plot({sin(x), BesselJ(0, x)}, x = 0 .. 4 * Pi);
```

Figure B.1 is similar in appearance to most of the two-dimensional plots used throughout this book. Now consider the same plot, but with the following options invoked:

```
plot({sin(x), BesselJ(0, x)}, x = 0 .. 4 * Pi,
              thickness = 2, axes = BOXED,
              title = 'Comparison of sin(x) and BesselJ(0, x)',
              font = [TIMES, ROMAN, 10]);
```

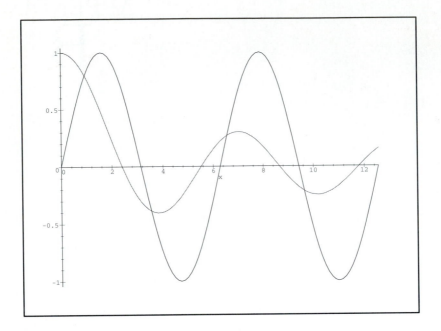

FIGURE B.1
Comparison of $\sin x$ and $J_0(x)$ on the interval $0 \le x \le 4\pi$. No special plotting options were used.

The `thickness` option sets line thickness from a value of 0 (the thinnest) to 4 (the thickest). In this example, both curves are drawn with a thickness of 2. The `axes` option `BOXED` tells *Maple* to draw a box around the axes. Other available `axes` options are `FRAMED`, `NORMAL` and `NONE`. The `title` option places the given character string on the plot as the plot title. Finally the font option takes a list with three components. The first component is the name of a font family, the second is the desired type style, and the third is the point size of the font.[1] Other plotting options are also available, and you should give the command `?plot[options]` to learn more about them.

B.2   THREE-DIMENSIONAL PLOTS

Now we take a brief look at some options that can enhance the appearance of three-dimensional plots. Consider the surface generated by the function $\cos(x + \cos y)$, shown plotted in Fig. B.3 with no options invoked.

---

[1] 1 point = 1/72 inch.

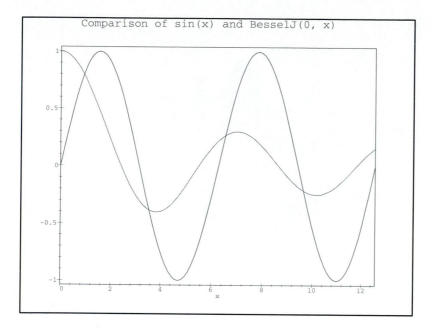

FIGURE B.2
Same basic information as in Fig. B.1 but with numerous options invoked.

```
> plot3d(cos(x + cos(y)), x = 0 .. 4 * Pi, y = 0 .. 4 * Pi, style = PATCH);
```

We now re-draw this figure with the following call to `plot3d()`:

```
> plot3d(cos(x + cos(y)), x = 0 .. 4 * Pi, y = 0 .. 4 * Pi, numpoints = 900,
         style = PATCHCONTOUR, axes = FRAME, orientation = [150, 110],
         labels = ['x', 'y', 'z'], title = 'cos(x + cos(y))',
         font = [TIMES, ROMAN, 10]);
```

The result is shown in Fig. B.4.

The first option called is **numpoints** which changes the resolution used in rendering the plot. In this case, 30 points are sampled in each coordinate direction, for a total of 900 points. The default is 625 which give a resolution of 25×25. Experience shows that 900 will often generate a very attractive plot.

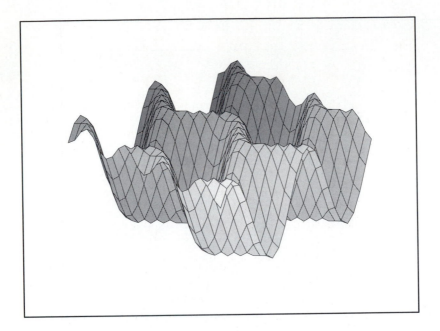

FIGURE B.3
Surface generated by $f(x, y) = \cos(x + \cos y)$ on the domain $0 \leq x \leq 4\pi$ and $0 \leq y \leq 4\pi$. No special plotting options were used.

Next we invoke the `style` option with a value of `PATCHCONTOUR` chosen causing the surface to be rendered with contour lines drawn in place. This can enhance the visibility of complicated surfaces.

The `axes` option is called with a value of `FRAME`, which results in the axes placed as shown in Fig B.4. The default is to draw no axes. The `orientation` causes the surface to drawn from the specified orientation, given in list form. Labels are assigned to each axis with the `labels` option. The list given to `labels` contains three strings used to label each axis. The `title` and `font` options work as they did with Fig. B.2.

We close this appendix by noting that there are many additional and very elaborate graphics capabilities built into *Maple*.[2] The interested reader should refer to the *Maple* book and the on-line documentation for additional details on the many powerful graphics abilities available to those who might need them.

---

[2]The ability to manipulate the color and placement of simulated lighting when rendering three-dimensional graphics would take a whole book in itself!

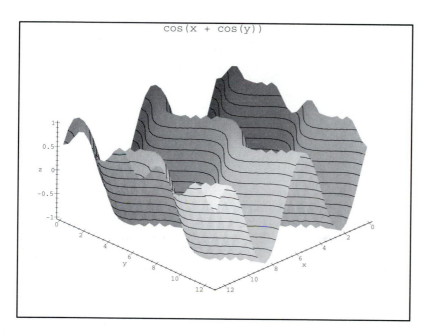

FIGURE B.4
Same basic information as in Fig. B.3 but with numerous options invoked.

APPENDIX
C

GENERATING FORTRAN AND C CODE

Maple contains features which allow its output to be easily used by other types of software that often find use in engineering mathematics. This appendix briefly explains how to use *Maple* in this fashion with both the FORTRAN and C programming languages.

C.1 FORTRAN EXAMPLE

Let $f(x) = \sum_{n=1}^{\infty}(1/n^2)\sin(n\pi x/L)$ be a Fourier sine series with $x \in [0, L]$. Suppose we require a FORTRAN statement which computes the ten-term partial sum for this series. First, we use the sum() to build the ten-term sum:

```
> tmp1 := sum((1 / n^2) * sin(n * Pi * x / L), n = 1 .. 10);

                Pi x            Pi x            Pi x            Pi x
   tmp1 := sin(----) + 1/4 sin(2 ----) + 1/9 sin(3 ----) + 1/16 sin(4 ----)
                 L               L               L               L

              Pi x            Pi x            Pi x
   + 1/25 sin(5 ----) + 1/36 sin(6 ----) + 1/49 sin(7 ----)
                L               L               L
```

```
       Pi x               Pi x                 Pi x
+ 1/64 sin(8 ----) + 1/81 sin(9 ----) + 1/100 sin(10 ----)
        L                  L                    L
```

The `fortan()` function can be used to express this result as the right-hand side of a valid FORTRAN expression:

```
> fortran(tmp1);

     t0 = sin(0.3141593E1*x/L)+sin(2*0.3141593E1*x/L)/4+sin(3*0.3141593
    #E1*x/L)/9+sin(4*0.3141593E1*x/L)/16+sin(5*0.3141593E1*x/L)/25+sin(
    #6*0.3141593E1*x/L)/36+sin(7*0.3141593E1*x/L)/49+sin(8*0.3141593E1*
    #x/L)/64+sin(9*0.3141593E1*x/L)/81+sin(10*0.3141593E1*x/L)/100
```

Note that *Maple* has properly indented the code to begin in the seventh column with continuation characters in the sixth column as appropriate. This result can be placed in a file for external editing using the `filename` option:

```
> fortran(tmp1, filename = 'foobar');
```

The file with name `foobar` now contains the Fourier expansion in FORTRAN format. This may then be included in a FORTRAN source file for use as appropriate.

C.2   C EXAMPLE

Suppose we are writing a C function which will compute the first two terms of the asymptotic expansion of $J_0(x)$ for $x \gg 1$. This expansion can be obtained be expanding $J_0(x)$ about the point at infinity with the `asympt()` function. Thus,

```
> tmp2 := asympt(BesselJ(0, x), x, 3);

              1/2                      1/2      1/2                          3/2
             2    sin(x + 1/4 Pi) (1/x)        2    cos(x + 1/4 Pi) (1/x)
    tmp2 := ------------------------------ - 1/8 ------------------------------
                       1/2                                  1/2
                       Pi                                   Pi

              1/2                      5/2
             2    sin(x + 1/4 Pi) (1/x)               7/2
    - 9/128 ------------------------------ + O((1/x)   )
                       1/2
                       Pi
```

This can be converted into C code with the `C()` function. Note that we first load this with a call to `readlib()`. The result is

```
> readlib(C):

> C(tmp2);

        t0 = sqrt(2.0)/sqrt(0.3141592653589793E1)*sin(x+0.3141592653589793E1/\
4)*
sqrt(1/x)-sqrt(2.0)/sqrt(0.3141592653589793E1)*cos(x+0.3141592653589793E1/4\
)*
sqrt(1/(x*x*x))/8-9.0/128.0*sqrt(2.0)/sqrt(0.3141592653589793E1)*sin(x+
0.3141592653589793E1/4)*sqrt(1/pow(x,5.0))+O(sqrt(1/pow(x,7.0)));
```

This output can be captured in a file with the `filename` option as in the previous example.

Both the `fortran()` and `C()` functions have a variety of options for controlling things like precision and optimization. See the on-line help files for more detailed information.

BIBLIOGRAPHY

Anderson, Dale A., John C. Tannehill, and Richard H. Pletcher: *Computational Fluid Mechanics and Heat Transfer*, Hemisphere Publishing, Washington, 1984, p. 155.

Bertin, John J.: *Engineering Fluid Mechanics*, Prentice-Hall, Englewood Cliffs, 1984.

Char, Bruce W., Keith O. Geddes, Gaston H. Gonnet, Benton L. Leong, Michael B. Monagan, and Stephen M. Watt: *First Leaves: A Tutorial Introduction to Maple V*, Springer Verlag, New York, 1992.

Char, Bruce W., Keith O. Geddes, Gaston H. Gonnet, Benton L. Leong, Michael B. Monagan, and Stephen M. Watt: *Maple V Language Reference Manual*, Springer Verlag, New York, 1991.

Devore, Jay L.: *Probability and Statistics for Engineering and the Sciences*, Brooks-Cole, Pacific Grove, CA, 1991.

Greenberg, Michael D.: *Advanced Engineering Mathematics*, Prentice-Hall, Englewood Cliffs, 1988.

Kreyszig, Erwin: *Advanced Engineering Mathematics*, Seventh Edition, Wiley, New York, 1993.

Oneil, Peter V.: *Advanced Engineering Mathematics*, Wadsworth, Belmont, CA, 1991.

Redfern, Darren: *The Maple Handbook*, Springer Verlag, New York, 1993.

Waterloo Maple Software, *Maple V Release 3 Notes*, Waterloo Maple Software, Ontario, CA, 1994.

Wiley, C. Ray and Barrett, Louis C.: *Advanced Engineering Mathematics*, McGraw-Hill, New York, 1982.

Zill, Dennis G. and Cullen, Michael R.: *Advanced Engineering Mathematics*, PWS-Kent, Boston, 1992.